DO NOT REMOVE
CARDS FROM POCKET

Backgrounds for

Joyce's Dubliners

Backgrounds for

Joyce's Dubliners

Donald T. Torchiana
Professor of English, Northwestern University, Evanston, Illinois

Boston
ALLEN & UNWIN
London   Sydney

Allen & Unwin, Inc.,
8 Winchester Place, Winchester, Mass. 01890, USA

Allen & Unwin (Publishers) Ltd,
40 Museum Street, London WC1A 1LU, UK

Allen & Unwin (Publishers) Ltd,
Park Lane, Hemel Hempstead, Herts HP2 4TE, UK

Allen & Unwin (Australia) Ltd,
8 Napier Street, North Sydney, NSW 2060, Australia

First published in 1986

Library of Congress Cataloging in Publication Data

Torchiana, Donald T.
  Backgrounds for Joyce's Dubliners.
Includes index.
    1. Joyce, James, 1882–1941. Dubliners. 2. Dublin (Dublin)
in literature. I. Title.
PR6019.9D883 1985   823'.912   84–28349
  ISBN 0–04–800014–0 (alk. paper)

British Library Cataloguing in Publication Data

Torchiana, Donald T.
  Backgrounds for Joyce's Dubliners
1. Joyce, James, 1882–1941. Dubliners.
I. Title
823'.912   PR6019.09D/
  ISBN 0–04–800014–0

Set in 10 on 11 point Palatino by Columns of Reading
and printed in Great Britain by
Billing and Son Limited, London and Worcester

For Katherine, David, and William

Joyce to Cyril Connolly: "I am afraid I am more interested, Mr. Connolly, in Dublin street names than in the riddle of the Universe."

Cyril Connolly, *Previous Convictions* (London: Hamish Hamilton, 1963), p. 271

Contents

	Acknowledgments	xiii
	Introduction: James Joyce's Method in *Dubliners*	1
1	"The Sisters": the Three Fates and the Opening of *Dubliners*	18
2	"An Encounter": Joyce's History of Irish Failure in Roman, Saxon, and Scandinavian Dublin	36
3	"Araby": the Self-Discovery of a Double Agent	52
4	"Eveline": Eveline and the Blessed Margaret Mary Alacoque	68
5	"After the Race": Our Friends the French, the Races of Castlebar, and Dun Laoghaire	77
6	"Two Gallants": a Walk through the Ascendancy	91
7	"The Boarding House": the Sacrament of Marriage, the Annunciation, and the Bells of St George's	109
8	"A Little Cloud": the Prisoner of Love	125
9	"Counterparts": Hell and the Road to Beggar's Bush	141
10	"Clay": Maria, Samhain, and the Girls Next Door in Drumcondra	150
11	"A Painful Case": the View from Isolde's Chapel, Tower, and Fort	165

12 "Ivy Day in the Committee Room": Fanning the
    Phoenix Flame, or the Lament of the Fianna   176

13 "A Mother": Ourselves Alone   188

14 "Grace": Drink, Religion, and Business as Usual   205

15 "The Dead": I Follow St Patrick   223

    Conclusions: Joyce, Dublin, *Dubliners*, and After 258

    Index   274

Acknowledgments

My deepest gratitude is for the help of three old friends: Wallace W. Douglas, John V. Kelleher, and Desmond Kennedy. They read this book in typescript and saved me from many errors of fact and infelicities of style. I have also been helped by several libraries and their staffs: the British Library, the Newberry Library, the New York Public Library, the Northwestern University Library, and the Trinity College, Dublin, Library. I am indebted most of all, however, to the National Library of Ireland. The United Arts Club in Dublin also has my gratitude for offering me help and service.

For further aid in writing this book, I am also grateful to Richard Ellmann, John Feeley, Richard J. Finneran, Patrick and Monica Henchy, Brendan Kennelly, Frank Kinahan, Edward MacLysaght, Augustine Martin, the late Glenn O'Malley, Steven Putzel, Patrick Rafroidi, Hugh B. Staples, and Jacqueline Tyson.

For permission to quote materials from Joyce's work, I also wish to thank the James Joyce Estate, Oxford University Press, the Viking Press, and Macmillan Publishers Ltd, London.

Portions of my introduction, and Chapters 1, 4, 5, 6 and 15 have appeared in *The Irish Short Story*, ed. Patrick Rafroidi and Terence Brown (Lille, 1979), *The Irish Writer and the City*, ed. Maurice Harmon (Gerrards Cross: Colin Smythe, 1984), and in *Eire-Ireland* and the *James Joyce Quarterly*. Bruce Bidwell and Linda Heffer in their *The Joycean Way* (Baltimore, Md: The Johns Hopkins University Press, 1982) have been kind enough to note three of my articles in their bibliography but somehow missed my 1979 essay (*The Irish Short Story*, pp. 127–40) that was to become the introduction to this book. There I made a number of points they were to make later. Don Gifford's *Joyce Annotated* (Berkeley, Los Angeles and London: University of California Press, 1982), 2nd ed., came to my notice after my own book had gone to press. He and I have made similar identifications of a number of details in *Dubliners* but disagree sharply on Joyce's method in using them.

A National Endowment for the Humanities–Newberry Library Fellowship, grants-in-aid from the Committee on Research of Northwestern University, and a Fulbright lectureship in American literature at University College, Galway, permitted me to do the research necessary to complete this book.

Not the least of my indebtedness is to A. G. Larson, my patient and superb typist.

I have dedicated this book to my children.

D.T.T.
Evanston, Illinois
May 1984

Introduction:
James Joyce's Method in Dubliners

Most critics remind us that in *Dubliners*, his first major publication, Joyce held up a mirror to the average Irishman. The ending of the famous letter to Grant Richards is usually cited to good advantage: "I seriously believe that you will retard the course of civilization in Ireland by preventing the Irish people from having one good look at themselves in my nicely polished looking-glass." Aside from this mirror-image of paralysis, commentators also point to Joyce's frequent use of the epiphany, especially at the end of his stories, to cast sudden illumination, a kind of radiance, which distinguishes the whatness of the story. Other critics insist on autobiographical interpretations. These stories, so the account goes, follow Joyce's four divisions of childhood, adolescence, maturity, and public life. Recent critics increasingly stress the psychosexual slant. Yet Joyce himself in his letters frequently reveals an almost obsessive demand for accuracy in the details of *Dubliners*, as though only the accurate fact ensured the meaning. Even when on the Continent, he seems to have had almost daily access to Irish newspapers, maps, and even John T. Gilbert's three-volume history of Dublin. In this regard, his final effort, "The Dead," may well sum up and conclude the entire volume, for it has, simply put, the most facts and details. Now, all these hints, speculations, and approaches go a long way to help a general reading of *Dubliners*. Yet they don't go very far in clarifying Joyce's method—one that is oddly enough neither the method of literary naturalism, a term early settled on him, nor that of the mere symbolist, the identity that graces him in so much American criticism. The insistence on a mirror, the details in what he called his nicely polished looking-glass, and the epiphanies at the end of the stories all suggest to me something else. But let me quote Joyce himself on the first story. As he once told Adolf Hoffmeister:

1

"In the first story in *Dubliners*, I wrote that the word 'paralysis' filled me with horror and fear, as though it designated something evil and sinful. I loved this word and would whisper it to myself in the evening at the open window. I have been accused of making up some words influenced by the conception of a universe that I never have seen. Perhaps my weak sight is to blame, so that my mind takes refuge in pictures evoked by words, and certainly it is a result of a Catholic education and an Irish origin."

Dubliners strikes me, then, as a series of representative pictures—or mirror-images, if you will. That is, they catch a permanence in Irish life that has a timeless quality as though each detail in any story had about it a built-in significance that no educated native Irishman could really miss and no outsider, armed with a guide to Ireland and a bit of imagination, could fail to detect. Yet these stories are also startlingly new, for all their occasional resemblance to Turgenev's *Sketches*, a scene from an Ibsen play, or the forceful truth of Tolstoy's short novels. This newness, as I take it, comes largely from Joyce's writing of Dublin as she had never been viewed before and, at the same time, writing against the mode of the Irish Literary Revival. Before, then, turning to the many-sided permanence that *Dubliners* pictures in such telling detail, let me first pursue this matter of literary strategy.

I

As I will argue later, the opening story, "The Sisters," pictures a boy's fate, his likely future defeat as a priest of the imagination—something like the fate of Father Flynn, a genuine and no less scrupulous priest. Misunderstood by his sisters and the boy's aunt, condemned by the uncle and Mr Cotter, the priest in his relationship to the boy serves as an ironic parallel to the figure of Father Christian Rosencrux—in fact Flynn means "ruddy" or "red" in Irish—Yeats's symbol for the imagination dormant for some two hundred years in both his 1895 essay "The Body of the Father Christian Rosencrux"

2

and the later poem "The Mountain Tomb." Yeats frequently went on to speculate that a like imaginative rekindling in literature would soon break out in Ireland, the hoped-for effulgence of the Irish Literary Revival. I hold Joyce's first story to be a strong demurrer against such a possibility in the Dublin of 1895 and after. Part of Joyce's method would then seem to be his setting his face against such extravagant hopes. For example, his derision at the publication of AE's *New Songs* in 1904 figures powerfully in his letters and in his probing the character of Little Chandler in "A Little Cloud." We recall that Chandler contemplated signing his name "T. Malone Chandler" in hopes of recognition as a poet of the Celtic Twilight, much like the writers in AE's gathering. It is just possible that one of the more egregious among the mediocrities that contributed to *New Songs*, George Roberts, a man who was to give Joyce trials enough in the publication of *Dubliners*, is openly glanced at in the character of Little Chandler himself. For, while he recognizes himself as "a prisoner for life," he does not recognize that he is also enacting the role of the famous Prisoner of Chillon, in Chandler's case a mean, loveless marriage, perhaps made doubly ridiculous if we recall the inclusion of Roberts's poem "The Prisoner of Love" in *New Songs*.

Nor have critics been slow to recognize the spoof of the Revival in the story "A Mother." The Kathleen of the story is betrayed partly by Holohan, and partly by her own mother's outraged propriety and legality. Yeats's play may certainly be mocked, no less his poem "Red Hanrahan's Song about Ireland"; Kathleen is not the daughter of Holohan. One might even go on to say that by the time we reach "The Dead" the boy of the first story has dutifully grown into the nervous yet complacent Gabriel—reviewer, teacher of languages, Continental traveler, critic, but not imaginative poet. His speech at table is clearly derived from the last of Browning's poetic volumes, *Asolando*, which Gabriel probably reviewed earlier in 1903. Gabriel's speech, very close to the easy sentiments of the "Epilogue" to that volume, also serves as something of a dramatic monologue to expose him at his most fatuous. The method, then, in part, has been to mock the literary ideals of the Revival and to show instead the paralysis of the imagination in Ireland.

II

But Joyce's larger method—a laying on of national, mythic, religious, and legendary details, often ironically, as we may also see—can discover itself in the simplest of references and place-names. For instance, early in the pages of "Two Gallants" we behold a mournful harpist playing "Silent, O Moyle" not far, we are informed, "from the porch of the club." Unobtrusively, Joyce has placed the key to the interlocking scenes of the story in our hands. For, instead of aimless wanderings through Dublin that the story seems at the best to afford, we recognize a landscape some two hundred years old. The club is the Kildare Street Club, bastion of a declining Ascendancy, and an offshoot from the older Daly's Club, where half the land of Ireland was said to pass through the gambling hands of a sporting nobility and gentry. In Corley (Lord Corley in *Ulysses*) and Lenehan we get the Garrison remnant of those former Ascendancy Bucks, still exploiting Ireland and getting paid for it to boot. As Joyce once said of British rule, and its instrument the Ascendancy in Ireland, "She enkindled its factions and took over its treasury." Consequently, every place-name in the story speaks of that Williamite and Georgian period and its profitable betrayal of Ireland's interest. From Rutland Square to the Shelbourne Hotel to Hume Street, the half-sovereignty, exposed in the small gold coin at the end, merely attests to that formula.

In the same mode, more briefly but no less powerfully, I would call attention to Farrington's final steps home upon alighting from the Sandymount tram in "Counterparts," then to the furniture in Mr Duffy's room in "A Painful Case," no less to the dead priest's books in "Araby," and last to the death-notice in "The Sisters." All these objects seem to me charged with a significance that goes to the heart of the stories and illuminates their pictures as though we unrolled a canvas.

If indeed a counterpart can be a legal document, a duplicate, or a like person, it can also be for Farrington himself another whose complement makes for a completeness. From first to last we see Farrington—whether at work, at play, or at home—in hell. Most readers recognize that he in fact commits all seven of the deadly sins. Tom his son pleads vainly that he'll say a Hail

4

Mary for his father—of no avail for a man in hell. Yet we sympathize with Farrington, and Joyce in a letter has expressed the same sympathy—he may be more sinned against than sinning. Hence, as we watch Farrington enter Mr Alleyne's office at the onset, a place centered by "the polished skull which directed the affairs of Crosbie and Alleyne," we are also in the place of a skull, Golgotha. At the story's end, when Farrington steps from the tram at Shelbourne Road, we hear of him propelling "his great body along in the shadow of the wall of the barracks." This is the famous Beggar's Bush Barracks, still standing today but no longer used by the military. A famous eighteenth-century engraving by Giles King shows the real meaning of the area before the barracks was built: a haunt of beggars, thieves, footpads and rapparees. In his way, Farrington is one of them, yet he, too, has suffered crucifixion that day and may, like the fortunate thief in St Luke's Gospel, his counterpart, receive some release from his hell.

Mr Duffy has another counterpart. Perhaps enough has been said about his library in "A Painful Case," but no one has looked at the fact that "he himself had bought every article of furniture in the room." That furniture includes "a black iron bedstead, an iron washstand . . . a coal scuttle, a fender and irons . . . a black and scarlet rug. . . . A little hand-mirror . . . a white-shaded lamp." All these may seem of a piece when we realize that Mr Duffy's counterparts are the two slow trains, one from Kingstown that knocked Mrs Sinico down, the other from Kingsbridge moving laboriously toward Cork, parallel on its track to the Liffey but puffing in the opposite direction. Yes, Mrs Sinico had tried, as Joyce tells us, to "cross the lines," had died of "shock and sudden failure of the heart's action," and "had gone out at night to buy spirits." So she had also sought out Mr Duffy after their first meeting, so she had crossed the lines when pressing his hand to her cheek, and so he had rebuffed her and broken her heart. Chapelizod, South George's Street, and the Magazine Hill, identified with the beginning, middle, and end of the story, are also Dublin's three associations with Isolde, her chapel, her tower, and her well, all underlining the ironic application of the Tristan and Isolde story to Mr Duffy's mistake.

Just as quietly, the dead priest's books perused by the boy in

"Araby" are all about or by double agents. Vidocq is perhaps the most celebrated, yet he must also vie with Pacificus Baker, compiler of the *Devout Communicant*, he who brought the young Edward Gibbon into the Catholic church, Gibbon who was to become one of her greatest enemies. *The Abbot*, despite its title, settles on a supposed waif, taken up by Protestant nobility, who later, in disguise, spies upon Mary Queen of Scots, but not without sympathy, and only at the end does he return to find himself indeed the scion of that Protestant nobility. Accordingly, only at the end of "Araby" does the boy, earlier aware of his "confused adoration," learn the futility of transferring his love of the Virgin to Mangan's sister, who so much resembles the girl in the charity bazaar on the Saturday after Whit Monday. He is in a world of double agents that include himself, his father surrogate, the uncle, Mrs Mercer, "a pawnbroker's widow who collected used stamps for some pious purpose," and the Irish girl making up to bank-holiday visitors from England. Perhaps the same boy, the boy in "The Sisters," will also reflect, after his telling silence at the end of the story, on the implications of a death-notice that makes Father Flynn's life virtually correspond with the church in Ireland since Catholic Emancipation in 1829, attaches his death to the defeat of another James at the Boyne on the same day, holds up the Feast of the Precious Blood for a man who fancied himself responsible for a broken chalice, and may point to another St Catherine's Church where Emmet was executed. To these enemies of promise one is bound to add the detail that the good father had also retired to a shop in Great Britain Street where articles were sold to keep water from infants. Even an unscrupulous priest might have found himself disappointed and crossed before his death in such an ethos. The opposite irony springs from Mrs Mooney's decision in "The Boarding House" to "catch short twelve at Marlborough Street;" for she will be going to the Pro-Cathedral, the Church of the Immaculate Conception, only after ensuring that Polly her daughter, a pregnant and "perverse madonna," will be married.

How much and how deep the most pedestrian and ordinary details flashed out meanings to Joyce is a subject usually reserved for discussion of *Ulysses*. Yet even the titles alone of the above stories suggest that meanings may be more than one, as we shall see in titles like "Clay," "Grace," "A Mother," and "The Dead." Yet I would continue here to show how Joyce's method also makes for an expansion of his effects by linking the paralysis of Dubliners to all Ireland and insisting that its impress is from something more than a contemporary malaise. Joyce's frequent appeals to a historical memory strike an almost timeless note for the bane that has always afflicted Ireland.

III

For instance, during the boys' wanderings in "An Encounter," time and again we happen on places of historical encounters where the Irish always ultimately lost, however apparent the victory might have seemed. Following the North Strand Road and then the Wharf Road, the boys also trace the line of the battle of Clontarf, a famous Irish victory over the Norsemen, yet also a Pyrrhic victory because of the loss of Brian Boru. Their final encounter with the pervert is in part a meeting head-on with a cruel twisted puritanism going back to Cromwell's time and not unknown to the Catholic church in Ireland. Cromwell also landed at the Pigeon House, the boy's failed destination. Yet they are also encountering a perpetual figure in Irish life, the combination of priestly and political repression that stretches back further than Cromwell. More-over, the field where the boys come to rest, within sight of the River Dodder, is very close to the confluence of that river and the River Liffey. This place, given its shallow beach, was the site of the original Scandinavian landings in Dublin. In just such a field, the Norsemen would often construct a Thingmote where trials were held before a combined priest and magistrate, a *godi* as described in Haliday's *Scandinavian Kingdom of Dublin*. A convicted malefactor's only chance to escape execution was to run the gauntlet of surrounding warriors and escape the ring of bystanders. So the boy in the story goes over the slope, escaping his goggle-eyed pious sadist with silence, cunning, and something like exile. An encounter on ancient grounds turns out to be an encounter with a possible conqueror of himself, given religious and political forces, if he stayed. Stephen Dedalus' weapons will be his. Thus one historical reference.

No less drastic historically appears the likely necessity of defeat when, as in "After the Race," an Irishman gains the allegiance of the French in any contest with the English. The sense of triumph that flushes the face of James Doyle while riding in a winning French car after the 1903 Gordon-Bennett Cup Race sharply recalls Irish enthusiasm after another such famous race won by the French. I speak, of course, of the notorious Races of Castlebar, the jibing appellation affixed to the British rout by a small French and Irish force under General Humbert in 1798 after the landing at Killala. But it's the aftermath, as Joyce's title suggests, that must preoccupy us. In the story, aboard the yacht in Kingstown harbor, the Englishman Routh wins the final game of cards over the Frenchman Ségouin. But the heaviest losers are the Irish-American Farley and the Irishman Jimmy Doyle. Just so after the Races of Castlebar. A second engagement lasted but a half-hour when the French surrendered. Their officers and men were well treated, even feted in Dublin. The Irish were massacred on the spot and their officers summarily executed. "Our friends the French," the traditional slogan, said to link patriotically Catholic France to Catholic Ireland in their joint enmity toward England, turns out to be inevitably disappointing, perhaps even collusive in Ireland's usual defeat.

But defeat at home or exile abroad may be much the same. Surely neither is much different historically, or so a story like "Clay" might insist. While Maria is clearly a symbol of Ireland—the Little Old Woman who appears to be ugly— she has for her reward in this story a remembrance of her mortality in the neighbor girls' trick. But beyond this a neighbor girl also wins the ring in the games while, of the four Donnelly children, one receives a prayer-book and the others get the water. In other words, the predominant likelihood for children in such a family is either the church or emigration. Might it be too much, then, to think of those mischievous girls next door as somehow resembling Caledonia and Britannia? The evening is not just Halloween or Allhallows Eve. It is also the beginning of Samhain, the Irish winter, when the druidical god of death sets evil spirits abroad in the darkness without disguise—such a history and such a time of year play nicely into Joyce's hands.

IV

The timelessness of Irish paralysis reinforces what I might call mythic, religious and legendary patterns that Joyce seems to place so frequently at the very center of each story or picture. This method is openly visible in books like the *Portrait* and *Ulysses*, but I strongly believe that Joyce has invested very similar paradigms in most if not in all these *Dubliners* tales. John Kelleher's justly famous essay "Irish history and mythology in James Joyce's 'The Dead,'" cleverly establishes the mythic center of the final story as the fate of King Conaire in the saga "The Destruction of Da Derga's Hostel." But more on the ramifications of this piece must wait on my concluding discussion of "The Dead." For the moment let me show Joyce's method in other stories as equally likely to lay on religious and legendary imprimaturs.

In "Eveline," for instance, if we can accept the title as directing us to a little Aoife as well as to a little Eve, we may strongly question Eveline's rejection of Frank. To be a little Aoife is to emulate a number of legendary and mythic women, none a very great friend of the Irish family. To be a little Aoife may mean to be like the mother of Conla, or to be like the wicked stepmother of the Children of Lir, or even to follow Dermot MacMurrough's daughter and marry Strongbow in the smoking ruins of Waterford. In the same story, "Eveline," the religious pattern is taken ironically from the life of the Blessed Margaret Mary Alacoque, whose colored print is on the wall. Her sufferings led to her meeting with Christ at the grille, the merging of his burning heart with hers, and the eventual founding of the Order of the Sacred Heart, so dear to family life in Ireland. Yet, in the name of that order and the promises made to the Blessed Margaret Mary, Eveline dumbly refuses to accompany "openhearted" Frank to Buenos Aires. In short, she who left a home consecrated to the Sacred Heart for that very cause refuses a similar call to her own heart and soul. A heritage of Christ's blazing love for man, caught in the visions of a provincial French girl of the seventeenth century, now denies the heart and renders chastity trivial in a later provincial and Catholic Dublin.

Sometimes Joyce's audacity in pursuing the ironies of religious assumptions in Dublin almost surpasses belief. If we count the moneylenders, questionable political figures, and ordinary run of failed businessmen and castle officials attendant upon the red-faced Father Purdon in "Grace," they add up to a round twelve. We might well call the group apostles enough, if not children of light, as they ingest the Word, the sanctifying grace from a businessman's Christ. Another example: one critic, Joseph Blotner, has detailed the many parallels with the Crucifixion to be found in "The Boarding House." But he has neglected Joyce's clear-cut division of that story, the second part assuming less than a page of text yet seemingly equivalent in weight to the first. Here Joyce appends his sequel to the crucifixion that is any Irish forced marriage, that is, he gives us the likely drama of the Annunciation. In *Ulysses* we learn that Bob Doran on his yearly bender had identified himself to prostitutes as Joseph. Now here at the end of "The Boarding House" Polly suddenly drifts into a dream full of "hopes and visions" until her surroundings fade from her mind before she's recalled by her mother's voice. If her role has been that of a magdalen in most of the story, now—pregnant, dreaming and hopeful—she may be no more than "a little perverse madonna" yet she is in the same human predicament as her saintly sister of old, the Mother of Christ. To observe further the threats of Mrs Mooney, a butcher's daughter, and the implacable attitude of Doran's employer, a great Catholic wine merchant, toward Doran, should he be exposed and refuse the sacrament of marriage, in no way lessens the ironic pertinence of the birth and crucifixion of Christ for another loveless Irish marriage sanctified by a mass.

Just as pertinent, though more muted as befits legend, is Joyce's use of Dun Laoghaire, at the time called Kingstown, in "After the Race." To contemplate Doyle senior, the former butcher and merchant prince, and his son Jimmy is also to glance at the continuing fates of Niall of the Nine Hostages and his son Laoghaire. Niall had embraced the hag Royal Rule to get the kingship at Tara; he had sought to advance himself on the Continent; one story has it that he was slain by a Saxon arrow shot by a rival Leinsterman backed by the Franks. Laoghaire was known for his attention to Irish law, his formulating the Senchus Mor, and then for also imposing the Boromean Tribute—cattle, sheep, and swine—originally forced by King Tuathal on Leinster. Captured during Leinster's resistance, Laoghaire swore by the four elements never to repeat his attempt. He broke his oath, however, and was immediately struck down by those elements. In the face of this legendary account, the flickering ironies in the fortunes of the Doyles, whose money and position are dependent upon meat, need not be drawn out. Yet the father is a kind of prince collaborating with royal rule; despite his patriotism, police contracts had allowed him to expand his business. He is also a parent who has sent his son to college and then to Cambridge in England. The son in turn has lost him a good deal of money to a Briton while in the company of Frenchmen in whose enterprise the father had encouraged the son to invest, thus hoping to extend both their social lives into Continental circles. Jimmy had dabbled in law at Trinity and now has returned to the family stronghold, formerly Dun Laoghaire, after a foray near Naas, once King Tuathal's base in forcing the Tribute. Breathless and excited, Jimmy is struck by the dawn's light on a body of water, Dun Laoghaire/Kingstown harbor, where, disarmed, relieved of his money, slumped toward earth, his head in his hands, he must nevertheless face his friends, the French.

In like manner, the expanding shadow of old Jack on the wall as his fire momentarily brightens may also set us thinking as we begin "Ivy Day in the Committee Room." For in fanning the flame he unwittingly stirs memories of the Phoenix Flame associated with Parnell and, before him, with the Fenian efforts to rid Ireland of England. Interpretations of the story that identify Parnell with Moses and the martyred Christ are well enough known. Yet the enlarged shadow of a decayed old man may also be juxtaposed not only with Parnell and the Fenian tradition but also with the original Finn and his Fianna. Finn and his warriors also cruelly contrast with the mayor-maker Fanning, his tool Dicky Tierney, and their seedy vote-canvassing underlings in the Committee Room. The popping of corks from Guinness bottles may also contrast with the real meaning of the Irish words behind the misnamed Phoenix, that is, *fionn-uisge*, "pure water."

Joyce's method tends to the hard and accurate facts of Dublin obviously enough. But it also appeals to the farthest reach of the Irish imagination, especially when excited by the illustrious dead in religion, legend, myth, history, place-name, and literature. The resulting picture or mirror-image is permanent.

V

But Joyce's method is also highly conventional as the practice of short story writing goes, so much so that I doubt that he could get *Dubliners* published today. The stories are simply too well done. The *New Yorker*, for instance, would probably rather accept a piece by someone like the late Frank O'Connor for its supposed Irish tone. Yet, though I may have dwelt overmuch on the interior intricacies in *Dubliners* for this introduction, Joyce's stories are just as rewarding if we but pay attention to their external events. So much on the level of mere narration is hit off brilliantly and even slyly, although that surface appears to be a rather formal, naturalistic one. Hence I ought to say a few things about Joyce's use of the more conventional methods of short fiction, and look for a moment at such important considerations as the matter of structure, tone, character, plot, action, and the like.

Joyce's structure tends to be the expected tripartite one: introduction, body, and what often appears to be an unfinished conclusion. But when he wishes to gain emphasis or effect a sharp contrast he will often interrupt his pages with a line of dots or make sure that a considerable space lies between two paragraphs as if to insist that the reader pause. "Eveline," "The Boarding House," and "A Little Cloud" are supreme examples of the first practice. The Eveline who lives under the protection of the Blessed Margaret Mary Alacoque and the Eveline who resists a secular imitation of the founder of the Order of the Sacred Heart are sharply contrasted: Eveline at home and at the North Wall, Eveline without Frank, then with him, and at last without him. So, too, with Little Chandler. We view him at Corless's and then at home, first under the gaze of Ignatius Gallaher, then with his wife and child. While the contrast is a glaring one, we also may mark the common elements in both scenes. In "Counterparts" and "A Painful Case," extra space brings us to the conclusion of both stories. Like Mr Duffy, we look up after the newspaper account of Mrs Sinico's death. At that point his changing reactions begin. Similarly, a line of dots heralded the end of Farrington's day at the office, but his awaiting the tram is rendered more subtly by the slightlest increase in space that nevertheless helps us fix the increased anger and loathing that will explode into violence at the end. I am not sure that other critics have observed this practice, simple though it is, but when Joyce combines it with his multiple-meaning titles, his apparently innocent but loaded first paragraphs, and then his lingering yet truncated conclusions, usually the moment of epiphany, then one may realize how very scrupulously Joyce adheres to the structure of a short story. He does so much with so little.

A further example of this economy is Joyce's characterizations. I am especially impressed to find that his most powerful characters are often those who are barely seen, if seen or heard at all. The priest, Father Flynn, in "The Sisters," for instance, exists largely as a matter of confused memories or the uncertain impression of his corpse. Yet his presence is a haunting one from first to last and, by my account, shadows the boy as one personage or another in all first three stories, and then again in "The Dead." On the other hand, unpleasant characters like Corley, O'Madden Burke, Mr Henchy and Jack Mooney nevertheless engage our attention, even hold it, not just by what they utter but also by their physical presence, so very close somehow not only to what they say but also in fact to what they do. We meet or hear of them, no less incorrigible than ever, in *Ulysses*. Yet even in *Dubliners* Henchy's shortness, bustling nature and briskly rubbed cold hands somehow fit him most appropriately as hypocritical friend and back-stabber of Joe Hynes, who himself probably understands best what Ivy Day means and the continuous betrayal that it commemorates. No less, Jack Mooney's stubby arms and then the long look he casts on Bob Doran from the top of the stairs suddenly recall us to his determined mother and murderous, drunken father as another major threat to Doran. Corley walks like the policeman, his father; O'Madden Burke's stance with his umbrella matches his pompous name and imperious talk, natural covers for his shaky finances; Holohan's limp implies, however unfairly, something of his deviousness. Mr Fitzpatrick of the vacant expression, the askew hat and flat accent remains a startling foil yet also a goad to the increasingly ferocious Mrs Kearney.

Part of Joyce's success in striking off such memorably complex characters, sometimes in only a glance or two, may also lie in his controlling tone, one that can also seem at such great odds with itself. Joyce has the maddening talent of being both satirical and sympathetic, comic and tragic, malicious and sentimental, cynical and thoughtful both or all at once. As soon, for instance, as we begin to sympathize with Little Chandler, we also recognize him for the fool that he is. The child-beater, Farrington, whom we ought to hate, nevertheless gains a modicum of our sympathy for his retort to Mr Alleyne and his defeat by the English sponge Weathers. The boy in "Araby" is doubtless a victim of puppy love, a comic casualty of the onset of puberty, yet who will not admit as a reader the terrible seriousness of the same boy's self-discovery at the story's end. Polly Mooney may indeed resemble "a little perverse madonna," yet something close to the ethereal touches her as she falls into a reverie of hopes and visions just before the story's end. Which side, we still ask, after finishing "A Mother," are we meant to be on, Mrs Kearney's or that of her detractors? And when will the arguments end on how we are meant to take Gabriel at the end of "The Dead"? Given Joyce's brilliant admixture of tone, I hope the answer is never.

As far as their actions go, most characters are caught up in the toils of a paralysis as much of their own making as it is of any burden handed down to them. Yet a heavy sense of determination hangs over all the stories—a determinism, whether religious, racial, political, or historical, that is seldom clearly recognized. Thus, not much happens in *Dubliners*, and what does happen appears to be part of a chain of causation that is habitual and age-old. In almost every story, the past lends great weight to the frustration of present action. In the first of the three opening stories alone, a dead priest has been

14

misunderstood and will continue to be misunderstood. In the second, two boys fail to arrive at the Pigeon House but, willy-nilly, failure from the past has confronted them at every turn. In the third, a gift is not bought at the charity bazaar, largely for religious, historical, and only lastly sexual reasons. Drinking habits, traditional drinking habits, render more than one Dubliner foolish and disappointed—the boy's uncle, Eveline's father, Farrington, Mrs Sinico, old Jack and his son, Mr Kernan, to name but a handful. The church serves as a like inhibitor, as every story attests. Love, freedom, altruism, adventure, genuine struggle, all these dominions of spontaneous action and life are in very short supply.

At the risk of being overly paradoxical on this subject of determinism I must nevertheless add that, however abated their actions and characters, the stories do brim with excitement. The unsaid, the half-said, the undone or barely done, these halting movements also afford sharp glimpses of the extreme tensions, the desperate resolves, the chilly resignations, the nearly inhuman rages that invest what I have called this pictorial record or series of mirror-images that emerges as the total *Dubliners*. The buried life is, after all, the pulsing subject of this book. I shall seek it out by looking at ancient patterns that give an iron though dim structure to the merging of action, character, and tone in story after story. The nervous, pathetic, malicious, and tragicomic Irish life that beats within these patterns I shall try to show, no matter how unrelenting Joyce's method can be, as human, all too universally human.

VI

Here at last I ought to speak briefly of my own method in reading *Dubliners*. Basically, I have tried, perhaps impossibly, to combine the virtues of American and Irish readers. Americans tend to be subtle readers without being very knowledgeable about Ireland. Irish critics know Dublin well enough but read Joyce sometimes as might a literal-minded historian. I have tried to do justice to both, to Joyce's subtlety yet also to his considerable, if not scholarly, knowledge of Dublin and Ireland, for Joyce's way is not the scholar's way, even in his final, detailed presentation of the West of Ireland in "The Dead."

In the hope that I may not be accused of attributing far too much information to Joyce, I have, accordingly, taken my cues from his inquiries to his brother Stanislaus on Dublin fact and lore, the kind an intelligent Dubliner on the scene would be expected to know, the kind Joyce found in the "Dublin annals," in Gilbert's *History of Dublin*, or in Irish newspapers that he seemed to have in his possession almost daily, even when abroad. After all, Joyce was also the son of a father who seemed to know all Dublin—faultily—and Joyce also once called *Ulysses* itself his father's book. Thus, I have often presented rather shallow but no less relevant evidence for my interpretation of *Dubliners*. Such evidence would nevertheless be the standard knowledge of his frequently still uncomprehending Dublin readers. Tourist guides, newspaper reports and advertisements, accounts of Dublin and County Dublin by such as F. Elrington Ball, D'Alton, Weston St John Joyce, Gilbert, Falkiner, and Dillon Cosgrave, to name but a few, are such repositories of received opinion at its best. In some ways they offer just the materials for Joyce's mind, the Irish mind at its most typical and impressive—of capacious memory, often identified by the world with the antiquary or genealogist, and then sharpened by a Jesuit education that taught it organization, placement, and presentation of the stuff of memory.

When possible, I have also tried to cite materials Joyce would have known as he was writing *Dubliners*. I have not always been successful in holding to this principle of general information. It is not just a matter of dates. Nevertheless, my greatest risk has been my use of Father Patrick Woulfe's 1923 edition of *Irish Names and Surnames*. In his preface he tells us that this edition is sixty pages longer than the 1922 edition. How very much longer, then, are both editions than the desired first edition of 1906 that turns out to be little more than a list of Irish forms of English names and surnames in Ireland. The reader should recognize this lack.

Finally, since I have read most of the interpretations of *Dubliners*, I have tried to single out those critics for praise who have helped me most. This book doesn't aim at controversy— who writing on Joyce in any new manner can be that certain of his own conclusions? Thus, I have also maintained a tentative air about my statements as the only truly befitting air, though I am in no real doubt about my general findings. But, since my text accents backgrounds first and interpretations only second, I have occasionally digressed to suggest the depth and the consistency of Joyce's selection from Dublin's urban details. I have even indulged from time to time in what may seem far-fetched speculation, if only to point at further possibilities in these stories that other scholars may wish to pursue. Finally, in taking this tentative, empirical, local, historical, even socio-logical approach, I also maintain a perhaps singular position, namely the assumption that the Joyce who wrote *Dubliners* was also the Joyce who wrote *Ulysses* and *Finnegans Wake*. To be sure, his style changed, his range broadened, his allusions became more intricate, and his thinking developed, yet the basic method of all three books impresses me as remaining very much the same in kind. As we all know, Joyce finally revealed his hand by giving detailed explanations of his last two books to Budgen, Gilbert, and Beckett. I suspect, however, that something like the unrelenting artistic independence of his youth kept Joyce from making such like admissions about *Dubliners*, although *Ulysses* does clear up much in that book. If any of my claims is true, then the following pages are an attempt to get on with the job.

1

"The Sisters":
The Three Fates and the
Opening of Dubliners

"The Dead" continues to be admired as the best story in *Dubliners*, indeed perhaps the best in English in this altogether deadly century. Yet "The Sisters," the story opening the volume, the first of three stories treating the theme of childhood, is no less important with its insinuating first paragraph offering that strange concatenation of paralysis, simony, and gnomon, not to mention the story's constant push of inconclusive dialogue and seemingly anticlimactic ending. What's more, Joyce's first published story, which, highly revised and expanded, came to serve as the first step to "The Dead," remains even today his most controversial piece in *Dubliners*.

I shall review briefly some predominant interpretations of "The Sisters," then pause to show how details of the story partly bear out these theories, and finally offer my own speculations on the story by concentrating on four important words in it—*Rosicrucian, gnomon, simony*, and *Providence*—the last absent from the final version, the first three new to it. By way of conclusion, I shall try to face up to the implications of my reading.

The dominant reading of the story is more or less shared by the critics Kenner, Tindall, Magalaner, and Kain.[1] With Tindall tending to push these points to extremes, their account, considerably trimmed, discovers difficulty in the title; sees Father Flynn as somehow symbolic of God, the Pope or the Irish Catholic church; detects in the cream-crackers-and-sherry episode a rather truncated or shadowy version of the Eucharist;

senses that the three words in the first paragraph are somehow
significantly connected; puzzles over the oriental motif; and
generally gives the story over to the boy. Tindall's reading is
the most suggestive in its promise for a closer scrutiny,
especially in his puzzling over the "Rosicrucian boy" and his
associations with Yeats.

Of course more intricate readings have always been available,
especially those that suspect a homosexual relationship between
the boy and the priest, or see the latter as a kind of paralyzed
Christ, an unrisen Lazarus, and even a gnome or gargoyle.
One interpretation discovers in old Cotter's mumbled hostilities
an ignorant concern over the boy's masturbation—a secret sin
against which he is adjured to take cold baths lest his head,
too, go soft.[2]

As an alternative to such articles, Thomas Connolly published
in 1965 his important essay "Joyce's 'The Sisters': a pennyworth of snuff."[3] Wielding Occam's razor in the fashion of a
poleax, Connolly clears the board of any hint of simony,
transubstantiation, popery, defrocked priest, homosexuality,
gargoyles, or sacrilege.[4] Thus far Connolly's article comes as a
breath of critical fresh air. But when he reduces the story to
merely a general theme—the response that the boy makes to
the death of his old friend—and finally concludes, with the
figure of the gnomon in mind, that incompleteness is the real
paralysis in the story I must part ways with him.[5] Consequently, apart from a subdued objection from Bernard
Benstock,[6] we are more or less back where Joyce left us in 1914.

But not quite. Since writing these words, I have also read
Florence L. Walzl's two further contributions to the subject.
Both perform a service for Joyce scholars, and one offers an
original contribution toward understanding the story. Let me
review them for a moment.

The first is an omnibus essay that loosely brings together
just about all that has been said on "The Sisters."[7] Long-
winded and occasionally wandering as her essay may be,
Professor Walzl provides a judicious synthesis on such
matters as changes in the text, the characters of the priest
and the boy, the importance of the story for the beginning of
the volume, and so on. Along the way Professor Walzl explains
for the first time the uncle's wish that the boy "learn to box his

corner" as an important phrase in carpentry—and, I might add, for which a carpenter's rule is needed, but more on that later.

Her second essay, written in conjunction with Burton A. Waisbren, MD,[8] attempts to establish Father Flynn's death as caused by paresis, or what was then called general paralysis of the insane. They conclude that "in his [Joyce's] final version of 'The Sisters,' he used a medical symbol for what he believed was the social and psychological situation of the Irish people."[9] While the authors provide some analogous phrases from Osler's description of paresis for passages in the story, the real source for their argument is Stanislaus Joyce's entry in his diary for 13 August 1904:

> He [James Joyce] talks much of the syphilitic contagion in Europe, is at present writing a series of studies on it in Dublin, tracing practically everything to it. The drift of his talk seems to be that the contagion is congenital and incurable and responsible for all manias . . .

This is where the authors stop quoting. But Stanislaus goes on to say: "and being so, that it is useless to try to avoid it. He even seems to invite you to delight in the manias and to humour each to the top of its bent."[10] While there is more, the obvious questions immediately come to mind. Are we to believe that as many as ten of the stories are probably based on congenital syphilis, as in *Ghosts*? And how is paresis here symbolic? Is it to indict Dublin for clandestine sin and sex, as the authors imply? What, if so, has the point to do with the title, the broken chalice, and the priest's dying old? Are we truly meant to take seriously old Cotter's and Uncle John's hints of the priest's sinfully sexual nature or that of one of his parents? If paresis has addled his wits, why, then, the insistence on Father Flynn's scrupulosity? When so many more questions might be raised, I'm afraid the Walzl and Waisbren essay may well turn out to be a mare's nest.

I

Yet the details of the story do indeed hint that the characters are suffering from something more than incompleteness. Consider the much revised death-notice of Father Flynn:

1st July, 1895
The Rev. James Flynn (formerly of St. Catherine's Church, Meath Street), aged sixty-five years
R.I.P.[11]

This notice, a typical unsmiling set piece in Joyce's work, as usual quietly hints so very much. Initially, the death of a priest on the day of the Feast of the Most Precious Blood is more than mildly ironic, especially since he felt responsible for a broken chalice. Something of the same irony at the expense of the Catholic church in Ireland may reside in the fact that 1895 is the centenary year of the founding of Maynooth; moreover, Father Flynn's death at the age of 65 gives him a 50 per cent chance of having been born in the year of Catholic Emancipation, 1829. His life may yet be that of the resurrected Catholic church in Ireland. In addition, the *Freeman's Journal*, which supposedly bore the announcement of Father Flynn's death on 1 July, also recorded a more famous death for 29 June, that of the great English agnostic Thomas Huxley. To have been retired from St Catherine's Church in Meath Street is in some sense to repeat an earlier sundering, for in the thirteenth century the parish of St Catherine was separated from the original parish, St James's; or, as the parish historian has put it, ". . . it was deemed advisable to dismember St. James's from St. Catherine's, and to erect the latter into an independent Parish."[12] Moreover, the earlier St Catherine's Church was on the northwest corner of Thomas Street and Bridgefoot Street.[13] In Thomas Street, Robert Emmet was executed in front of the porch of the Protestant St Catherine's Church. As one guide to Dublin puts it, "From that time, this spot has been regarded as a holy place by the people of Ireland."[14] Combining these memories of patriotic and religious moment, we may also recall that 1 July, Old Style, memoralizes the defeat of another James in 1690. Who, we might ask, now rests in peace?

Generalizing from these flashes of the past compressed in Father Flynn's death-notice, we might also ask what it meant to live in Great Britain Street behind a shop selling goods to keep water off infants? Or what might portend in being one of three children born in Irishtown, all three named after British sovereigns? And what pain did such a death bring, denying as it did the priest's last wish to revisit the place of his birth, Irishtown, that locale south and east of Dublin where the native Irish momentarily fled after being ordered out of Dublin by the Lord Deputy in 1655?[15] To speak to the boy of the catacombs, of the Irish College in Rome, and of Napoleon may have been for Father Flynn also to brood over the rumor that the Pope was a supposed prisoner of the Freemasons in the catacombs—a theme in Gide's *Les Caves du Vatican*—and over Pius VII's virtual imprisonment by Napoleon, who had also closed the Irish College in 1798. What, finally, are we to think of the ignorant condemnation of Father Flynn from the mouth of a red-nosed former distiller of other spirits, a bore with the socially dubious name of "old Cotter," the English equivalent of "cottier" in Ireland?

A like tragedy remains to be mentioned. Professor John Kelleher has been kind enough to remind me in a letter of the important social background in this story, the title alone suggesting the ruin that has fallen not only on Father Flynn but also on his sisters as well. Apparently, a promising boy from a poor family in Irishtown, especially if he went to the Irish College in Rome, might expect two of his sisters to earn money and help put him through his training. After serving as his housekeepers when he went up the ecclesiastical ladder, his sisters might expect their rewards: a decent chance at good marriages. We know of Father Flynn's accomplishments and learning, yet we are also made aware of his sisters' flat accents and malapropisms. The conclusion must be that his scruples, his breakdown, and then his strokes have been the wreck of all his promise and their rewards, since the Flynn sisters had to care for their brother until his death and are left ignorant, near-destitute, aged spinsters, victims themselves of wrong choice. On this level—that of the easily expendable priest, no matter how brilliant—the boy also might ponder well Father Flynn's "great wish for him."

Thus, the suggestions surrounding the priest alone hint of mighty forces past and present hostile to Ireland, the faith, and Father Flynn's own unimpaired existence, and his sister's also. Even an unscrupulous man might have found himself disappointed and crossed in such an ethos. Yet the question remains: how are these intimations of national and religious disaster in Father Flynn related to other episodes—the boy's dream of Persia, the visit to the death-room ablaze with tawny gold light, the memory of the good father dozing or bespattered with snuff, even the seemingly endless and halting dialogue between Eliza and the boy's aunt that concludes the story?

II

Perhaps I should try to answer these questions by first posing another of my own. Given Father Flynn's painful antecedents, what kind of impression are we meant to imagine he makes on the boy, especially if we recall old Cotter's last words on the ill results of the boy's friendship: "It's bad for children because their minds are so impressionable. When children see things like that, you know, it has an effect . . ." What effect does such a mentor have on a boy in whom he inculcates the niceties in distinguishing among sins or impresses with "the duties of the priest towards the Eucharist and towards the secrecy of the confessional"? One such effect or influence may be largely aesthetic: to inculcate writing as a transforming ritual with the power of creating a conscience—in short, the literary theory behind the volume itself. Consider four important words that may make particular this claim.

The first is found in the phrase directed at the boy by his uncle—"that Rosicrucian there." In the year of Father Flynn's death appeared also W. B. Yeats's essay "The Body of the Father Christian Rosencrux." Yeats's subject is the death-sleep of the imagination in literature and its hoped-for reawakening in the near future. By my theory, Joyce's subject is the imagination's awakening in the boy and its likely demise, after the example of the inspiring priest. Let us consider a few passages from this extremely short essay. The first sentences catch its essence:

> The followers of the Father Christian Rosencrux, says the old tradition, wrapped his imperishable body in noble raiment and laid it under the house of their Order, in a tomb containing the symbols of all things . . . and set about him inextinguishable magical lamps, which burnt on generation after generation, until other students of the Order came upon the tomb by chance. It seems to me that the imagination has had no very different history during the last two hundred years, but has been laid in a great tomb of criticism, and had set over it inextinguishable magical lamps of wisdom and romance, and has been altogether so nobly housed and apparelled that we have forgotten that its wizard lips are closed, or but opened for the complaining of some melancholy and ghostly voice.

In at least three other junctures of the essay, Yeats expands on the negative of this theme:

> . . . but now it is not the great persons or the great passions we imagine which absorb us . . . but the wise comments we make upon them, the criticism of life we wring from their fortunes . . .

> I cannot get it out of my mind that this age of criticism is about to pass, and an age of imagination, of emotion, of moods, of revelation, about to come in its place . . . we will learn again that the great passions are angels of God, and that to embody them . . . is more than to comment, however wisely, upon the tendencies of our time, or to express the socialistic, or humanitarian, or other forces of our time, or even "to sum up" our time, as the phrase is; for art is a revelation, and not a criticism . . .[16]

In September of that year, Yeats published "Irish National Literature, III" in the *Bookman*, beginning the essay with the above words in their full context and adding: "This revolution may be the opportunity of the Irish Celt, for he has an unexhausted and inexhaustible mythology to give him symbols and personages, and his nature has been profoundly emotional from the beginning."[17] Most, if not all, of the criticism of Father Flynn, and of the boy by association, may be likened to the pragmatic comment—as when the priest is summed up by sisters and aunt at the end—that remains uncomprehending before the revelation or golden blaze of the imagination.

But for the moment we might recall some more specifically relevant facts about the Rosicrucians. Founder of the order in 1408, an order supposedly not made public for two hundred years, Father Rosycross, as he is generally named, was a German nobleman and former monk initiated into the wisdom of Arabia looking back to the tradition of Hermes Trismegistus, ultimately the wisdom of the Egyptian god Thoth, inventor of speech and writing, magician of words and patron of writers.[18] Rosicrucianism as a doctrine closely parallels Joyce's own aesthetic theory, even to sharing strong anti-papal sentiments; for to see the macrocosm in the microcosm, the whole human world in a Dubliner, and then to mark a man's exterior as the signature of things—to allow the trivial event or remark to light up an inner significance—are principles as germane to Joyce as they are to the Rosicrucians.[19] Also to stress the imagination as the great agent of magic is to find Joyce and a Rosicrucian master, Paracelsus, in accord; for Joyce the imagination had "magical powers."[20] Here is Paracelsus: "Man has a visible and invisible workshop. The visible one is his body; the invisible one his imagination."[21] Nor should the Rosicrucian symbolic belief in the transmutation of baser metals into gold disguise its close approximation to Joyce's theory of literary art as that of the transubstantiation of the Eucharist. In fact the very grail chalice itself—so important to the story—is as pertinent to the Rosicrucian veneration of the vase as was the chalice to the Knights Templars or to the Mass of the Precious Blood.[22] Nor is the quest after the Lost Word or even the veneration of King Solomon's Temple and the rite of Hiram very distant for a boy who sets out on a quest to the Pigeon House in the next story and discovers the real meaning of an apparently oriental temple in the third. The fact that every Rosicrucian in early days was expected quietly to initiate his successor before his own death is no less relevant for priest and boy.[23] Since Flynn means "red" or "ruddy" in Irish, the priest's very name may point to a Father Rosycross.

More pertinent, however, is the connection of the Rosicrucian order to the Masons, however much the supposed origins of the relationship have been disputed. For since the mid-eighteenth century Master Masons have been eligible to join the Rosicrucians, while both orders claim eastern origins and share an occult and alchemical vocabulary. For both groups life itself represented a distillation process quite apart from the muttered platitudes of the ex-distiller old Cotter. Master Masons, the Juniores of the Brotherhood, were termed "Masters of the Appearance of Light, otherwise Masters of the Dawn of Light and of the Lost Word."[24] Such is the magical alchemy that purifies a conscience and prepares for the reception of light.[25]

I see Father Flynn, then, as initiating the boy into the discriminations of ritual and conscience that will allow him in turn to refine the rough materials of the world into something like the permanence of alchemical gold. But here is Yeats again on the alchemists:

> I had discovered, early in my researches, that their doctrine was no merely chemical fantasy, but a philosophy that applied to the world, to the elements and to man himself; and that they sought to fashion gold out of common metals merely as part of a universal trans-mutation of all things into some divine and imperishable substance; and this enabled me to make my little book [*Rosa Alchemica*] a fanciful reverie over the transmutation of life into art, and a cry of measureless desire for a world made wholly of essences.[26]

The blazing light of the priest's death-room, so reminiscent of the light his followers discovered surrounding Father Rosycross's tomb and unaltered body, may also mark the boy as his successor or one of the illuminati-to-be. Moreover, he has his bread, so to speak, the world of daily experience he is released into by the priest's death; perhaps that is why Joyce has him sip wine only—a reminder of the Most Precious Blood and the quest he will inherit. Perhaps, too, Joyce's original choice of St Ita's Church for Father Flynn was based on the legend of the saint's being discovered as a child in a blaze of light.

In keeping with this Masonic overlay with Rosicrucianism, especially as Father Flynn resembles the figure in Yeats's essay, consider the second term, *gnomon*, notably as it occurs in the boy's Euclid. Instead of the parallelogram with a similar parallelogram removed from it and, by extension, any such incomplete figure, we discover that even more primary meanings attach to the word: "a thing enabling something to be known," and then the "term used of a mechanical instrument for drawing right angles"[27]—a carpenter's square. Such a square is a prime symbol of craft masonry (quite visible on the Masonic Hall in Molesworth Street, close to the National Library), the insignia for a Master Mason and a symbol of the great allegory of Masonry, the legend of the Master Builder, Hiram Abiff.[28] In this sense, Father Flynn is also a kind of master builder—and the title from Ibsen's play may also be echoed—and mentor for the boy, the future literary craftsman.

In the same manner, the word *simony* is related to both *Rosicrucian* and *gnomon*, for a high grade among Rosicrucians—who originally aimed at purifying the Catholic church—has the title Magus.[29] For Father Flynn to be called a simoniac, then, may merely be for him to resemble Simon Magus, who also learned his magic, it is said, in Egypt.[30] Among the legends clinging to his name, one is particularly apt for Joyce's purposes. It finds him disputing his divinity with Peter and Paul before the Emperor Nero. In an effort to prove his powers, Simon Magus then attempted to fly but fell to his death, surely a Daedalian theme dear to Joyce. One recalls that Stephen's father in both the *Portrait* and *Ulysses* is named Simon.[31] Nor is such a fall without its imaginative appeal to a student of Ibsen's *Master Builder* like Joyce. Those, then, who exonerate Father Flynn from any act of simony may well be right. He has nevertheless assumed the magical role of Simon Magus in furthering the literary bent of a boy who will someday contend with Peter and Paul before a new Roman Authority, and finally take it upon himself to fly to preserve his artistic integrity, or call it his literary magic. One might also speculate that the scrupulosity of Father Flynn—his hope to be spirit-borne in Dublin—also came to grief over the accident of a broken chalice, not to mention the earthy insistence of the confessional.

How, then, do these three terms—*Rosicrucian, gnomon* and *simony*—tie in with the all-important word *Providence* repeated four times in the first two paragraphs of the story printed in the *Irish Homestead* for 13 August 1904? First, the use of *Providence* in these four instances is a narrowed one. We are told that Providence had led the boy's feet to the lighted window only for him to discover the priest still alive. Then Providence, called "whimsical" this time, led him to a far side of Dublin, not to the priest's house when the latter actually did die. A third reflection by the boy asserts that such a capricious Providence may well have taken him at a "disadvantage." Finally, the very first sentence of the story had already read "Three nights in succession I had found myself in Great Britain-street at that hour, as if by Providence." In our version of the story the word has disappeared, yet an even more sinister sense of Providence hovers about this story and the next two to come; for Joyce had already hinted in the *Homestead* story that Providence is actually Fate, but in the story we read Fate's appearance is both more dramatic and subtler.

One need go no further than the Myth of Er in Plato's *Republic* to learn how close Joyce has kept to the classical idea of Fate or the Fates. Thus, structurally, in "The Sisters" the priest and the boy are joined in their careers by the sisters, not two but three. For the boy's aunt and the sisters Flynn between them in fact spin out the boy's fate, almost unknown to him, in recounting or pointing to the priest's passage from life to death. Fatal sisters all, the three prophetically utter the doom or slow paralysis to come for another Dublin youth of intelligence, sensitivity, and scrupulosity who will be a disappointed priest in another realm.

Hence by gesture, command, and conversation the three women unwittingly spin, allot, and make inevitable the boy's fate. Clotho, the spinner, who traditionally holds the distaff and represents the present time, probably lives in Nannie. She beckons the boy up the stairs and into the death-room. The slovenly and decayed present unavoidably forces itself upon the boy's sight as he gazes at her skirt and boots when he ought to be praying. Something like the present circumstances in Joyce's Dublin, Nannie is deaf and remains silent before the maudlin gossip over the priest's past put in the mouths of the aunt and Eliza at the end. The second fatal sister, Lachesis, the allotter, representing the past and doing the actual spinning, inhabits by this account Eliza. She it is who divulges the accident of the broken chalice and the subsequent laughter in the confessional and, in doing so, foretells the ruin of the boy's own hopes as an artist. She rightfully dominates the two-way conversation that closes the story. Logically, then, Atropos, the inevitable, who stands for the future and cuts the thread, is of course the boy's aunt. Like old Cotter and the boy's uncle she will be among the uncomprehending ones that will ensure the boy's paralysis as a literary man or priest of the imagination in later Dublin life.

But the question remains: how may these speculations help a reader of "The Sisters"? Let me, then, turn to the last sentence of the story. Originally it read, coming as the penultimate sentence, "Then they knew something was wrong." With the halting yet somewhat overinsistent final version—"So then, of course, when they saw that, that made them think that there was something wrong with him . . ."—Joyce if not Eliza makes clear to the alert reader the strong suggestion that there might indeed be something wrong with *them.* I take this utterance as the epiphany of the story, the final statement that will lodge within the boy and doubtless be recognized for its irony in some future moment. "They"—those including Father O'Rourke, who came upon Father Flynn laughing in the confession-box—or old Cotter and the boy's uncle, who sum up the priest, to use Yeats's term for unimaginative literature again, personify the oppressive fate that will paralyze the grown boy. Significantly, the golden dawn of Yeats's Rosi-crucian order has become a highly dubious sunset for a boy marking a death to which he was led by a faintly lighted square, another symbol of a Master Mason.

So the powerfully negative forces visible even in Father Flynn's death-notice suggest an implacable Fate pitted against the imaginative impetus roused in the boy. The dream, in which his soul "recedes into some pleasant and vicious region," is Arabian in setting and betokens the awakening life of the senses in their most acute form, the dense life of earth, sex and the sensuous that will be the boy's priestly realm. To seem to absolve the confessed magus is tentatively to accept that hitherto forbidden life. Indeed, according to Yeats's interpretation of Father Rosycross, and along with Joyce's pointed display of golden light in the death-room where clings the odor of flowers, we are several times reminded that to the three women and the boy Father Flynn apeared to be alive. He was resigned to his fate; there was no telling the exact moment of his death; in fact he was a beautiful corpse, as if only sleeping. All listen near the story's end for him to repeat his laughter until they catch themselves. However, he will live for a time in his successor, who will nevertheless succumb in his imaginative brotherhood. So Fate and one version of the Golden Dawn in Dublin.

III

The general reasons for reading "The Sisters" in this way may seem all too obvious, but they may be worth listing before passing on to the more specific ones. The growing importance of Yeats to the young Joyce beyond the mere biographical encounters is paramount. Yet his determined disdain for Yeats's Irish Literary Revival is no less powerful. The rebirth of a European imagination under its aegis must have struck Joyce as absurd. Second, the double, even triple, meaning of all the stories in *Dubliners* is certainly signaled in this the first story. The concern in his first published fiction with the theme of the artist not only serves to tighten the bond between *Dubliners* and the *Portrait* but also asks that we re-examine the prospects of Stephen in *Ulysses*. Again, for all the frequent acerbity in Joyce's satire from story to story, we cannot help remarking his deep imaginative sympathy here, as so many critics have not detected, for a priest of his own abandoned church whose paralysis is drawn as the crowning fate in Dublin.

Yet the strongest implications are for the next two stories in the book. In "An Encounter" a reluctant Indian is reduced to virtual silence, cunning ("let you be Murphy and I'll be Smith"), escape and future exile by a man "chewing one of those green stems on which girls tell fortunes." Fate and fortune become one for a boy of literary bent when he encounters a likely edition of his future self around one of the oldest contested grounds since Scandinavian Dublin flourished, the confluence of the Liffey and the Dodder. In "Araby" what appears to be the same boy has unwillingly turned into a double agent; his confused adoration intermingles the holy and the sensual. His quest eastward results, by accident, in his breaking a chalice (the ideal image of Mangan's sister) that he had till then successfully borne "through a throng of foes." The discovery gnaws at his rectitude no less powerfully than it did at Father Flynn's. The boy who had watched the lighted window of one exemplar of Father Rosycross unresurrected now discovers the lights out in the temple. The vicious and pleasant region is no longer a dream but the real world of a seedy bazaar.

Let me conclude, then, where I started with a reference to "The Dead." There Gabriel Conroy, a magus of a minor kind, helps celebrate 6 January, the Feast of the Epiphany—the day of Old Christmas, as it is called in Ireland. As a magus on that eve, it is right that a revelation should come to him. He is also the guest of three women whom he chooses to designate the Three Graces. This story, too, is about Fate, usually seen in Ireland as the breaking of *geasa* or taboos. (John V. Kelleher has already traced the shadowy parallels between Gabriel Conroy and King Conaire, both breaking one by one those taboos that stand between themselves and death.)[32] Yet, curiously enough, the movement of this story runs counter to the first three. The movement east is now translated into one toward the West of Ireland, the sacred Ireland of a peasantry thought by both Joyce and Yeats to be Asiatic. In other words, Gabriel's eyes are directed to the real locus of the literary and moral imagination, the most Irish part of Ireland, Connacht beyond the Shannon, not without its oriental mysteries, and not without its dead singer still alive in Gretta's heart.

Hence I take it that the spell is broken. Gabriel—conceivably the boy of "The Sisters" grown older—devotes himself to teaching and reviewing; if we recall Yeats's essay again, to something very like the criticism and comment that stand in lieu of imaginative creation. Yet one sees him as at least morally reborn by an act of imagination that gets him outside himself in his sympathy for Michael Furey. In doing so, Gabriel completes Father Flynn's prospective trip to Irishtown, that despised, run-down, non-English part of Dublin. And Gabriel's quest is charitable, the Word has not been lost after all. The scrupulous Father Flynn, ruinous as he may have become, shines through Gabriel's selfless feelings for a boy from Oughterard. No matter what Fate has in store for him, Gabriel may have snapped the thread with his concern, much like Father Flynn's concern for the sins of this world also and variously expressed by the Poor Clares of Nun's Island, the Trappists of Mount Melleray, the Knights of St John who first settled Usher's Island, and St Catherine herself from whom Father Flynn had been so long separated.

NOTES: CHAPTER 1

1 Hugh Kenner, *Dublin's Joyce* (Bloomington, Ind.: University of Indiana Press, 1956), pp. 50–3; Marvin Magalaner and Richard Kain, *Joyce: The Man, the Work, the Reputation* (New York: New York University Press, 1956), pp. 71–5; Marvin Magalaner, *Time of Apprenticeship: The Fiction of Young James Joyce* (London/New York/Toronto: Abelard-Schuman, 1959), pp. 72–86; and William York Tindall, *A Reader's Guide to James Joyce* (New York: Noonday Press, 1959), pp. 13–17.

2 See, for instance, Edward Brandabur, "'The Sisters,'" in *Dubliners: Text, Criticism, and Notes*, ed. Robert Scholes and A. Walton Litz (New York: Viking Press, 1969), pp. 333–43; Fritz Senn, "'He was too scrupulous always.' Joyce's 'The Sisters,'" *James Joyce Quarterly*, vol. 2, no. 1 (Winter 1965), pp. 66–71; Peter Spielberg, "'The Sisters': No Christ at Bethany," *James Joyce Quarterly*, vol. 3, no. 2 (Spring 1966), pp. 192–5; David R. Fabian, "Joyce's 'The Sisters': gnomon, gnomic, gnome," *Studies in Short Fiction*, vol. 5, no. 2 (Winter 1968), pp. 187–9; William Bysshe Stein, "Joyce's 'The Sisters,'" *Explicator*, vol. 20, no. 7 (March 1962), item 61; Michael West, "Old Cotter and the enigma of Joyce's 'The Sisters,'" *Modern Philology*, vol. 67, no. 4 (May 1970), pp. 370–2.

3   Thomas Connolly, "Joyce's 'The Sisters': a pennyworth of snuff," *College English*, vol. 27, no. 3 (December 1965), pp. 189–95.
4   One must also praise W. F. Gleeson, Jr, "Joyce's 'The Sisters,'" *Explicator*, vol. 22, no. 4 (December 1963), item 30, for ridding Father Flynn of the agnosticism, apostasy, and simony foisted on him by his non-Irish critics.
5   Connolly, op. cit., p. 195.
6   Bernard Benstock, "'The Sisters' and the critics," *James Joyce Quarterly*, vol. 4, no. 4 (Fall 1966), pp. 32–5.
7   Florence L. Walzl, "Joyce's 'The Sisters': a development," *James Joyce Quarterly*, vol. 10, no. 3 (Summer 1973), pp. 375–421.
8   Florence L. Walzl and Burton A. Waisbren, "Paresis and the priest: James Joyce's symbolic use of syphilis in 'The Sisters,' " *Annals of Internal Medicine*, vol. 80, no. 6 (June 1974), pp. 758–62.
9   ibid., p. 761.
10 *The Complete Dublin Diary of Stanislaus Joyce*, ed. George H. Healey (Ithaca, NY/London: Cornell University Press, 1971), p. 51.
11 At least three commentators have discovered that 1 July is the Feast of the Most Precious Blood of Our Lord Jesus Christ. See Florence L. Walzl, "A date in Joyce's 'The Sisters,'" *Texas Studies in Literature and Language*, vol. 4, no. 2 (Summer 1962), pp. 183–7; William Bysshe Stein, "Joyce's 'The Sisters,'" *Explicator*, vol. 21, no. 1 (September 1962), item 2; and Michael S. Reynolds, "The Feast of the Most Precious Blood and Joyce's 'The Sisters,'" *Studies in Short Fiction*, vol. 6, no. 3 (Spring 1969), p. 336. Stein also notes that 1 July commemorates the battle of the Boyne, but he forgets that James II was also the loser there.
12 Fr N. Donnelly, *A Short History of Some Dublin Parishes* (Dublin: Catholic Truth Society, [1913]), vol. 2, p. 202.
13 ibid. Also information from the Rev. L. O'Donoghue of St Catherine's.
14 T. D. Sullivan, *A Guide to Dublin* (Dublin: A. M. Sullivan, n.d.), p. 55.
15 John T. Gilbert, *Calendar of Ancient Records of Dublin* (Dublin: Joseph Dollard, 1889), pp. 280–1. See also J. P. Mahaffy, "Irishtown, near Dublin," *Hermathena*, vol. 14 (1906–7), pp. 165–7, and "Irish local legends," *Irish Builder*, vol. 38, no. 872 (15 April 1896), p. 79.
16 W. B. Yeats, "The Body of the Father Christian Rosencrux," *Essays and Introductions* (London: Macmillan, 1961), pp. 196–7.
17 *Uncollected Prose by W. B. Yeats*, ed. John P. Frayne, vol. 1 (London: Macmillan, 1970), p. 377.
18 William York Tindall, "James Joyce and the hermetic tradition,"

Journal of the History of Ideas, vol. 15, no. 1 (January 1954), pp. 23–39, demonstrates Joyce's knowledge as a young man of *The Tables of the Law* and *The Adoration of the Magi* by Rosicrucian Yeats. Tindall also notes that Joyce had signed and dated his own copy of Walter Marsham Adam's *The House of Hidden Places: A Clue to the Creed of Early Egypt from Egyptian Sources*. As his review of J. Lewis McIntyre's *Giordano Bruno* in October 1903 suggests, Joyce may have also acquired a good deal of his hermetic knowledge from that neglected heretic. See also "The Bruno Philosophy," *The Critical Writings of James Joyce*, ed. Ellsworth Mason and Richard Ellmann (London: Faber, 1959), pp. 132–4. Equally relevant is Frances M. Boldereff, *Hermes to His Son Thoth: Being Joyce's Use of Giordano Bruno in Finnegans Wake* (Woodward, Pa.: Classic Non-Fiction Library, 1968), passim.

19 Arthur Edward Waite, *The Real History of the Rosicrucians* (London: George Redway, 1887), pp. 201, 204.
20 "Catalina," *Critical Writings of James Joyce*, p. 101.
21 Waite, op. cit., p. 206.
22 Arthur Edward Waite, *The Holy Grail: Its Legends and Symbolism* (London: William Rider, 1933), p. 182. See also Hargrave Jennings, *The Rosicrucians, Their Rites and Mysteries*, 3rd edn (London: John C. Nimmo, 1887), vol. 1, pp. 225–9.
23 "Rosicrucians," *The Catholic Encyclopaedia* (London, 1912), vol. 13, p. 193.
24 Arthur Edward Waite, *The Brotherhood of the Rosy Cross* (London: William Rider, 1924), p. 444.
25 Arthur Edward Waite, *Lives of the Alchemistical Philosophers* (London: George Redway, 1888), p. 12. See also Leonard Albert, "Ulysses, cannibals and Freemasons," *AD*, vol. 2 (Fall 1951), pp. 265–83.
26 W. B. Yeats, "Rosa Alchemica," *Mythologies* (London: Macmillan, 1959), p. 267.
27 *The Thirteen Books of Euclid's Elements*, translated from the text of Heiberg with introduction and commentary by T. L. Heath (Cambridge: Cambridge University Press, 1908), Vol. 1, pp. 370–1.
28 *The Laws and Constitutions of the Grand Lodge of Free and Accepted Masons of Ireland* (Dublin: S. Underwood, 1898), p. 141, and Arthur Edward Waite, *A New Encyclopaedia of Freemasonry* (London: William Rider, 1921), Vol. I, pp. xxiii, 366–7.
29 Waite, *The Real History of the Rosicrucians*, p. 416.
30 E. M. Butler, *The Myth of the Magus* (Cambridge: Cambridge University Press, 1948), p. 75.
31 Julian B. Kaye, "Simony, the three Simons, and the Joycean

myth," *A James Joyce Miscellany*, ed. Marvin Magalaner (New York: James Joyce Society, 1957), Vol. 1, pp. 20–36, though accusing Father Flynn of outright simony, nevertheless notes the Simon Daedalus–Simon Magus identification in the *Portrait* but concludes that the elder Daedalus is really the Icarus whom Stephen must not follow.

32 John V. Kelleher, "Irish history and mythology in James Joyce's 'The Dead,'" *Review of Politics*, vol. 27, no. 3 (July 1965), pp. 414–33.

2

"An Encounter":
Joyce's History of Irish Failure
in Roman, Saxon,
and Scandinavian Dublin

In a speculative essay on "An Encounter," Fritz Senn includes mention that Cromwell is linked to the boys' advance into Ringsend as were also more generally the Vikings. Senn then goes on to summarize: "In their own struggle for independence, largely abortive, the two boys are, on a very small scale, imitating history, and especially a great deal of Irish history."[1] At another point, without revealing precisely why, he states that the so-called pervert of the final encounter "is a spectre of what the boy himself may one day become."[2] Like many of the worthwhile generalizations in Senn's disjointed essay, these are surrounded by a good many dubious assertions. For instance, John Pidgeon, who gave his name to the Pigeon House, is branded a member of the paralyzed establishment oppressive to the boys; the Vitriol Works are somehow indicative of the vitriolic nature of the story; the unruly Dodder suits a day of miching and misrule among the boys; and so forth. For all its value, then, Senn's essay is a clutter of general, tentative insights and a host of hit-or-miss associative conjectures. Superior in its way to most other comments on the story,[3] Senn's piece at best needs refining. His general perspective of Roman, English, and Scandinavian encounters with the native Irish over the centuries demands elaboration if the story is to be something more than a pursuit of adventure culminating in endless wandering and terminal flight. For instance, the man with the bottle-green eyes concludes the story yet is also in it from the first. The boy's final escape, by something like silence and cunning, will have exile added to it someday. The narrator might well become something like the reader of Tom Moore, Sir Walter Scott, and Lord Lytton, but he is escaping much more than a possible future self at the end. The overwhelming hints of betrayal, censorship and punishment early in the story all come to a head in what, as usual, appears to be the anticlimactic thoughts of the boy penitently awaiting the once despised Mahony. And therein, as I shall try to prove, lies the final illumination of the story.

I

Ireland enthralled by Rome is one of Stephen Dedalus' more snide rejoinders to Haines in the opening pages of *Ulysses*—yet it also applies to the boy's first encounters with the Dillon brothers. Not only the Roman tyranny but also its future Irish priest, Joe Dillon, master with his brother of sham battles, dominate the first page of this story. As Joyce once pin-pointed the issue in his essay "Ireland, Island of Saints and Sages": ". . . I confess I do not see what good it does to fulminate against the English tyranny while the Roman tyranny occupies the palace of the soul."[4] The ferocity of Joe Dillon and the betrayal inherent in the later actions of his brother Leo nevertheless derive quite normally from parents strict in their daily religious observances in the Jesuit chapel of St Francis Xavier, the adventurer turned priest, in Upper Gardiner Street. Why, then, should not the fierce Indian, Joe Dillon, like St Francis Xavier himself, become a priest, a future pacifying influence among once pugnacious yet sometimes reluctant Indians? Why should not a warrior and priest become a leader? Did not the chapel of St Francis Xavier have its first stone laid in the year of Catholic Emancipation?

This chain of faint connections relating Rome to Irish soil also includes English links. Joe Dillon, for instance, had got his ideas of the Wild West from his library of English boys' weeklies, back numbers of *Pluck*, the *Union Jack* and the *Halfpenny Marvel*, the last boasting in 1895 that "This journal was founded to counteract the pernicious influence of the Penny

Dreadfuls." Already, then, Joyce brings together the bizarre train of Wild West, Rome, England, and Ireland in the boy's first encounter. The time of the story might suggest, however, something more than boys' games in this train of oppressive associations.

The Wild West, after all, is also a name for the West of Ireland. The name Dillon might also point to another denizen of that Wild West, John Dillon MP for East Mayo (1885–1918), who declared against his leader—or chief—Parnell in August 1891.[5] Moreover, Leo himself cannot help but suggest the Pope of the time, Leo XIII, opponent of Home Rule in Ireland, an ecclesiastic strenuously set against social reform in Europe, a staunch supporter of English government in Ireland, and later honored in 1903 by a visit from another idler, the dubiously pious Edward VII.[6] Most readers will also recognize the irony in Father Butler's condemnation of *The Apache Chief*, especially when discovered in Leo's copy of the *Halfpenny Marvel*, though how four pages of Roman history might be any less bloody than the pitched battles of the American West remains unstated. Even the name Butler is not without its significance, a name appropriated from what was a most distinguished family among the earliest English conquerors of Ireland, those who bore arms in the Ormond title. The Anglo-Norman Ormonds, stemming from Theobald Walter Butler, were second only to the FitzGeralds in renown. Moreover, the Butler boast was that they had never become hibernicized. Their most distinguished representative, James Butler, First Duke of Ormond, for all his loyalty to Ireland as her lord-lieutenant, saw her as first submissive to the English Crown. Father Butler, then, with his mockery of National schools, with his disdain for writers of adventure stories for Irish boys, and with his touting of Roman history, appears to be very much in the mold of his illustrious forebears of the later English Protestant persuasion.

Thus far, then, down to Leo's failure to turn up for the day's miching, Joyce has quietly shown an Irish boy restive under the feared and conservative domination of Rome, whether enduring lost battles, a tense schoolroom patterned on the English system, or the failure of a comrade to keep his promise, not to mention that spiritual restlessness common to all his friends.

II

The beginning of the boys' peregrinations is probably Clarke's Bridge on the Royal Canal. As the bridge closest to North Richmond Street, it also lies close to a thoroughfare with trams bearing "business people up a hill," which street, Summerhill, becomes Ballybough Road on the other side of the bridge.[7] The story also mentions a mall nearby, doubtless the Charleville Mall. The boys must have passed through the mall, turned left at the first lock of the canal at Newcomen's Bridge, and then walked northeast on the North Strand Road until they came in sight of the Vitriol Works on the left. John D'Alton in his *History of the County Dublin* lists it as a former flint-glass factory, recently transformed, on the city side of the Tolka. *Thom's Directory* (1895) suggests that Joyce's reference is to a manure works in Poplar Row, W. & H. M. Goulding Ltd, manure- and acid-manufacturers in a street that intersects the North Strand Road on the boys' left and then becomes the Wharf Road where they turn right. Bearing south on this road, now called the East Wall Road, they encounter the ragged children, pause at the Smoothing Iron, where they had hoped to engage in a mock siege, and finally direct themselves to the North Wall, the quays, and the Liffey.

To what end, a reader may query, all this pavement? Why these detailed observations on what must seem but the preliminary route to the Liffey before the boys cross and catch sight of their goal, the Pigeon House in Ringsend? I would answer that Joyce is merely preparing us in these encounters for the final encounter with a perverted representative of the English and Scandinavian tides that have washed over Ringsend in Irish history.

For instance, the North Strand Road, not to forget the Wharf Road, was under water as late as 1673 according to Sir Bernard de Gomme's famous map. In other words, the boys have so far propelled themselves along reclaimed land, formerly the shore that witnessed one of Ireland's greatest battles, the battle of Clontarf that had its center point at Ballybough Bridge at the Tolka and was contested bloodily most of Good Friday, 1014, until the tides floated away the ships that were the last hope of the Scandinavians.[8] Yet, all too typically, it was a Pyrrhic victory for the Irish, since Brian Boru and two of his sons were killed in the course of the battle. No less a losing encounter was the cancellation of O'Connell's proposed monster meeting on 8 October 1843 in Clontarf. On the other hand, the boys' contention with the ragged children has in it the lowest level of the continuous religious contention in Ireland, prolonged to this day, and even fostered inadvertently at the time by the so-called ragged schools, Protestant and Catholic.[9] Once again, then, I would underline the consistent reminders of Irish failure on the site of each of these boyish encounters.

But British oppression and Irish national failings always seem to go hand in hand, and the North Strand Road ought to be testimony enough for the doubting. That road also borders an old duelling-ground,[10] a particularly notorious Irish enthusiasm from past years. Most of the bridges the boys cross, like the Newcomen on the Royal Canal or the Annesley on the Tolka, celebrate the names of the British conqueror. The first commemorates a director of the Canal company when the canal was opened in 1791, and the second recalls Lord Annesley, Viscount Glerawley, husband to the sister of the all-powerful John Beresford, the Commissioner of Revenue who virtually created the northeast Dublin that Joyce knew.[11] Moreover, of necessity the boys must have crossed Upper Sheriff Street on their way to the North Wall and thus skirted the locale of the former prison where Ireland's friends the French were held captive from the time of the French Revolution to the defeat of Napoleon.[12] No less, when the boys make a right turn at the Vitriol Works, they tread a ground long known for its grisly encounters yet also a ground early established by three brothers dispossessed during the Plantation of Ulster. Running west of the road, from Nottingham Street to Newcomen Bridge, and extending to Ballybough Road, Mud Island, as it was called, was for two hundred years, down to the mid-nineteenth century, the haunt of robbers, smugglers, and rogues under the rule of a leader virtually immune from the law, the King of Mud Island. Dead bodies, usually those of appendages of the law, frequently turned up in its backstreets. Unless accompanied by a powerful military force, constables or bailiffs usually avoided the place.[13] The same background of religious oppression stands behind the flint-glass factory that had preceded the Vitriol Works, for it was established after the Treaty of Limerick by an Irish Catholic gentleman, Captain Philip Roche, kept from government service by his religion and thus forced into commerce where he succeeded well enough.[14] I could also add that in this Clontarf area alone legends still remain of the marauding Knights of St John, the disappointed heroics of Silken Thomas FitzGerald, and the raid, disastrous to the Irish, in 1641 by Sir Charles Coote.[15] From every side, before they even cross the Liffey, tragic embroilment stares at the boys.

III

An interlude in the story appears to follow, for the boys do little more than gape at the commercial bustle along the streets near the Liffey. By noon they have stopped in their journey to eat along the quays, and they even speak of running away to sea. Then they take the ferry from the North Wall Quay and cross the river. Exactly why Joyce transports the boys "in the company of two labourers and a little Jew with a bag" remains an enigma to me. Perhaps we are meant to heed the further exploitation of Ireland by the stranger as we contemplate a juxtaposition of pedlar and worker, Jew and Irishman on the Liffey water, since the Liffey Ferry Service, still in use, dates from a charter granted by Charles II in 1665.[16] When the boys alight on the south side of the Liffey, probably at Sir John Rogerson's Quay, they watch for a time a Norwegian three-master discharging lumber. Here Joyce makes two observations that ought to alert us to the importance of this apparently trivial scene. First, the narrator can't distinguish the "legend" on the ship and, second, he looks for a sailor with green eyes—exactly why we are never told, but the hint is that green betokens adventure and presumably escape. The only man with green eyes, however, is a sailor who amuses the crowd by uttering "All right! All right!" when the planks of lumber hit the ground. But for the alert reader the word "legend" will soon take on a different meaning derived from the Scandinavian occupation of Ireland. As for the repeated "All right! All right!" we may be persuaded to recall other triumphant voices from other ages, voices of the conqueror obtruding himself on the Irish coast, denuding Ireland of her trees, or opening an alien parliament or lawcourt.

This seeming digression from the boys' itinerary, for all its mystery, nevertheless strikes me as relevant. The encounter with a green-eyed man later on has now been prepared for, especially for one who is devoted to the literature of adventure and escape in his own peculiar way. As I shall also argue, we will discover him in a most mysterious historic setting.

IV

As the boys enter Ringsend in hopes of reaching the Pigeon House, they encroach upon one of Dublin's oldest and most highly traveled grounds.[17] For all of the phallic and Christian symbolism bestowed on the Pigeon House by American critics, the place is a most logical destination for the boys, for it was in 1895 still a fort for an artillery detachment, full of soldiers, cannon, military stores, and an armory on a tip of land stretching into a bay once full of packet ships, historic comings and goings, and many a sea adventure, battle, military landing, or native departure. In a letter to Stanislaus, Joyce relates how his solicitor Lidwell urged him to "write another story about Ringsend" if "An Encounter" remained unacceptable to Roberts, and Joyce completed the sentence with the phrase "which has many historical associations". [18] Let us contemplate them.

Before it was sold in 1897 to the Dublin Corporation for £65,000, before its beginning in 1813, and before the construction fo the Pigeon House harbor and hotel in 1790, the fort had been a watch-house at the end of the pilings forming the South Wall. The caretaker and watchman was a man named Pidgeon who slowly turned the rude structure into a resort for the quality during the second half of the eighteenth century. Ringsend itself, however, from which the South Wall, the Pigeon House fort and, by the time of the story, the Poolbeg lighthouse projected, had long ago become the entrance and exit for Ireland's conquerors. Thus, the boys could not have picked a likelier spot for encounters that brought frustration or defeat for Ireland and triumph for England. For example, here landed the Parliament army in November 1646. In August 1649, Oliver Cromwell himself landed with an army of 12,000 men and considerable artillery and munitions. Already Parliament soldiers had been quartered at Ringsend preparatory for the battle of Rathmines. Henry Cromwell landed at Ringsend in 1655 to assume the governorship of Ireland, as did Lord Berkeley the Viceroy in 1670. No less, in 1689 adherents to James II's cause arrived in Ringsend, while James himself on Good Friday 1690 gazed from Ringsend's shore at the daring foray against one of his frigates by Sir Cloudesley Shovel. For the other side, General de Ginkel took his departure from conquered Ireland in 1691 at Ringsend. In the eighteenth century lords-lieutenant continued to disembark here. When the Pigeon House was used as a temporary depot and barracks in the rebellion of 1798, Wolfe Tone, who lived in nearby Irishtown just before it, had hoped to gain access to the enormous store of arms for the United Irishmen. That was also a frustrated plan of Robert Emmet's and, after him, of Thomas Henry Hassett in 1864 for the Irish Republic Brotherhood. All to no avail.

Thus the military heyday of Ringsend and its port, even before the Pigeon House became a fort in 1813 and in many cases before its first rude construction shortly after 1735. Despite the melancholy decline of Ringsend in their own century, the boys clearly have headed, almost instinctively, toward the gateway to many a disappointing Irish encounter.

V

Yet they make one more move—to a field described as having "a sloping bank, over the ridge of which we could see the Dodder." There they experience their last encounter, the most serious and the most ancient. At this point, we might hark again to Stanislaus' brief but pregnant note on the story:

> . . . "An Encounter" is based on an actual incident that occurred to my brother and me when we planned and carried out a day's miching together. He was about twelve

and I was about ten years of age at the time, and we did not understand what kind of individual we had encountered, but our suspicions were aroused. We thought he was a "queer juggins"—some kind of escaped lunatic— and we gave him the slip. *Later my brother put him into the book as a by-product of English educational methods.* (My italics)[19]

This "captain of fifty," as Stanislaus also once called him— he of the good accent and English education—approaches the boys in the story, all the while chewing "one of those green stems on which girls tell fortunes," that is, predict their future husbands with such singsong as

> Tinker, tailor,
> Soldier, sailor,
> Rich man, poor man,
> Farmer's son, etc.

while they remove the leaves from the stem. Then, of course, the man reverts to his own schooldays and his reading of Moore's poems and the literature of Sir Walter Scott and Lord Lytton. As many critics have noted, Joyce offers the real hint from the start that the narrator may be encountering his own likely fate in the sinister, romantic reading and behavior of him whom Mahony later calls "a queer old josser," perhaps meaning an old roué.[20] After all, Lord Lytton, against whom the stranger most warns the boys, had had an affair with Lady Caroline Lamb, separated from his Irish wife Rosina, and could write such stuff as *The Roué; or, The Hazards of Women*, a story treating the adulterer Sir Robert Leslie.[21] For a boy preferring American detective stories, where reigned "fierce and beautiful girls," to the usual Wild West urbanities, his future identity might almost be assured. Meanwhile, this grizzled romantic passes deliberately from talk of school and books to girls, especially their hands and hair in what approaches a neurotic religious ritual. After taking himself off to a corner of the field to masturbate, he returns to speak again, this time of punishing and whipping boys, most severely boys with girlfriends. As he continues his virtually uninterrupted monologue, Mahony himself leaves to chase a cat and then to wander "aimlessly" at another end of the field. Meanwhile, the narrator remains silent before the man's speech that turns ever more circular, insistent, and monotonously mysterious. At last the boy says goodby, fearfully takes his way up the slope, calls out to Mahony as "Murphy," and is himself recognized by his friend running toward him.

As Senn and others have affirmed, on an obvious level Joyce presents us with a recrudescence of the sinister puritanism recalling Cromwell and his sadistic cruelties in Ireland—the Curse of Cromwell has been with us since. The jerry hat with the pronounced crown, the cane like a pilgrim's staff, and the religious intonation and ritualistic recital betray a decayed puritanism that gloats over forbidden pleasures, condemns sex as evil yet resorts to masturbation, and fantasizes on the sadistic reprisals due those who would act otherwise. The puritanical code of the Roman Catholic church in Ireland was almost a byword at the time. Moreover, the imploring, beseeching look the pervert directs to the boy may also remind us of other English conquerors—lord mayors, viceroys, generals, and prelates who landed at Ringsend—in their loving hope of sternly persuading Irish life to another course than its own. Father Butler and Joe Dillon, priest and priest-to-be, cause no less terror by their persuasions at the beginning of the story. Yet such a figure may also render for the boy a judgment and encounter from history even more arresting, ancient, and implacable.

For, if we pay heed to the boy's surroundings, we discover ourselves very close to the confluence of the Liffey and the Dodder, in early times more a delta than a direct link, the site of the Steyne on the land southward from the Liffey to the Forty Acres.[22] The Steyne derives from the ancient Scandinavian pillar or stone formerly standing in that area, "a flat piece of ground extending southwards from the strand of the Liffey to 'the lands of Rath,' and eastward, from near the city walls, to the river Dodder".[23] Relevantly enough, this land early came into the hands of the Butler family after the Norman invasion. Charles Haliday in his *The Scandinavian Kingdom of Dublin*, a favorite book of Joyce's, describes this ancient point for Viking incursions and their purpose in choosing it:

. . . the point of land here referred to may be described as an elevated ridge near the confluence of the Liffey and the Dodder, forming what the Scandinavians termed a "Noes", or "neck of land between two streams," and was the place where the Dublin Northmen generally landed.[24]

On the next page, Haliday explains:

. . . the Northmen had a peculiar object in selecting their landing place. Their ships were long and shallow, lightly built, and for the greater part without decks. These they ran ashore, when about to land, and in winter drew them up the beach, there to remain until summer enabled them "to keep the sea." The bank of a river, a flat sandy strand, such as the north side of Stein presented, was, consequently, best adapted for their purposes, and at all times was preferred to a deep-water anchorage.[25]

Haliday includes a map of this area made from the Down Survey of 1654 showing the stone itself between "Lowsy Hill" and "The Colledge" along with the increasingly lateral span of the Liffey as it widened into Dublin Bay and the Dodder at Ringsend.

Equally notable for our story seems to be the Norse custom of setting up a Thing—an assembly of the people to elect a king, make laws, try a criminal or effect a legal judgment—at a Thingmount or, as it became known, and Joyce so denominated it in the *Portrait*, a Thingmote. Here a hereditary magistrate, a *godi*, usually presided, a combination of priest and chief, Christ and Caesar, in one authority. These Thingmotes, places of law and judgment, were of necessity close to the shores of rivers or seashores, often set off by a circle of stones on a slope. The Thingmote of Dublin, as Haliday tells us—and I've been summarizing his account—"was at the angle formed by Church-lane and Suffolk-street nearly opposite the present Church of St Andrew . . . It was here this remarkable mount the Thingmote of Dublin stood until the year 1685."[26] A gallows hill and a temple where blood sacrifices were made usually adjoined a thingmote. One may speculate on the relevance of the slums of Ringsend and of the Pigeon House itself as dim analogies, especially since both hanging-place and house of worship were easily transformed to suit the exigencies of Christian civilization. But Haliday's further account best pinpoints what I take to be the ancient power of popular judgment confronting the silent boy in the all-but-empty field overlooking the Dodder:

> It is scarcely necessary to state that every act of the Northmen from the election of a king and the promulgation of a law to the trial of a criminal, or the decision of a title to land, was governed by the judgment of the people assembled at a Thing. Hence we read in the Sagas of Court Things, House Things . . . At Things, assembled on an emergency, the chieftain then present presided, but at the permanent court a "godi," or hereditary magistrate sat. The form of the court also varied with circumstances.
>
> On sudden emergencies an open space was fenced by stakes round which the verbond, a sacred chord, was tied. Sometimes the fence was a circle of stones, the centre being reserved for those who were to be the "Lagmenn," and who alone were permitted to enter. But all permanent settlements appear to have had fixed places of judicature, raised on plains like the Stein accessible by water . . . On such plains a mount of earth was sometimes raised whereon the godi sat with his "lagmen," the armed "bonders," and freemen standing around. Not far from this mound was another hill used as a place of execution . . . when these Things were used for criminal trials . . . In the Shetland Islands, on a tongue of land at Loch Tingwell, is the "Law Ting" from which it is stated that according to the "custom of the Northmen it was allowed to the condemned criminal to endeavour to make his escape to the kirk of Tingwall; in attempting this his way led through the crowd of spectators, and if he effected his escape, either by their favouring him or by superior swiftness or strength, and reached the kirk he was freed from punishment, this was a kind of appeal to the people from the sentence of the judge."[27]

Thus, going beyond the obvious puritanical threat of a Cromwell *redux*, alive ever since the mid-seventeenth century in Catholic Dublin, I speculate that Joyce offers us just as powerfully the fruits of one of the earliest Irish encounters, the intimidation of Viking priest and governor combined, in the adolescent trial of a boy and his precipitous retreat into silence and cunning preparatory to his fearful escape. The earlier mention of Norwegian three-master, the indecipherable legend, the alignment of green eyes with adventure and running away from school and home, and the first green-eyed crowd-pleaser have prepared us for this last and earliest circle of judgment and execution.

VI

Why, then, the ending? In maintaining that Roman, Saxon, and Scandinavian tyranny combine in the military gentleman, I have not forgotten the boy's own predilections for "unkempt fierce and beautiful American girls," romantic literature, and social superiority—doubtless his accent is also good and he could pass muster for an English-educated Smith, also an English name. To this extent he does indeed encounter what may be a more determined edition of his fate in Ireland. Man and boy, both are a different sort from Mahony—even the stranger notes the difference between the boys. Yet the narrator's last encounter is with Mahony, also part of himself. For Mahony had come at his call, in this case at the behest of a truant boy—in one pair of green eyes an escaping criminal in collusion with another Irish boy on the run from authority. The boy is then rightly penitent for despising a mere Irish with whom, after all, he is one. While every previous encounter has provided hints of defeat, loss, exile, or death, in this final one the boy has at least found another Irishman responsive to himself. While no Leopold Bloom, Mahony, who used slang freely, didn't funk it. Murphy has seemed to serve the boy better than Smith.

Yet I may well be too sanguine. Mahony's dark complexion, his catapult, his chasing a cat, his being mistaken for a Protestant because of his cricket badge, and his wandering away from the narrator during his greatest trial—all these acts leave an impression, perhaps no more, yet still an impression. After his encounter with the aged product of English education, the boy will probably no more hide behind the name of Smith. Yet his giving Mahony the name Murphy may still lend the story the final somber turn it demands. The crux, then, for me lies in the penultimate sentence: "He ran *as if* to bring me aid" (my italics). Such a return of one Irishman to another is also not without its surprises as a historical encounter, for Murphy is the anglicized version of the Gaelic surname for the father of Dermot MacMurrough,[28] the infamous king of Leinster who fled Ireland only to return with something less than aid—the Norman invaders whose heritage still surrounds the restless Irish boys and sets Ireland against herself.

NOTES: CHAPTER 2

1 Fritz Senn, "'An Encounter,'" *James Joyce's Dubliners: Critical Essays*, ed. Clive Hart (New York: Viking Press, 1969), p. 34.
2 ibid., p. 31. Earlier, Tindall had imprecisely made the same point when he spoke of the boy's "meeting himself for the first time . . . suddenly knows himself, his sin [pride], and his folly—and maybe the nature of Dublin" (*A Reader's Guide to James Joyce* (New York: Noonday Press, 1959), p. 19).
3 For example, Sidney Feshback, "Death in 'An Encounter,'" *James Joyce Quarterly*, vol. 2, no. 2 (Winter 1965), pp. 82–9, and A. M. Leatherwood, "Joyce's mythic method: structure and unity in 'An Encounter,'" *Studies in Short Fiction*, vol. 13, no. 1 (Winter 1976), pp. 71–8.
4 *The Critical Writings of James Joyce*, ed. Ellsworth Mason and Richard Ellmann (London: Faber, 1959), p. 173.
5 F. S. L. Lyons, *John Dillon* (Chicago, Ill.: University of Chicago Press, 1968), p. 142.
6 See, for instance, "The Pope and Ireland," *Irish Times*, 25 January 1889, p. 5, and "The Vatican and Ireland," *Freeman's Journal*, 6 February 1889, p. 4.
7 D. A. Chart, *The Story of Dublin* (London: Dent, 1907), p. 326.
8 ibid. See also Weston St John Joyce, *The Neighbourhood of Dublin* (Dublin: H. M. Gill, 1939), p. 246, and M. J. Tutty, "Clontarf," *Dublin Historical Record*, vol. 21, no. 1 (March–May 1966), pp. 2–13.
9 *Thom's Directory* (1895), p. 1311.
10 Chart, op. cit., p. 327.
11 Dillon Cosgrave, *North Dublin—City and Environs* (Dublin: Catholic

Truth Society of Ireland, 1909), pp. 90–1.

12   ibid., p. 100, n. 1.

13   St John Joyce, op. cit., pp. 244–6. See also "Memorials of Mud Island," *Irish Builder*, vol. 12, no. 254 (15 July 1870), pp. 163–4.

14   St John Joyce, op. cit., p. 246.

15   John D'Alton, *The History of the County of Dublin* (Dublin: Hodges & Smith, 1838), pp. 82, 85–8.

16   Photograph and caption, *Irish Times*, 7 February 1976, p. 1. See also E. MacDowell Cosgrave and Leonard R. Strangways, *Visitors' Guide to Dublin and Neighbourhood together with Supplemental Guide to the Irish International Exhibition of 1907 Giving a Complete Dictionary of Dublin* (Dublin: Sealy, Bryers & Walker/London: Simkin, Marshall, Hamilton, Kent, n.d.), pp. 101–2. Alas, the ferry service stopped in the spring of 1984.

17   For this general survey of Ringsend and the Pigeon House, I am indebted to the following: Chart, op. cit., p. 326; F. Elrington Ball, *History of the County of Dublin*, Pt 2 (Dublin: A. Thom, 1903), pp. 33–42, and *An Historical Sketch of the Pembroke Township* (Dublin: A. Thom, 1907), pp. 39–45; D'Alton, op. cit., pp. 849–59; Weston St John Joyce, *Rambles Near Dublin* (Dublin: Evening Telegraph Office, 1890), pp. 36–7, and *Neighbourhood of Dublin*, pp. 1–18; T. E., "The Pigeon House," *Dublin Penny Journal*, vol. 2, no. 65 (28 September 1833), pp. 99–101; *Whammond's Illustrated Guide to Dublin and Wicklow* (Dublin: Robertson, 1875), pp. 90–1; Kevin P. O'Rorke, "Dublin's Mount Herbert," *Dublin Historical Record*, vol. 30, no. 2 (March 1977), pp. 71–3; B. H. Blacker, *Brief Sketches of Booterstown and Donnybrook* (Dublin: George, Herbert, 1861), pp. 21–3, 54–6, 67, 87, 94, 192, 195; "A torpedo station at the Pigeon House," *Irish Times*, 2 October 1889, p. 5; and "Dublin Corporation Electricity Works," *Irish Builder and Engineer*, 5 November 1904, pp. 730–4.

18   *Letters of James Joyce*, ed. Richard Ellmann (New York: Viking, 1966), vol. 2, p. 307.

19   Stanislaus Joyce, "The background to *Dubliners*," *Listener*, 25 March 1954, p. 526.

20   Eric Partridge, *A Dictionary of Slang and Unconventional English* (London: Routledge & Kegan Paul, 1977).

21   *Brother Jonathan*, vol. 23 (29 March 1843), pp. 1–48.

22   Ball, *Pembroke Township*, pp. 9–13. See also "Irish local legends," *Irish Builder*, vol. 38, no. 872 (15 April 1896), p. 79.

23   Charles Haliday, *The Scandinavian Kingdom of Dublin*, ed. John P. Prendergast (Dublin: A. Thom, 1881), pp. 144–5.

24   ibid., p. 148.

25   ibid., p. 149. See also John Charles FitzZachery, "The Dodder; its

history, traditions, and associations," *The News and Dublin Lantern*, 11 January 1902, n.p.

26 Haliday, op. cit., pp. 162–3; cf. George A. Little, "The Thingmote," *Dublin Historical Record*, vol. 13, nos 3 and 4 (1953), pp. 66–71.

27 Haliday, op. cit., pp. 159–61.

28 Patrick Woulfe, *Irish Names and Surnames* (Dublin: H. M. Gill, 1923), pp. 394–5.

3

"Araby":
The Self-Discovery of a
Double Agent

If we leave the many, many pages of Harry Stone's essay on "Araby" to his patient corrector,[1] this story concluding the three on childhood has been sensibly approached by at least two critics who have thus made my own path to the Royal Dublin Society showgrounds in Ballsbridge much easier.[2] Stressing as they do the confused adoration in the boy's love for Mangan's sister, these commentators have also fastened on his disillusion. I may be left, then, to marshall the evidence not only for the boy's chagrin—against the background of a charity bazaar—but also to explain that "anguish and anger" as a discovery of himself and other characters in the story as double agents. For this major point I am especially indebted to the suggestions of my late colleague, Professor Glenn O'Malley. I shall try to convince the skeptical by taking a very hard look at the religious, literary, social, and historical details that cling to the growing boy. "The Sisters" touches on a blighted faith, "An Encounter" pictures frustrated hope, "Araby" points to the bafflement of charity for a boy nevertheless literary to his fingertips.

I

The easiest place to start is with the boy's favorite book among the three owned and probably read by the dead priest. In "The Sisters" we remarked the boy's sensitivity to words, especially strange ones like "paralysis"; in "An Encounter" his reading tended toward detective rather than Wild West fiction; here in 1894 he prefers a book because its pages are yellow, the literary color of the nineties that implied decadence. That favorite book, *The Memoirs of Vidocq*, was penned by a double agent. François Eugene Vidocq (1775–1857) had early fled the paternal coop and, as the introduction to his *Memoirs* admits,

> . . . after various, rapid, and unexampled events in the romance of real life, in which he was everything by turns and nothing long, he was liberated from prison, and became the principal and most active agent of police. He was made Chief of the Police de Sûreté under Messrs. Delavau and Franchet, and continued in that capacity from the year 1810 till 1827, during which period he extirpated the most formidable of those ruffians and villains to whom the excesses of the revolution and subsequent events had given full scope for the perpetuation of the most daring robberies and inequitous excesses.[3]

What more likely reading for a boy enamored of detective stories than the personal account of a police spy, sometimes called the world's first detective, who moved nimbly from the underworld to that of the literary salon and back, a total master of disguise? Perhaps just as pertinent in the context of Joyce's story, Vidocq, after removal from his post, established himself as a paper-manufacturer near Paris where he employed for the most part ex-convicts who had served their sentences. Of course his *Memoirs* speaks primarily of his criminal days and subsequent turnabout and success as a double agent in brilliant accord with the motto, "It takes a thief to catch a thief." But this reverse talent never endeared him to the police. Unhappily, the conclusion to the *Memoirs* laments that the original strain of the double agent prevailed in Vidocq's final return to the prison Sainte Pelagie for debts incurred by his passion for gambling. Now, Vidocq did manage to live on, return to the proper side of the criminal ledger, and die peacefully, though in and out of jail again. But in 1829 the matter of debtors' prison is put delicately but no less pointedly by his translator: "Vidocq . . . could not resist the fell temptation which has brought him to distress and a prison."[4] The boy in "Araby" clearly favors a book that unfolds the doubtful triumph of the flesh in the disguise of the ideal detective—and because its pages are yellow.

But the dead, enigmatic, important, and now familiar priest (three stories, three priestly readers) had two like books in his possession. One is *The Devout Communicant; or, Pious Meditations and Aspirations, for Three Days before and Three Days after Receiving the Holy Eucharist*, a tract by the Reverend Pacificus Baker. Sometimes known as Father Bernard Baker, he was the Franciscan who reputedly received the 16-year-old Edward Gibbon into the Catholic church. Though the full title of his work virtually explains its contents—meditations and aspirations for before and after taking Holy Communion[5]—the volume's relevance to the idea of the double agent obviously lies in the strong likelihood, according to the *Dictionary of National Biography*, that Father Pacificus Baker, chaplain to the Sardinian ambassador in London and later provincial of his order, received one of the church's greatest foes, Edward Gibbon, into the faith, in the Roman Catholic Chapel, Lincoln's Inn Fields, 8 June 1753.

More political yet no less ecclesiastical in its turnabout runs the main story in the second book, Sir Walter Scott's *The Abbot*. Let me pinpoint this central action. Roland Graeme, apparently an orphan, has been turned over to Lady Avenal by his fanatically Catholic grandmother and brought up as a page in the Avenal household. As a youth, he attends the unfortunate Mary Queen of Scots in order to spy on her. But his love for the Catholic Catherine Seyton, attendant to the queen, and the urgings of his grandmother turn him into a double agent. He secretly helps plan the queen's escape. His grandmother, however, also reveals that Roland is an Avenal on his father's side. Julian Avenal was his father and has left Roland the last male heir of the house. Rescued by his grandmother from the battlefield where his parents died, Roland had also befriended Father Ambrose, the abbot of the title, in fact Edward Glendinning, brother to Sir Halbert, husband to Lady Avenal. True to the theme of the double agent, Roland, upon his return to Avenal and after the abbot's departure for France, abandons his attachment to the Catholic church for the so-called reformed faith, although he ultimately married one of the older persuasion, Catherine Seyton.

These books, then, had been in the dead priest's possession, a man of whom we hear no more. Yet he is of the greatest importance to a story treating the revelation that comes to a boy at the end of a charity bazaar. The first paragraph of the story informed us of the noise when the Christian Brothers "set the boys free" at what was the O'Connell Schools.[6] The next sentence points to an uninhabited house. The third and last contrasts it with the houses containing "decent lives within them," houses that stand acknowledging those lives "with brown imperturbable faces." The boy's is one of those houses. As if by elaboration, the next paragraph is given to the priest, his reading, the garden, and his charities.

Perhaps enough has been said about the tangled garden and its "central apple tree," along with the priest's "rusty bicycle pump." Doubtless something of our fallen nature and failure of spirit may be implied, as so many have written. But the equal emphasis on waste room, musty air, useless papers, and former dead tenant glances back strongly to that empty house in the first paragraph. Moreover, the rusted bicycle pump, and then the curious if not strange reading—the pages were *curled*—might also describe a priest who no longer made calls and might have been hesitant about his calling. We have no more than slight hints. I would also counter the prevailing reading of the priest's charity as but ironic mockery. Though the details of the paragraph may point to a world unkind to the priest, his real charity shines through his selfless willing of money to institutions, and only secondarily in willing his furniture to one of his own, his sister. He has thought of his neighbor in Christ first, perhaps mistakenly but nevertheless selflessly. The love of Christ came before the love of self.[7] Such will be, supposedly, the purpose of the nondenominational charity bazaar, Araby, on behalf of the Jervis Street Hospital. To give money to an institution is something like being an instrument of God. I hazard the guess, then, that the story will show more than one empty house, more than one pious reader at odds with the world and, finally, more than one believer who will give his money to an institution—the boy's shilling to gain entrance—but will not bring anything to someone's sister. For a double agent, if not for the charitable priest, charity might otherwise have begun at home, empty as that home might be.

II

Mysterious priest and random yet significant books are a prelude to the boy's confused adoration—that phrase commentators have seized upon so readily. Such adoration is apparent in the boy's calling Mangan's sister his image, ultimately his chalice. He gazes at her from railings, her name is a summons, she is part of his prayers, and so on. But dress, body, hair, and petticoat are the real sources of his confusion. I would argue, nevertheless, that his quest for a gift at Araby continues his role as a double agent, even though the East, the splendor of imagination, a sacred gift, the Grail, even an initiation into manhood are all combined in his lonely journey from Amiens Street Station on a special train to the makeshift station in Ballsbridge. Altogether fittingly, his aunt, the Atropos of the first story, has uttered a truth in her suspicions that the fete might be a Freemason affair. Indeed, the General Hall of Araby has more about it of the Masonic temple than it does of the Catholic church that all critics smell out.

Consequently, let's take a harder look at the bazaar itself and perhaps spy out more clearly the double role fixed on the boy. Most critics are also satisfied to mention the existence of the official catalogue for Araby that reposes in the National Library of Ireland, but none has gazed very steadily at the importance, size, length, and day-to-day progress of the event. A digression on such matters and how they played into Joyce's hand may be no digression at all.

The first point to make is that the Araby Bazaar began on Bank holiday, Whit Monday, and was officially opened by the Lord-Lieutenant on Tuesday, 15 May 1894. The immediate charity was in aid of Jervis Street Hospital, rebuilt for £55,000 in 1886, of which £14,000 remained to be paid. Dating from 1718 and known as the Charitable Infirmary in Cook Street, the hospital had also been aided in 1742 by the first performance of Handel's *Messiah* in Fishable Street. The hospital in Jervis Street in 1894 was sometimes called the accident hospital and catered largely to the unfortunate employed in the neighborhood of Dublin's docks and railway terminals. The charity bazaar was the third in Dublin, the first being the Masonic Bazaar in 1892 and the second the Kosmos Bazaar in 1893. Because of bad weather, Araby was continued on Monday and Tuesday, 21 and 22 May, of the next week. For months plain posters had adorned all Dublin featuring the word "Araby" in brown letters on a yellow background—the two colors of the story's first page. Most stores also had photographs or cards signaling the coming bazaar. In fact promotions extended to the entire British Isles with most railways advertising Whitsuntide excursions heading their bills with the notice "Araby in Dublin." The fete itself cost between £5,000 and £6,000; in all, over 92,000 persons attended. A special searchlight was set up on the Central Hall whose beam would connect with another from the top of the charity hospital. Inexpensive return fares for special trains—in one of which the boy rides alone on what was thought to be the last night of the event—brought an enormous number of people every half-hour over the Loop Line from Amiens Street. After the opening, all entry tickets were a shilling.[8] I ought to add that the fete narrowly missed being called Chaos, but the proposer of that name was reminded by the planners that Kosmos or Cosmos followed Chaos in natural order of events. As I have suggested all along, this third story, resolved in a charity stall, had also its real-life difficulties with those of a different notion of charity or, in the stilted words of the *Irish Times* reporter:

> . . . the only thing the committee had to contend against was an incursion towards the end of last week, of a number of people who ought to be respectable, with roulette tables, which they ran for the benefit, not of the hospital but of their own pockets. Possibly they were of opinion that charity begins at home.[9]

Next, then, perhaps I ought to cite some of these descriptions of the event that mirror the applauded, vulgar, and trite magnificence that Joyce counters with the final disappointment of the story. Thus Tuesday, 15 May, the official opening:

> The scene was one of bright bustle. It was a tonic for wearied folk, fatigued in the ordinary humdrum of life. Brilliancy of many colours, beauty of construction and form, and devices of ingenious art, and fancies dramatic, and enjoyments dainty or gay, and things novel to see,

and people curious in costumes to admire, and the paths of an Orient to pace, the illusion was sufficient and simple . . . Araby is a reality for extent and grandeur of conception.[10]

On that Tuesday, when the Lord-Lieutenant made his presence known, the reporter for Ireland's foremost Unionist paper of the day went into paroxysms of delight:

His Excellency the Lord Lieutenant of Ireland raised the curtain, figuratively speaking, yesterday afternoon in the great theatre at Ball's Bridge disclosing to the eyes of thousands of admiring spectators a scene of rich Oriental beauty and splendour that has surely never before been seen in this little corner of the Empress Victoria's broad domains. And somehow, when one thought for a moment of the plain brick building hidden away in a narrow street in a mean quarter of the city, and of the suffering sick in its quiet and almost severely bare wards, contrasting it with the animation and the vivid colouring of the thronging multitudes, the brilliant spectacle assumed yet another feature. All this wealth and art and stir we were reminded was in the cause of charity. Between the suffering at Jervis Street Hospital and the gaiety at Ball's Bridge there was an unseen yet undoubted sympathy; a direct link just as apparent as when an electric searchlight flashed from the summit of the hospital across the dark city last night, and blended with the brilliant beam which scintillated from the lofty tower in the bazaar grounds.[11]

The Lord-Lieutenant himself had stressed that the bazaar demonstrated that all lived in "an age which was devoted to annihilation of distance" and with a rather unthinking pun declared to great laughter that he pronounced Ballsbridge "an acutely congested district."[12] In something of the same vein, the reporter accented the magic carpet theme, the contrast between a Royal Dublin Society of the spring show full of cattle and barking dogs, and the present transformed scene of oriental beauty and stuffed camels:

Well, the citizens of Dublin are just as happily placed as though they possessed the magic carpet, for the one moment they may be in the city, and, hey presto! they find themselves in sunny Araby, brushing skirts with dusky sons of the desert, closely-veiled houris of the harem, and travellers from every part of the East . . .[13]

Nor is this oracle without the poetic strain. Taking on those who feared a falling-off in attendance if the rain of the early part of the week continued, he turned to lines from *Lalla Rookh*, a poem which serves as an antidote and ironically an unwitting parallel to Joyce's story:

The spectacle within the Oriental city was if possible more gorgeous than on the opening day, and those who have the success of the fete at heart need not despair and quote, as they are likely to do by reason of their Eastern surroundings, these pessimistic lines by Moore, which we venture to report—

> I knew, I knew, it could not last,
> 'Twas bright, 'twas heavenly, but 'tis past,
> Oh ever thus from childhood's hour
> I've seen my fondest hopes decay.[14]

In similar vein, on Friday the writer testifies in no less fruity a voice to the poetry of Araby:

There must be something in the name of Araby that causes the divine afflatus to descend upon those who study its manners and customs. Moore's "Lalla Rookh," with its resplendent and vivid imagery and perfect poetry, was the wonder of the age, for the Irish songster's experience of the East was confined to his reading of the Arabian Nights and Oriental literature generally. With the advent of Araby in Dublin there has been a passion for producing Arabian poetry and music, and already Herr Gmur, of Cork, and others have written songs and waltzes pertinent to the subject. Last night little Miss Ethel North, aged nine years, sang a song at the Mansion House Smoking Concert, the words of which were written by her father, Mr. W. S. North, the well-known tenor. The chorus is—

> If you want it, come to Araby.
> If you want it, come to Araby.

59

'Tis a jolly spot.
And anything you haven't got,
If you want it, come to Araby.

There is more literary merit about the verses of course.[15]

But, of course, enough. If none of these vulgar particulars lodged in Joyce's mind, I nevertheless submit that the generally trite, overblown carnival atmosphere of the charity bazaar, however worthy, is no small part of the boy's pained recognition at the story's end. Most anticlimactically, perhaps, because the attendance at Araby had been impaired by rain on the first three days, Saturday was not the last day. The bazaar was rumored to continue into the next Monday and Tuesday.[16] And it did.

III

At the realistic level, then, the boy enters the Central Hall of the Royal Dublin Society premises devoted to a charity bazaar on behalf of the Jervis Street Hospital whose motto was "Soli Deo Gloria." The evening is Saturday, 19 May, and the bazaar is still officially to end at 10:30. The clock reads ten minutes to ten. He enters the Central Hall through a turnstile, having paid a shilling—no sixpenny entrance is described in the catalogue. The interior resembles a grand oriental fair, with stalls still open. The sign in silver lamps for the Café Chantant, out on the grounds, appears on a curtain. The boy would seem to choose the premier stall, the Civic Stall, presided over by the Lady Mayoress of Dublin, assisted by a bevy of girls, most bearing obviously Irish surnames. If Joyce has a specific stall in mind—and each tended to specialties—this first-named stall in the program is described as "decorated in the Moorish style, is stocked with Clocks, Gladstone Bags, Work Tables, Work Boxes, Umbrellas, Books, Lamps, Vases, Gongs, Cigars and Cigarettes, and a variety of other articles too numerous to mention."[17] Stalls like the Eastern Temple, Algeciras (the Galway Stall), and the Arabian Nights are also possibilities. In any case, the setting is oriental, the atmosphere half-darkened, the resemblance a palace or temple, the workers weary, the crowd few, the hall quiet, the money being counted. But the drama is one of initiation.

Let me quote the description of a like initiation from Waite's *Encyclopaedia of Freemasonry*:

> The place of initiation is a Sanctuary, and to know the meaning and purpose of initiation it is necessary that the Sanctuary should be entered. But we can enter by the Gate only. There is a root sense in which this gate is always the same and the Sanctuary is the same also. In different orders of initiation they are variously adorned and vested, for the modes of symbolism are many; yet there is invariably an outward sign that the Candidate is crossing a threshold, and that beyond this threshold he shall pass into a world of knowledge from which he is debarred otherwise . . .

> The manner of his entrance is that which is proper to a Postulant praying for gifts, humbly soliciting advantages, and to illustrate this position he may permit himself to be denuded of vested dignities attached to his place and grade in organized society.[18]

The account goes on to detail the movement past the gate into the heart of the mystery and the coming of illumination:

> The threshold is crossed by the Candidate as one who cannot walk alone, for as yet he has not eyes to see in the light of the secret knowledge. He is hoodwinked without because he is blind within. He is thus admitted unawares into the Secret Presence of the Sanctuary and therefore is restored to light . . .[19]

While many a critic has discovered elements of the grail quest in the boy's visit to Araby[20]—and I would suggest the Irish legend of the Cauldron of Dagda as equally pertinent—the actual initiation has remained a troublesome point. Yet the boy has come seeking a gift. He has entered a hall described as resembling a church after the service; up to this point he has been inwardly blind. He appears to enter the stall only to examine the wares. He must in fact walk alone and need go no further. The jars at the darkened entrance to the stall resemble

61

Eastern guards. That is enough. The growing darkness around him is really a kind of light. Gate, Central Hall, and Eastern stall have brought him to a discovery of himself. And his aunt had hoped that the bazaar wouldn't be "some Freemason affair."

IV

How does he discover himself—that is the natural question. Perhaps a key sentence is the one following "At the door of the stall a young lady was talking and laughing with two young gentlemen." It reads: "I remarked their English accents and listened vaguely to their conversation." I take it that "their" in both cases refers to the "two young gentlemen," for the make-up of the bazaar, as I have shown, was overwhelmingly Irish, while the possibility of two English visitors at the end of Whit week for the last night of Araby was most likely. In other words, an Irish girl (called a "young lady" four times), probably Catholic if she merely tends the stall before closing on the last night, is making up to two young Englishmen. All seem older and socially superior to the boy. The second question to be asked is what is the conversation about, the subject of the story's epiphany? It sounds like a promise, or the hint of a promise, real or imaginary, which she would or would not deny—not a lie but a fib, perhaps no more than sheet banter yet also something very much like the romantic illusion of a charity bazaar where Irish maidenhood has a chance to display its beauty under the aegis of the Lord-Lieutenant. The boy was vain to think otherwise. Not unlike the priest of the first story, his chalice has been broken. But, instead of laughing in the dark, he very nearly weeps. His anguish and his anger define his dilemma: anguish that he must return empty-handed, anger for idealizing what has turned out to be a trivial flirtation, a mockery of his own idealized lust. Like most double agents, he is caught between both sides.

Just as visible have been the patriotic hints in his devotions to a girl called Mangan's sister. Clearly his confused adoration is couched not only in the language of the liturgy but also in

something of the same language, not less ideal, that Ireland
traditionally bestows upon Dark Rosaleen and Kathleen Ni
Houlihan. Most commentators have seen some such resemblance in Mangan's sister and have pointed to James Clarence
Mangan's "Dark Rosaleen." But the even more pertinent poem
may be Mangan's "Kathleen Ny-Houlahan" which contains the
conventional insistence that the lady is in fact no hag but
instead a beautiful girl:

Think her not a ghastly hag too hideous to be seen . . .

Young she is, and fair she is, and would be crowned a queen
Were the king's son at home here with Kathleen Ny-Houlahan . . .

Sore disgrace it is to see the arbitress of thrones
Vassal to a Saxoneen of cold and sapless bones!

I suggest that the boy witnesses the reverse of this process.
The flirting Irish girl from whom he might seek a gift becomes
something ugly before his eyes and very much a vassal at
home with the Saxoneen. Moreover, Joyce's earlier mention of
Jeremiah O'Donovan Rossa, whom Pearse later called the most
typical Fenian of his generation, refers to a man who had
nothing of this female compliance about him and had suffered
exile since 1871.[21]

Like Joyce, Rossa was uncompromising, stubborn, and
resolute in his ideals. His hatred and contempt for the English
were based on what he took to be their intellectual and moral
inferiority. During his six years of penal servitude, he was
tortured, left in solitary confinement for thirty-five days, forced
to eat his food from the prison floor with his hands manacled
behind him. His reaction was to jest, sing, and laugh.[22] Such
was the man Pearse was to eulogize at the grave-site in
Glasnevin on 1 August 1915 as the representative of Gaelic
Ireland.[23] Just how representative may be seen in one of
Rossa's typical outbursts against what he took to be the
timidity of Parnell:

New York, Friday
O'Donovan Rossa was seen this afternoon by a representative to whom he expressed himself as follows:—"I am
disgusted with the child's play of O'Brien and Parnell. I
am so disgusted that I am resolved to go to Ireland and

take up the cudgels myself. I shall not preach a dynamite policy publicly, but I shall reassert the opinion which caused me to be locked up twenty years ago. To-day I wrote to Mr. Blaine, the Secretary of State, asking him for a passport, and telling him of my intention. When I arrive in Ireland if I receive a nomination for Parliament I will accept it, though I take no stock in Parliamentary agitation, but if I am elected, I will refuse to take the oath of allegiance, and when a chance offers, I will give my reasons in pure Gaelic tongue, in the House of Commons itself. I am a good Gaelic scholar, and I might say a great deal about dynamite and they would not understand me. If they should want to understand me they will have to get a good interpretation. The only possible delay in my going to Ireland would be caused by my having to make provision for my family.[24]

He was not to return alive. But the boy has come for a gift that would be no gift, seen the light that was darkness, has witnessed a flirtation that mockingly underlines the real basis of his own infatuation, and has beheld an Irish girl responsive to England and barely to him—only out of duty did she feign an interest in his presence. Yet which side is he on? The answer must be both. He has been deluded by vanity, as Rossa was not.

V

Nor is the boy different from most of the other characters in the story. Let me for a moment recall a central passage that concentrates these three realms, the religious, the patriotic, and the artistic:

> Her image accompanied me in places the most hostile to romance. On Saturday evenings when my aunt went marketing I had to go to carry some of the parcels. We walked through the flaring streets, jostled by drunken men and bargaining women, amid the curses of labourers, the shrill litanies of shop-boys, who stood on guard by the barrels of pigs' cheeks, the nasal chanting of street-singers,

who sang a *come-all-you* about O'Donovan Rossa, or a ballad about the troubles in our native land. These noises converged in a single sensation of life for me. I imagined that I bore my chalice safely through a throng of foes.

By the story's end, however, he had not. That is to say that at a place seemingly most conducive to romance, a charity bazaar called Araby, the boy has been delivered into the hands of a daughter of those flaring streets, she who would carry on with his country's traditional foes, and barely grant him the courtesy of recognition. No great effort, then, is demanded of us and the boy to see these same contradictions in an old woman with the surname Mercer, "a pawnbroker's widow, who collected used stamps for some pious purpose"; in an uncle as substitute father whose drunkenness frightens children; in a Christian Brothers school where children seem to be incarcerated; in a priest who may have stopped making calls long before he died; in a charity bazaar that dwindles into darkness and weariness, more like the hospital whose building cost it would supply; in a boy whose puberty had tricked him into what he had taken as an escape from that world; in a single sensation of life that is drunken, cursed, and bargaining, no matter what litanies, images, or chalices one may imagine there. The boy's street is blind, his own house empty, and the only truly charitable creature dead. Thus Whitsuntide in Dublin.

NOTES: CHAPTER 3

1 Harry Stone, "'Araby' and the writings of James Joyce," *Antioch Review*, vol. 25, no. 3 (Fall 1965), pp. 375–410. See the reply by Robert P. ap Roberts, "'Araby' and the palimpsest of criticism or, through a glass eye darkly," *Antioch Review*, vol. 26, no. 4 (Winter 1966–7), pp. 469–89.
2 Ben Collins, "Joyce's 'Araby' and the 'extended simile,'" *James Joyce Quarterly*, vol. 4, no. 2 (Winter 1967), pp. 84–90, sees the importance of the garden, the grail quest, and the confused adoration; Frank Turaj, "'Araby' and *Portrait*: stages of pagan conversion," *Modern Language Notes*, vol. 7, no. 3 (March 1970), pp. 209–13, also sees that adoration as confusing passion and

piety. Most to my liking is J. S. Atherton, "'Araby,'" in *James Joyce's Dubliners: Critical Essays*, ed. Clive Hart (New York: Viking Press, 1969), pp. 39–47, with his keen attention to the particulars of the story.

3 *Memoirs of Vidocq, Principal Agent of the French Police, until 1827; and Now Proprietor of the Paper Manufactory at St Mande. Written by Himself*, Vol. 1 (London: Whittaker, Treacher & Arnot, 1829), p. x.

4 ibid., Vol. 4, p. 270.

5 Rev. Pacificus Baker, *The Devout Communicant* (New York: Catholic Publication Society, n.d.). The London edition, which I haven't seen, is dated 1813.

6 Popularly known in Joyce's youth as the O'Connell Schools, the Christian Brothers School may have seemed narrow and mediocre to Joyce and his brother Stanislaus but has since retained some fame in its 150th year. That a school founded by the Liberator on 9 June 1828, St Columba's Day, should daily set boys free is not without its irony. See Dillon Cosgrave, *North Dublin: City and Environs* (Dublin: Catholic Truth Society of Ireland, 1909), pp. 60–1; "The Christian Brothers Schools, North Richmond Street," *Irish Times*, 8 January 1891, p. 5; "Christian Schools, North Richmond Street, Dublin," *Irish Builder and Engineer*, 13 February 1904, p. 74. For praise of the school, see C. P. Curran, *Under the Receding Wave* (Dublin: Gill & Macmillan, 1970), pp. 32–4.

7 J. F. Sollier, "Love, theological virtue of," *Catholic Encyclopedia* (New York: Encyclopedia Press, 1913), vol. 9, pp. 397–9. See also "A Roman Catholic clergyman's will in dispute," *Irish Times*, 26 March 1890, p. 3, for a typical case of a family's disputing such a will, and the jury's decision within five minutes against them.

8 Sheila O'Dea, "Historic Irish Hospital—2: Jervis Street, Dublin," *Irish Hospital*, vol. 1 (August 1962), pp. 19–20; *The Official Catalogue of 'Araby,' Grand Oriental Fête . . .* (Dublin: Brown & Nolan, 1894), p. 5; and "Araby. How it was organized. How it was advertised. The closing scenes," *Irish Times*, 23 May 1904, p. 6.

9 "Araby," *Irish Times*, 23 May 1894, p. 6.

10 "Araby," *Irish Times*, 16 May 1894, p. 6. For an equally insipid text and pictures of the more glamorous stalls, see "Araby," *Illustograph*, June 1894, pp. 113–16.

11 ibid.

12 ibid.

13 ibid.

14 "Araby," *Irish Times*, 17 May 1894, p. 6.

15 "Araby," *Irish Times*, 18 May 1894, p. 6.

16 "Araby," *Irish Times*, 19 May 1894, p. 7.

17 *Official Catalogue of "Araby,"* p. 17.
18 Arthur Edward Waite, *A New Encyclopaedia of Freemasonry*, with a New Introduction by Emmett McLoughlin (New York: Weathervane, 1970), Vol. 1, p. 304.
19 ibid., p. 305.
20 See John Freimarck, "'Araby': a quest for meaning," *James Joyce Quarterly*, vol. 7, no. 4 (Summer 1970), p. 366, and Jerome Mandel, "Medieval romance and the structure of 'Araby,'" *James Joyce Quarterly*, vol. 13, no. 2 (Winter 1976), pp. 234–7.
21 P. H. Pearse, "A character study," *Diarmuid O Donnabain Rosa, 1831–1915: Souvenir of Public Funeral to Glasnevin Cemetery* (Dublin: 1 August 1915), p. 5.
22 ibid., pp. 5–6.
23 *Collected Works of Padraic H. Pearse* (Dublin/Cork/Belfast: Phoenix Publishing Co., 1924), pp. 127–37. See also *Rossa's Recollections* (Mariner's Harbor, NY: O'Donovan Rossa, 1898), passim.
24 "O'Donovan Rossa and Mr Parnell," *Irish Times*, 3 January 1891, p. 5.

4

"Eveline":
Eveline and the Blessed
Margaret Mary Alacoque

Interpretations of Joyce's "Eveline" continue to appear, some sensible, some fantastic, fixing on the heroine's decision to escape her home, and on her failure to do so, as the crux of the story.[1] Yet no one, so far as I know, has been able to offer a reading that accounts for the many significant details that surround that failure. I have in mind not only the symbolically oppressive dust and weariness that overwhelm Eveline but also the story's insistence, despite its few pages, on growing nightfall; the hallowed tradition of Irish family and home; the palpitations of Eveline's heart; the shadowy figures associated with Melbourne and Italy; the signal accent on height and freedom suggested by the proper names Buenos Ayres, Melbourne, and even Eveline Hill; and finally the arresting figure of Frank, especially at his departure from the North Wall.

Most critics begin considerations of the story by showing Eveline to be linked to our original mother Eve. To be a diminutive Eve, as the name implies, often includes for them the further connotation of original sin.[2] Hence her final refusal of escape is read as Joyce's altogether proper corrective to what might have been but one more female fall. Yet the Hebrew meaning of Eve is "life" or "lively."[3] As a little Eve or potential giver-of-life, then, Eveline Hill's rejection of Frank may also be said to be ironic. For after several readings of the story might one not wish that she had indeed fallen, so to speak—fallen rather than returned to her squalid Irish lower-middle-class home? Moreover, in

Ireland, Eve or Eva has many special connotations that may underline this irony even more tragically.

As the *Oxford Dictionary of English Christian Names* points out, Eva or Eve "in Ireland and Scotland . . . was used to represent the Celtic Aoiffe [sic]."[4] This and another source further demonstrate how Eveleen and Eveline are diminutives of Eve or Eva.[5] Despite the fact that the name Eveline might have also had an independent Gaelic and Norman derivation,[6] a little Eve or Aoife may also conceivably recall the wicked stepmother in the well-known tale of the Children of Lir, a sorceress responsible for their transformation and ultimate death, or even that Aoife who tricked Cuchulain and later presented him with a son Conla to be killed by the hero in battle. Finally, if one remembers, as most Irishmen would, that Dermot MacMurrough, King of Leinster, gained Strongbow's support for an invasion of Ireland by promising him the hand of his daughter Eva—the marriage was celebrated—then powerfully national in addition to mythological tragedy may be said to lurk behind Eveline's name. In other words, Eveline's failure to leave with Frank may compel us to see her act as more than an ironic commentary on her namesake, whether we regard the original fall as sinful or fortunate. For, in dumbly turning her face against marriage and children of her own, Eveline accepts the traitorous destiny of at least three Irish women of the fabled past and, as I shall try to show, rejects the example of her who had protected the Irish home by rejecting her own.

I

I refer to the Blessed Margaret Mary Alacoque. She, though mentioned briefly, seems to me the ghostly presence that unifies the otherwise disparate details of the story. Keeping the tragic and ironic overtones of the name Eveline in mind, we might seek with renewed curiosity the possible relevance of a suffering that strangely parallels Eveline's yet a suffering that also led to sainthood and the founding of an order celebrating Christ's special love for mankind—that is, the career of the Blessed Margaret Mary, now canonized. On this score Marvin Magalaner, offering in a general footnote a few facts of her life, has let things stand with the inconclusive statement: ". . . whether Joyce intended any identification of the saint with Eveline, who also becomes paralyzed at the docks and is thus recalled to her drab, celibate life, is a matter for the reader to decide."[7] Although these specific details from the saint's life strike me as irrelevant to the story, stressing as they do a straight, unironic parallel in lives, I shall nevertheless argue that the identification of Eveline with the Blessed Margaret Mary is central. It highlights in Joyce's Dublin a misguided young woman who denies the sacredness of the heart, largely because of her devotion to the Order of the Sacred Heart that lies behind the pious pretense of Irish family life—an order founded by a seventeenth-century French maiden whose tribulations curiously and ironically matched those of Eveline Hill, right down to the story's sharply divergent conclusion.

Born in a small village in Burgundy on 22 July 1647, Margaret Alacoque seemed a predestinated child in that she early practiced austerities that rivaled even those of the saints. Young she lost a parent and had to endure persecution from relatives who treated her little better than they would a servant. At the age of 20 she refused an offer of marriage and in her 24th year entered the Visitation at Paray le Monial founded by St Francis de Sales. So far the shadowy parallels with Eveline's hardships must be evident. Notwithstanding the glories conferred on her then and later, Margaret Mary Alacoque's years in the convent were attended by misunderstandings and even hostility from the rest of the religious community. Her chores, like those of Eveline, usually consisted in dispensing household stores and attending young children. Virtually addicted to suffering, she was corrected more than once for her singular notions or for her clumsiness and slowness, these corrections echoing those offered Eveline at home by her father and at the Stores by Miss Gavan.

However, the first great revelation came to her on 27 December 1673. Just as Eveline had first seen Frank before a gate, so Margaret Mary, kneeling before the grille in front of the sacrament on the altar, suddenly felt herself to be invested by the divine spirit. And then she was clearly told that she had been chosen to be the instrument by which His love for all men was to be made known. He lamented that mankind had coldly spurned His love. These revelations continued, and on at least one occasion the Lord took her heart and placed it within His own, returning it burning to her breast. Her emulation of His suffering—and now these singular revelations—were not destined to ease her position in the convent, especially when in one of her visions she was informed that she would be a sacrificial victim for the lack of charity among her sister communicants.

But she stood not entirely alone. For during her early revelations she was befriended and helped by Father Claude de la Colombière, of whom a voice told her at their first meeting: "This is your guide." His stay as spiritual director to the Visitation convent was but little more than two years old when he was sent to Protestant England to be chaplain to the Duke and Duchess of York, later King James II and Queen Mary, where his sufferings from religious persecution were intense. Nevertheless, the celebration of the Sacred Heart spread, and the saint-to-be, already reputed to be one of the Lord's sanctified, died in a fever of divine love and ecstasy on 17 October 1690. She was beatified in 1864 and canonized in 1920.[8]

II

Joyce's story itself is divided into three parts. All parts point to the family—more exactly to its center, the heart. The first third discovers Eveline home at the window as evening descends. The waning light will turn out to be prophetic. But at the moment she reminisces over her girlhood and adolescence, largely upon old faces now dead or gone. Arrested by this panorama of change and the fact that she, too, is on the point of flight, Eveline gazes about her at the few objects, so often dusted, that identify her home and that quietly hint broken promises, family discord, and escape to a better place. The objects are named—a picture of a nameless priest who had long before emigrated to Melbourne, a broken harmonium, and a "coloured print of the promises made to Blessed Margaret Mary Alacoque." Although Joyce does not name the promises, they and the print are still easy to come by in Dublin. These promises made to the Blessed Margaret Mary, and to those who believe in her and her order, radiate clockwise from a figure of Christ standing with His arms outstretched; beneath Him is space for the signatures of father, mother, children, and presiding priest, all to be signed under the caption "Consecration of the Family to the Sacred Heart." The promises read as follows:

I   I will give them all the graces necessary for their state of life
II   I will establish peace in their families
III   I will console them in all their difficulties
IV   I will be their assured refuge in life and more especially at death
V   I will pour out abundant benedictions on all their undertakings
VI   Sinners will find in my Heart a boundless ocean of mercy
VII   Tepid souls shall become fervent
VIII   Fervent souls shall advance rapidly to great perfection
IX   I will bless the houses in which the image of my Heart shall be exposed and honoured
X   I will give to priests the power of touching the most hardened hearts
XI   Persons who propagate this devotion shall have their names inscribed in my Heart, and they shall never be effaced from It
XII   I promise that those who receive Communion on the First Friday of nine consecutive months, shall not die under my displeasure.

Beneath Christ's feet, in an arc surmounting the chalice, sword, scourge, nails, and crown of thorns, appear two verses drawn, respectively, from the gospels of St Matthew and St John: "Come to Me all you that labour, and are burthened, and I will refresh you" and "I am the way, and the truth, and the life."

Needless to say, both these verses read somewhat ironically in view of the sickly and overtired Eveline. Nor do Christ's twelve promises seem to have much more efficacy, at least not for the Hill family in its consecration to the Sacred Heart. Eveline is virtually graceless. There is little peace in the family. Her consolations come from outside. She has known little of benedictions, mercy, or assurance. In the end her fervent love will not only become tepid; it will disappear and Frank with it. Despite this colored print of the promises, her house is not blessed. Her father's heart remains hardened against her and the remaining children. No priest has intervened, though her father's threat of violence had given Eveline heart palpitations. The accent of the print, its promises, and the order itself is on the integrity of the family. So far, however, Eveline's three memorials—print, harmonium, and photograph—silently comment on the bleakness of her home. The harmony of a well-accorded household is broken. If the word "Melbourne" suggests a better place, then the unknown priest may well have been her proper guide had she but heeded his example. He might indeed be said to have dimly filled the roles of Father de Sales and Father Colombière in his faded presence and reputed emigration to Australia. But his yellowing photograph has not softened her father's heart.

Her only salvation lies in her suitor Frank. I shall even be bold enough to liken him to the Christ who revealed Himself to Margaret Mary, for Frank is immediately described as "kind, manly, and open-hearted." He also would take her to a better place, this time Buenos Ayres, literally a better atmosphere, as his spouse. She had first encountered him, as has been said, at a gate, where his face, described as "bronze," had about it the appearance of an icon or image. He had taken her to that romantic operetta *The Bohemian Girl*, where the heroine promises to fly from her home with the hero if need be, although her father finally consents to the union. No less, Frank's singing of the lass that loves a sailor recalls the happy conclusion of *HMS Pinafore*. But Eveline is bitterly aware of the Irish family and community disapproval of a runaway marriage. Her father is adamant. More to his thinking would be Eveleen and her shame in Moore's melody, "Eveleen's Bower." Of course Margaret Mary had withstood both pressures in refusing marriage at 20. And Eveline is about the same age—just "over nineteen."

The second third of the tale tightens the forces pulling on Eveline. The day's illumination is gone. She harbors second thoughts about her brutal, drunken father. He is getting old. On occasion he has been bearable, even pleasant. But, as if to continue the motif of the broken harmonium, Joyce makes her hear a street organ playing. Earlier just such a one had offered "a melancholy air of Italy," drifting in from the street, to her dying mother. Her father, however, had sent the organ-player away. Crazed from the burden of daily sacrifices, her dead mother, recalled by the renewed music, now looms as a portent for herself. Escape she must. Now the pull of Frank as deliverer is overpowering:

> Frank would save her. He would give her life, perhaps love, too. But she wanted to live. Why should she be unhappy? She had a right to happiness. Frank would take her in his arms, fold her in his arms. He would save her.

Yet her promises to her mother, also jogged in memory by the music, had been to hold their home together. Predictably, the final third of the story will fix on the passion of her heart as it adjudicates between her promises to her home and to Frank. Will it be the example of Margaret Mary or the saint's living Irish memory that will prevail?

At the North Wall the darkness is complete, yet in the blackness of the ship along the quay hope may be said to gleam from the "illumined portholes." But the outcome of the story is hinted early in this last third with its charged naming of the boat as a "black mass." For so it comes to appear to Eveline as a vessel of escape. Does she see herself as the woman on the altar? Though she prays desperately and calls upon God for direction, when Frank's entreaty appeals to her spirit she remains dumb before him. Three times he calls her, and three times she denies him with silence, her hands bound to the railing. At another railing, Blessed Margaret Mary had merged her heart with Christ's and had had it replaced in her breast afire with love. Afterwards she had remembered her heart aglow like a furnace. A bell does sound in Eveline's heart, and she feels Frank's hand in hers. Nevertheless, instead of the flames of heaven, the seas of the world seem to surround her heart: "He was drawing her into them: he would

drown her. She gripped with both hands the iron railing."
Home pulls her back. She cries out against what she takes to be
the seas of this world. In other words, she rejects the call of her
savior, establishes the rail as a barrier, and turns the possible
sacrament or union of hearts into a black mass rather than any
elevation sacred to her own name and the connotations of
Melbourne and Buenos Ayres. A heavy body sinking, not a
spirit rising and refined, is her image. Instead of divine and
fiery ecstasy she offers her lover something less than bare
humanity: "She set her white face to him, passive, like a
helpless animal. Her eyes gave him no sign of love or farewell
or recognition." She who left a home consecrated to the Sacred
Heart had for that very cause refused a similar call to her own
soul. Unblessed, unsanctified, and unseeing, her final stance is
not of spiritual radiance but of animal acceptance, human
paralysis. Thus, a heritage of blazing love, so erotic in its
inception, that swept France in the seventeenth century
through the visions of a provincial girl has dwindled to
something hardened and dead, an order denying the heart and
rendering chastity trivial in a provincial Catholic Dublin that
refuses any elevation and demands a meaningless sacrificial
victim for a religious community lacking charity. To dark night
and dust Eveline will return, a prisoner in the heartless sanctity
of the Irish home. The final and insistent cry of her crazed
mother, however foolish-sounding, had warned her—
"Derevaun Seraun! Derevaun Seraun"—a cry that means in
West of Ireland dialect: "Worms are the only end."[9]

NOTES: CHAPTER 4

1 For instance, Marvin Magalaner, *Time of Apprenticeship: The Fiction
of Young James Joyce* (London/New York/Toronto: Abelard-Schuman,
1959), p. 120, feels that "Joyce does not imply any condemnation of
Eveline for not doing as he himself had done." Even more
fantastically, Thomas Dilworth sees her as a reluctant Helen—"the
story has an important matrix in the elopement of Helen of Troy"
("The numina of Joyce's Eveline,'" *Studies in Short Fiction*, vol. 15,
no. 4 (Fall 1978), pp. 456–8). For a fine background study, see also
Albert J. Solomon, "The backgrounds of 'Eveline,'" *Eire-Ireland*,
vol. 6, no. 3 (Fall 1971), pp. 23–38.

2 For an account that stresses Eveline as compounded of "self-assertive desires" that "illustrate the furtive operation of original sin," see William Bysshe Stein, "The effects of Eden in Joyce's 'Eveline,'" *Renascence*, vol. 15, no. 3 (Spring 1963), pp. 124–6. For a confused treatment of the same theme, see Ronald Rollins and Michael Coran, "Eden as field and fortress: a note on Joyce's 'Eveline,'" *Modern British Literature*, vol. 3, no. 1 (Spring 1978), pp. 78–9.
3 *The Oxford English Dictionary of Christian Names*, compiled by E. G. Withycombe, 3rd edn (Oxford: Clarendon Press 1977), p. 112.
4 ibid.
5 ibid., and Flora Haines Longhead, *Dictionary of Given Names* (Glendale, Calif.: Arthur H. Clark, 1958), p. 180.
6 For discussions of the matter, consult Charlotte Mary Yonge, *History of Christian Names* (London: Parker, Son & Bourn, 1863), Vol. 2, pp. 39–41; Helena Swan, *Girls' Christian Names: Their History, Meaning and Association* (London: Swan Sonnenschein, 1900), pp. 196–9; and Eric Partridge, *Name This Child*, 3rd edn (London: Hamish Hamilton, 1951), pp. 112–13.
7 Magalaner, op. cit., pp. 152–3.
8 Alban Butler (ed.), *The Lives of the Saints*, rev. Herbert Thurston and Donald Attwatter (London: Burns, Oates & Washbourne, 1936), Vol. 10, pp. 236–42; Patrick O'Connell, *The Devotion to the Sacred Heart of Jesus* (Wexford: John English, 1951), pp. 1–10; and the *Irish Messenger* pamphlet *St Margaret Mary Alacoque* (Dublin: 1957), pp. 3 ff. As a reviewer of George Tickell's *The Life of Blessed Margaret Mary*, 3rd edn, wrote in the *Freeman's Journal*, 16 January 1891, p. 2: "the name and the fame of Blessed Margaret Mary are amongst the most cherished belongings of the Catholic households of the world."
9 Information from John Garvin, Galway City, 1970. Professor John V. Kelleher informs me that the explanation of the phrase was made earlier by Tomás de Bhaldraithe in a lecture at Harvard. For further on Joyce's mistake in worms and such matters, see James MacKillop, "'Beurla on it': Yeats, Joyce, and the Irish language," *Eire-Ireland*, vol. 15, no. 1 (Spring 1980), pp. 138–48.

5

"After the Race":
Our Friends the French,
the Races of Castlebar,
and Dun Laoghaire

Professor Zack Bowen, in an otherwise imperceptive essay on the political and historical backgrounds of "After the Race," sums up one point by saying:

> Young Doyle comes to understand that the last "great" game lies between Routh and Ségouin, as history repeats itself in the struggle between France and England. Jimmy, Ireland, as in the days of Tone, having been an unimportant but involved bystander in the struggle, understands that "he would lose, of course."

In a note on the story, Bowen again appears unaware that the French ever did land in Ireland in 1798.[2] Bowen's later essay, little more than an afterthought, offers that Villona the Hungarian might after all derive from Arthur Griffith's *The Resurrection of Hungary*. Here Bowen expands Villona's role as "artist-leader" to include also "the lessons of Hungarian politics."[3] But, as I shall hope to show, the story recalls more immediately a race much more famous in Ireland than the Gordon-Bennett Cup Race. At the same time I shall suggest that "After the Race" also reflects on the success of many a national revolution, not just the Hungarian, to contrast with the Irish failures so obviously represented in the Doyles, father and son. Finally, the whole matter of race itself would seem, almost cruelly, to be an abiding issue of the story. These three themes, then, history, national independence, and racial fiber, may inhere, as we have begun to see, most properly in the very title itself.

I

The immediate background, however, is the 1903 Gordon-Bennett Cup Race in which the English were placed last. Perhaps I need not sum it up—the preparations, huge crowd, and celebrations thereafter—for the Irish press gave it close and extensive coverage. Most readers are also familiar with Joyce's interview with Henri Fournier, a French racer and automobile company manager who did not compete for the Cup, that appeared in the *Irish Times* as early as 7 April 1903 and set the tone for the story. But I might add that Joyce did stick pretty close to the facts of the race. Camille Jenatzy, the German winner, was indeed a Belgian, as rumor had it, and the French were the winning team, placed second, third, and fourth after the seven rounds of the course. Thus, the Gordon-Bennett Cup went to the German Automobile Club, while the Montagu trophy went to that of France.[4] More relevant to the story, however, might be the behavior of the French team and their reception by the Irish both before and after the race.

After the race, one French driver, Henri Farman who came in third, a reporter described as "gay, bright-eyed, and unconcerned." No less debonaire were M. Gabriel and the gigantic René, the chevalier de Knyff, both buoyant and talkative, who, along with Jenatzy, "chaffed each other good naturedly."[5] Although Gabriel and Farman left Ireland before the Automobile Club of Great Britain and Ireland dinner on Saturday, the already popular chevalier de Knyff, who took second place, "was vociferously called for" and responded to Scott Montagu's toast calling France "the motherland of motoring, the country which first of all taught us to build racing cars."[6] The French arrival was no less genial. In fact, given the Irish tradition of Gallic Catholic friendship, I cannot help but compare this landing to earlier ones in 1798.

As the first French racing driver alighted from the steamship *Ferdinand de Lesseps* and touched Irish soil at the Alexandra Dock, a great cheer went up and, when the first racing cars were disembarked, three cheers rang out for "the Frenchmen." Tipping their hats and bowing, the French and their ladies flung pennies and pressed cigarettes on the ever present Irish urchins. French mechanics time and again repeated the word "Paddy." As the special correspondent for *Motoring Illustrated* wrote, "At least half a dozen of the leading French motorists were wearing green ties and caps out of compliment to the Emerald Isle—a bit of tactful blarney, which was much appreciated." All in all, a crowd of two thousand greeted the French landing.[7] To catch up with the beginning of Joyce's story—and Joyce's quiet derision throughout it—let me finally conclude this preliminary note with the words of *Vélo*, the authoritative French motoring journal, on the Irish reaction to the French landing and subsequent team victory:

> "We shall never forget the thrilling welcome of the crowd and, above all, *the extraordinary scene on our return to Dublin*, our carriages going at a walking pace through thousands and thousands of persons massed on the pavement, and hailing the champions of the new loco-motion *as if they were victorious soldiers* returning to their country after whipping the universe."[8] (My italics)

II

The story itself, however, breaks into two major events. After the French win the race, one of the French cars containing the jubilant Irishman, James Doyle, roars into view. Finally, the driver of that French car, André Ségouin, loses to an Englishman in a card game, although this time Doyle is the greatest loser. Between these events we are more or less rewarded with James Doyle's pell-mell reactions—delusive joys, fears, enthusiasms, anticipations, and a final pervading knowledge of isolation—to his new-found friends, the French.

From the beginning we have hints of the magnitude of these delusions; for the opening paragraph of the story, always so pregnant with hints of the outcome in *Dubliners*, discovers the foreign cars "careering" home to Dublin on the Naas Road to the applause of the native Irish. Still full of opening hints, Joyce sums up the direction of the cars and the story and ends the first paragraph this way:

. . . through this channel of poverty and inaction the Continent sped its wealth and industry. Now and again the clumps of people raised the cheer of the gratefully oppressed. Their sympathy, however, was for the blue cars—the cars of their friends, the French.

The final aftermath of this episode leads to Jimmy's fatal card game aboard *The Belle of Newport* in Kingstown harbor. At the very end, Villona, his supposed Hungarian friend, announces the dawn—"Daybreak, gentlemen!" Yet one more glance at the story's beginning may show this abrupt announcement already prefigured. Returning to Dublin, Jimmy and his friends, each in his own way, may well be said to be "careering," and all at Jimmy's considerable expense. His money, in turn, derives from a "careering" father, who exults in his son's social climbing. That father in turn made his start as a butcher and fervid nationalist yet, despite his wealth and success, remains but little different from those watching the French cars—"the gratefully oppressed." Moreover, the senior Doyle, we are also informed, had been lucky enough to secure police contracts and thus had modified his patriotic views. Ironically, by the story's end, his son has reverted, at least momentarily, to the "poverty and inaction" of the first paragraph. Then, why, we may ask, must the story end with daybreak proclaimed?

III

As any Irish schoolboy knows, and no American critic has recognized, to allude to what happened after a famous race won by the French is almost surely to recall to mind the Races of Castlebar and their tragic aftermath, tragic for the Irish of course, not for the French. Mr Bowen in his essay cited above senses some irony in history's repeating the failure of the French to aid the Irish in 1690 and 1798. But such general irony is not usually Joyce's way nor does it go far in illuminating the otherwise mysterious ending of the story. On the contrary, the

Races of Castlebar, with their subsequent military disaster for the French and Irish, play a baleful light on the James Doyle who must face the dawn in Kingstown harbor.

The historical account depicts General Humbert's landing with little more than a thousand men at Killala on 22 August 1798. The source most familiar to Joyce was probably Lecky's *History of Ireland in the Eighteenth Century* or perhaps Maxwell's *History of the Irish Rebellion in 1798.*[9] In any case, the events leading to the English rout at Castlebar are general knowledge in Ireland and easily summarized. After securing Killala and passing out weapons and uniforms to many an Irish peasant, occasionally more bent on plunder than on any specific campaign, the French pressed on to Ballina with at least five hundred Irish auxiliaries. On the 27th this combined force confronted a vastly superior British contingent under Generals Lake and Hutchinson at Castlebar and routed them, some of the British reeling back as far as Tuam and Athlone. Flags, muskets, cannon, uniforms, and stores festooned the line of retreat after the British literally raced from the field. Their singular defeat has never been forgotten in Ireland and has lived on gloriously in the ironic title of the Races of Castlebar. But the immediate elation and victory were shortlived, for the French and Irish force was crushed by Lake and Cornwallis in a brisk fight on 8 September at Ballinamuck. The French prisoners, officers and men, were well treated. The officers themselves were regaled with a banquet in Longford, and then, all prisoners having been conveyed to Dublin by canal barge, were greeted by thousands of citizens, plied with Irish hospitality during their twenty-four-hour stay in the capital, and departed the Pigeon House with the strains of the "Marseillaise" in their ears.[10] The Irish were massacred on the spot, and their officers executed. Some like Captains Byrne and Teeling, aides-de-camp to Humbert, were torn from their French comrades and, despite the General's strenuous efforts, hanged.[11]

Beyond these cursory parallels to the story, odd yet strangely relevant bits of the campaign may well have found their way into Joyce's story. For instance, remembering Ségouin's toast to Humanity, we may also recall the French revolutionary slogans Humbert proclaimed upon landing at Killala, especially the proclamation beginning "Liberty, Equality, Fraternity." Humbert himself has not a few resemblances to Ségouin. The General was a handsome, vigorous master of war, a man of marked passions and feline cunning who, though of low origins, was well able to affect the role of a gentleman if need be. Other curious references in the story are no less reminiscent of the campaign. Thus, Farley's yacht, named after the port in Rhode Island, *The Belle of Newport*, may still remind us that one of the first towns taken by the French was Newport, County Mayo, locale of the legendary Irish pirate queen, Grace O'Malley. Ironically enough, from the safety of Dublin Bay while aboard *Van Tromp*, Humbert wrote a letter to the court at the Royal Dublin Barracks on behalf of his aide-de-camp, Captain Bernard Teeling, who was nevertheless condemned to be hanged. We even know that a Colonel Farley sat among the officers conducting his court-martial.[12] Pertinent also may be the no less curious fact that Naas, the first town mentioned in the story, was also the site of one of the initial engagements of the rebellion. Then, too, at the battle of Colooney, the fight before the final débâcle at Ballinamuck, a force of Hompesch Dragoons, most of them Hungarians, encountered a detachment of Irish. Assuming by their language that the Dragoons were French, the Irish attempted to join them and were in no time dispatched.[13] Perhaps, too, Jimmy Doyle's inclusion in an exclusive and closed card game at the story's end—a game in appearance more a frolic than the disaster it turns out to be—also poses a shadowy likeness to the many, many United Irishmen meetings aswim in wine, cards, dining, dancing and singing, and foreign presences—not to mention being riddled with informers who rendered such evenings in close and grim detail in secret reports submitted to Dublin Castle that resulted in so many executions.[14]

IV

Keeping this large outline and these curiously apt details uppermost in mind, we might now address ourselves to the flow of the story itself and ask how these two battles, one a stunning victory, the other a tragicomic defeat, give Joyce's mirror the kind of Irish depth we have come to expect, especially as regards the theme of betrayal and self-betrayal.

Jimmy's returning with the winning French amid the cheers of a people never very distant from the traditional peasantry might not be so very different from Matthew Tone's or Bernard Teeling's triumphant progress with the French after the British rout at Castlebar. More pointedly, all during Jimmy's ride to Dublin, right down to the climactic card game, a scheme seems to be afoot. Specifically, Ségouin, successful like Humbert in exacting from an Irishman an investment in his new enterprise, cannot be termed exactly altruistic or ingenuous in his Irish affections. Villona, hard-up musician that he is, something of a sponge, and clearly an ally in what turns out to be more a Franco-British cause than any conflict, openly patronizes Jimmy and his family and is very nearly insulting in hailing the patriotism of Jimmy's drunken speech. Jimmy's pleasingly delusive vision of Ségouin and Rivière in combination with the imperturbable Routh—"the lively youth of the Frenchman twined elegantly upon the firm framework of the Englishman's manner. A graceful image of his, he thought, and a just one"—embraces much more finely than he imagines the highly ambiguous contest to come. A reader may even query precisely how it is that Routh happened to turn up at Ségouin's supper, probably at the Shelbourne, not to mention the Dublin of the Cup Race, long before Horse Show Week. While this question is never raised, still everyone that Jimmy knows seems to have an understanding if not a conspiracy in mind.

In the same vein, Rivière, apparently not to be outdone, enlightens Jimmy with the superiority of French mechanics, "not," as Joyce adds, "wholly ingenuously." Meanwhile Villona plays up to Routh by injecting into the conversation the pleasing topic of "the beauties of the English madrigal," somewhat to the Englishman's surprise. Then, almost like an *agent provocateur*, Ségouin turns the talk to politics and rather surely inflames the age-old contention between Englishman and Irishman, thus ensuring a heated contest wherein the French cannot really lose. His toast to Humanity and his tactfully opening a window have about them something of the same depth of rhetoric as the revolutionary slogans proffered the amazed Catholic peasantry of Killala.

Nor does Kingstown itself stand at such great remove from

the last invasion of Ireland; for the place-name hints of Routh's triumph-to-be in that it celebrates George IV's leavetaking from Ireland in the royal yacht in September 1821 when his title was made to supersede the original Irish name, Dun Laoghaire, not to be restored until very nearly a hundred years later. Even the aged ticket-collector Jimmy encounters in the station—he who singles Jimmy out from his companions with the salute, "Fine night, sir!"—may well be but another version of himself, the Gaelic Catholic only recently removed from the peasantry and now making up to the quality supposedly among his own— after or according to the race. Appropriately, too, all five young men march off as soldiers singing "Cadet Roussel" with the mocking chorus "Ho! Ho! Hohé, vraiment!" No less appropriately, the song celebrates a foolish "bon enfant" who dissipates his fortune and ends in penury. Little wonder that Joyce judges the harbor to be "like a darkened mirror at their feet." For in it at least one reader discerns the faint traces not only of George IV's departure, the original landing in Mayo, and the final defeat at Ballinamuck, but even more the dreaded consequences of all those comings and goings from Irish soil.

Those consequences usually included an ignominious Irish death. Here the omens are also overwhelming, after a time even to Jimmy. With the renewed heavy drinking comes Villona's mock-enthusiastic "Hear! hear!" during Jimmy's protracted speechifying; then follows the consciously heavy clapping concluding with Farley's loud laughter, which Jimmy takes as a compliment; then last-minute toasts are drunk to the red queens—are they, too, polite references to England? Jimmy senses that he has lost his audience, and we might add his luck. Almost from racial instinct he knows that he will lose without, true to history, knowing who will win. His fate in the form of IOUs is settled of course by the winning contenders, his friends and foe, much like the fates of Byrne and Teeling, not to mention Wolfe Tone and the Sheares brothers, before him. Jimmy is condemned by his own folly. At dawn he is summoned to reality, a kind of execution, the consequence of so much betrayal or self-betrayal in Irish history, by a man he had mistaken for another friend among his friends the French.

V

Jimmy's actions so far have bent the meaning of the title to include at least two sempiternal follies of the Irish poised before the English—betrayal by self and by friends. Yet those toasts raised just before the final onslaught at cards may yet insist upon a third meaning no less racial, so to speak. That toast honored Ireland, England, France, Hungary, and the United States respectively. Still one asks what nation might be the interloper. If Jimmy will later feel that he has indeed lost his audience, one may suspect here that so has Ireland. Which is only to say that all the other nations had achieved a modicum of independence or democracy while Ireland had not. England in 1689, the United States in 1776, France in 1789, and Hungary in 1867 had all forced some kind of democratic independence. Ireland, however, had clung to her sullen dependence despite a flamboyant and paralyzed nationalism decked out in idleness, commercialism, dissipation, social climbing, and dismantling drunkenness. All are embodied in Jimmy Doyle in his high-flown wretchedness, the victim, even below the Irish-American Farley, of democratic empire-builders—British, French, American, and Austro-Hungarian.

These Irish racial weaknesses, traditionally true if not so in fact, also speckle the story as do the evidences of betrayal. From the first we witnessed Irish "poverty and inaction" agape at the "wealth and industry" of the Continent displayed in the trim racing cars. The collusion later insinuated in Jimmy's fate we had early also marked down in "the cheer of the gratefully oppressed." The butt of his new-found friends, Jimmy takes a back seat to those he virtually deified, the gods of fashion who become his tailor gods, and discovers his patriotism to be no more an embarrassment than did his father before him in the face of money-bought status. In Kingstown, for that matter, his father had amassed his wealth, with the aid of police contracts, and now Jimmy loses it there—with the aid of something like a police contract, a game with an Englishman. Jimmy's mask of patriotism and social superiority sits no less farci-cally on him than does Dublin's "mask of a capital" that evening. Of course he joins the later toast to the red queens. Given enough rope Jimmy hasn't pulled himself up, socially or otherwise. He has hanged himself.

It is right, then, that his financially pinched and compliant friend among his French, English, and American acquaint-ances—I speak of Villona, a man something like Jimmy in cherishing music and racing together—should recall him to the light of dawn, the setting of his symbolic execution. For Villona is what Jimmy might have been, especially if we see Villona as embodying the lesson of Hungary's resurrection as a free nation held up by Arthur Griffith to Ireland in the year following the motor race. But with the publication of the story in the *Irish Homestead* for 17 December 1904 such freedom for his own race must have seemed improbable to Joyce. As he was to write of young Irish nationalists in *Stephen Hero*:

> The orators of this patriotic party were not ashamed to cite the precedents of Switzerland and France. The intelligent centres of the movement were so scantily supplied that the analogies they gave out as exact and potent were really analogies built haphazard upon very inexact knowledge. The cry of a solitary Frenchman (A bas l'Angleterre!) at a Celtic re-union in Paris would be made by these en-thusiasts the subject of a leading article in which would be shown the imminence of aid for Ireland from the French Government. A glowing example was to be found for Ireland in the case of Hungary, an example, as these patriots imagined, of a long-suffering minority, entitled by every right of race and justice to a separate freedom, finally emancipating itself.[15]

VI

Before concluding, however, let us contemplate but one more dimension to the title, racial to be sure, yet possibly even more shadowy, suggestive, and dim as may befit its source in Irish antiquity. This grey reminder issues tremulously in the salute rendered Jimmy by the ancient ticket-collector—to this day one frequently sees him in baggy trousers, visored cap, and assumed military figure—a man whose greeting to Jimmy alone may hint the ancient Irish name of Kingstown: Dun Laoghaire, or Leary's stronghold. Though this background remains but a hint, a final glance at the Doyles, father and son, may yet be in order, if we recall Laoghaire, a fifth-century king of Ireland, and his father, Niall of the Nine Hostages. The elder Doyle, former butcher of Kingstown, now designated a merchant prince, had done more than approve his son's folly. He had vicariously lived in those new Continental associations himself. How, then, do the large outlines of Niall's and Laoghaire's careers in any way match the overlapping folly of the Doyles?

The late conqueror of the British, Niall, ruler at Tara (380–405), had a Saxon mother. One story has him alone among his brothers willing to embrace the hag Royal Rule, who immediately turned into a beautiful woman. He long sought to collect the Boromean Tribute—mainly cattle, sheep, and swine—originally imposed by King Tuathal on Leinster. One account, of at least four, has it that Niall, while seeking to advance his kingship in France and Italy, was slain by a Saxon arrow shot by a Leinster rival, Eochaid, who was backed by the Franks.[16] His son, King Laoghaire (429–58), came to no less bizarre an end. Remembered for his opposition to St Patrick and for his formulation of Irish law and custom in the Senchus Mor, Laoghaire was taken in a fight with the Leinster forces while also attempting to impose the Tribute and spared only after swearing by the elements never to enter Leinster again on the same mission, an oath he broke in two years. As a consequence he is described as being struck down by the elements—dying of sunstroke on the banks of a river where the earth received him after his breath left him. In his unabating rage against Leinster he demanded and received burial armed and standing upright facing his erstwhile foes.[17]

In the face of this half-legendary account, the flickering ironies in the fortunes of the Doyles, whose money and position are dependent upon meat, need not be drawn out. But I speculate that the father is a kind of prince collaborating with royal rule, a repulsive force that has provided him with beautiful contracts, and a parent who has sent his son first to college and then to Cambridge in England. The son in turn has lost him a good deal of money to a Saxon while in the company of Frenchmen in whose enterprise the father had encouraged the son to invest, thus hoping to extend both their social lives into Continental circles. Jimmy had dabbled in law at Trinity and now has returned to the family stronghold, formerly Dun Laoghaire, after a foray near Naas, once King Tuathal's base in exacting the Tribute. Breathless and excited, he is struck by the dawn's light on a body of water, Dun Laoghaire/Kingstown harbor, where disarmed (relieved of his money), slumped toward earth, his head in his hands, he must nevertheless face his friends, the French.

VII

However low Joyce's opinion of "After the Race" may have been, we might ourselves hesitate before denouncing the story out of hand, whether we condemn it as his "least realized" tale or relegate it to the level of "the sketchiest and most over-defined" in *Dubliners*.[18] The critical implication of such slights is that Joyce hardly knew what he was talking about. Whatever the reason behind Joyce's own estimate of the story, this specific charge might well be directed more tellingly against his critics. For at least Joyce seems to see the possibilities inherent in a title that could speak all at once of the century-old illusion of France's regard for Ireland—held, for instance, by Maud Gonne—and its consequence before the ubiquitous British in the summer of 1798 and in 1903 when the 1898 celebrations were still echoing.[19] Nor would the title seem to exclude pause over the persistent racial tactics of French, British, and Irish when haled together in whatever cause. As far as the expected mercurial instability and earthbound emotions of the Gael—left forever the prey of friends, foes, and self alike—well, of course they might still summon an accidental and feeble gesture in Kingstown befitting the latest actor in the continuous heroic comedy and dubious finales dating from the reigns of that stubborn King Laoghaire and his ambitious father before him.

NOTES: CHAPTER 5

1   Zack Bowen, "'After the Race,'" *James Joyce's Dubliners: Critical Essays*, ed. Clive Hart (New York: Viking Press, 1969), p. 59.

2   ibid., p. 173.
3   Zack Bowen, "Hungarian politics in 'After the Race,'" *James Joyce Quarterly*, vol. 7, no. 2 (Winter 1970), pp. 138–9.
4   For a full account, see for instance "The great motor race," *Daily Express*, 3 July 1903, pp. 5–6; "Gordon-Bennett Motor Race," *Irish Times*, 3 July 1903, pp. 7–9; "Motor racing. Gordon-Bennett Cup. Official placings. French team finishes complete," *Irish Times*, 4 July 1903, p. 9; and C. L. Freeston, "The Great Race: how Jenatzy won the Gordon-Bennett Cup," *Car*, no. 59 (8 July 1903), pp. 201–13.
5   "The Gordon-Bennett Race," *Motor News* [Dublin], vol. 4, no. 8 (8 July 1903), p. 264.
6   "Dinner to the competitors," *Car*, no. 59 (8 July 1903), p. 213.
7   "Gordon-Bennett Cup race. Arrival of the French cars," *Irish Times*, 29 June 1903, p. 8, and "Arrival of French team and cars," *Motoring Illustrated*, 4 July 1903, pp. 132–4.
8   "Irish race echoes," *Motoring Illustrated*, 11 July 1903, p. 188.
9   W. E. H Lecky, *A History of Ireland in the Eighteenth Century* (London: Longmans, Green, 1892), Vol. 5, pp. 38–68. Needless to say, this standard history is referred to in *Finnegans Wake*. See James S. Atherton, *The Books at the Wake* (London: Faber, 1959), pp. 91–2. Another account likely available to Joyce was W. H. Maxwell's *History of the Irish Rebellion; with Memoirs of the Union, and Emmet's Insurrection in 1803* (London: Baily, Brothers, Cornhill, 1845), pp. 223–54.
10 Richard Hayes, *The Last Invasion of Ireland* (Dublin: M. H. Gill, 1937), pp. 152–61.
11 Charles Hamilton Teeling, *History of the Irish Rebellion of 1798: A Personal Narrative* (Glasgow/London: Cameron & Ferguson, 1876), pp. 311–14. See also Hayes, op. cit., pp. 153–4.
12 Teeling, op. cit., pp. 307–14.
13 W. J. Fitz-Patrick, *Secret Service under Pitt* (London: Longmans, Green, 1892), p. 360.
14 John T. Gilbert, *Documents Relating to Ireland, 1795–1804* (Dublin: J. Dollard, 1893), pp. 104–46.
15 *Stephen Hero*, ed. John J. Slocum and Herbert Cahoon (New York: New Directions, 1955), p. 62.
16 *Silva Gadelica*, ed. Standish H. O'Grady (London/Edinburgh: Williams & Norgate, 1892), Vol. 2, pp. 368–9, 403–7; *Ancient Irish Tales*, ed. Tom Peete Cross and Clark Harris Slover, with revised bibliography by Charles W. Dunn (Dublin: Allen Figgis, 1969), pp. 509, 515–17. See also "The Gordon-Bennett course from an antiquarian and historical point of view," *Motor News*, vol. 4, no. 6 (June 1903), pp. 165–210.

17 *Silva Gadelica*, Vol. 2, p. 407; Eleanor Hull, *Early Christian Ireland* (London/Dublin: David Nutt, 1904), pp. 4–6; and Thomas W. H. FitzGerald, *Ireland and Her People* (Chicago, Ill.: FitzGerald Book Co., 1910), Vol. 3, pp. 25–6. Also Samuel Lewis, "Kingstown," in his *A Topographical Dictionary of Ireland*, 2nd edn (London: S. Lewis, 1840), Vol. 2, p. 226.

18 Warren Beck, *Joyce's Dubliners* (Durham, NC: Duke University Press, 1969), p. 123.

19 A newspaper account of the Napper Tandy demonstration in 1900 might be instructive. It speaks of Maud Gonne and John O'Leary leading the procession to a house in Cornmarket to unveil a tablet in memory of Napper Tandy from the Wolfe Tone Ninety-Eight Association. Maud Gonne urged the crowd to turn to the deeds of 1798 for present consolation. But the most striking event of the procession "was the presence of a contingent dressed in the French uniform. The French tricolor and the Stars and Stripes were the favorite flags . . ." ("Napper Tandy demonstration," *Irish Times*, 16 April 1900, p. 6). I cannot help also speculating on the relevance of Maud Gonne's play *Dawn*, an anti-English, Famine play that appeared in Arthur Griffith's *United Irishman* for 29 October 1904. If we recall the last words of Joyce's story— "Daybreak, gentlemen!"—might we not also match it ironically with the call to action against the English at the end of the play and its concluding song to the dawn:

> They have bright swords with them that clash the battle welcome,
> A welcome to the red Sun, that rises with our luck.

See *Lost Plays of the Irish Renaissance*, ed. Robert Hogan and James Kilroy (Newark, Del.: Proscenium Press, 1970), p. 84. For more on Maud Gonne, the Irish Joan of Arc, and her hopes of the French, see Chris Healy, *Confessions of a Journalist*, 2nd edn (London: Chatto & Windus, 1904), pp. 227–31.

6

"Two Gallants":
A Walk through the Ascendancy

Recent studies of "Two Gallants" have gone a long way in clearing up what seemed to Joyce one of his most important stories. The Reverend Father Robert Boyle pointed out the undoubtedly nationalistic theme,[1] while Florence L. Walzl has not only agreed with him but also gone on to distinguish the three levels of the story as "a study of betrayal, social, political, and religious."[2] Both Father Boyle and Miss Walzl identify Corley and Lenehan as members of the Garrison—or friends to it—in any case treacherously on the side of the Crown. If Lenehan shamelessly exemplifies a slack and indifferent nineteenth-century Irishry that stands by as the nation is defrauded, then Corley is rightly identified as the active force in bringing that nation willingly to her knees and getting paid for it to boot. Betrayal does indeed lie at the center of the story, as one might expect from Joyce, who dated Irish betrayal from the time of Dermot MacMurrough and branded it as especially egregious in the bribery that brought about the Act of Union.[3] However, since both of the above essays slight the timelessness or, better, repetitiveness that Joyce usually insists upon when playing on the viol or harp of history, I would like to ponder that earlier period, even more damning than the Garrison, which underlines the age-old duping of a collusive Ireland. Though I shall probably offer no more than an extended footnote—a collection of Georgian rumors, stories, legends, and hints of betrayal—such a footnote may nevertheless demonstrate just how clearly the mirror of "Two Gallants" reflects the historic pomp and grandeur of Ascendancy treacheries that cast long shadows behind the otherwise mean and stunted posturings of Corley and Lenehan near the end of Irish enslavement.

91

I

Father Boyle has opened his essay by drawing our attention to what he calls "the central image" of the story—"the exposed, heedless, weary harp, whose mournful music struck silent the two Dublin gallants."[4] This is as it should be. But both he and Miss Walzl miss one quiet mention, a reference that makes Moore's song and the harpist himself singularly arresting. I refer of course to Joyce's allusion to "the porch of the club," the backdrop for harp and harpist. It signals in this truly central passage what may be seen as Joyce's persistent reminder of a gallantry that had luxuriated in Ireland since the Norman conquest but never so brazenly as at its irresponsible worst during the Protestant Ascendancy, roughly from the battle of the Boyne down to Catholic Emancipation. The Kildare Street Club—for that is Joyce's hitherto unrecognized reference—can be said to have epitomized the religious, social, and economic callousness of that historical period perhaps pinpointed in the years leading to the 1798 rebellion, years that endured the haughty indifference of England through such of her creatures as the implacable John Scott, Earl of Clonmel and Lord Chief Justice, and the unspeakable Francis Higgins, the Sham Squire made famous by FitzPatrick's oft-reprinted volume—both in some ways prototypes for Corley and Lenehan, as we may come to see.

The founding of the Club (in 1782), its membership and allegiances, and the reaction to it by the Irish populace all spell out its role as a perfect foil to a harp "weary alike of the eye of strangers and of her master's hands." Until recently, the Club was under suspicion as the home of the Stranger or friends of the Stranger, that is, the English. Long the haven of Unionism in Ireland, the Club in this century still attracted the fading, country, colonel types whose last great contribution to Irish life may have been the Gregory family. Characteristically for Joyce's story, the founding of the Club grew out of something like betrayal among men of extravagant habits—aristocrats, parliamentary leaders, members of the Hell-Fire Club. These had made up the parent organization, Daly's Club at numbers 2 and 3 Dame Street, opened between 1762 and 1765, a resort where "nearly half the land of Ireland is said to have changed owners," and where gentlemen of fashion, the self-styled Dublin Bucks—Buck Whaley, Buck Lawless, Buck English *et al.*—took *their wanton way among the gaming-tables.*[5] From this promising beginning stemmed the Kildare Street Club. The occasion was the blackballing of the Rt Hon. William Burton Conyngham. Consequently, he and his friends from Daly's formed their own club in 1782 and purchased, through their treasurer, David La Touche, a site on Kildare Street. Relevant to the financial drift of Joyce's story is not only the fact that Conyngham was Teller of the Exchequer but also that the Club lands ultimately purchased came from the estate of Sir Henry Cavandish, former Teller of the Exchequer, who had died in 1776 in debt to the government for an unexplained £67,305 7s 2d. In any case, the original premises burned down in the next century (1860), and the new Club was located further down the street at numbers 1, 2 and 3. Victoria's visits usually brought a volley of stones through its windows; in recent years some of its space had been taken by the Phoenix Assurance Company, while the membership itself remained the occasional butt of the feeble wit of *Dublin Opinion.*[6] And now the Club is gone, having combined with the University Club on Stephen's Green.

This mention of the Club, then, is but one glimpse of a highly suggestive backdrop of street- and place-names that Joyce sets behind the seemingly aimless wanderings of the two men. Marvin Magalaner has commented on their journey that "Joyce is very careful to trace realistically the wanderings of the two 'friends' through Dublin in this story."[7] But something more than realism is in the Dublin air they take. There can be little aimless or wandering in their peregrinations for an informed Dubliner. This litany of streets and places is one of almost unrelievedly black hints of betrayal and extravagance repeated at every turn Corley and Lenehan make. Moreover, the journey ends fittingly with Lenehan and the reader fixing their eyes on a gold coin. Joyce once summed up English rule in Ireland, and that of its instrument the Irish interest, that is, the Protestant Ascendancy, with this succinct pronouncement: "She enkindled its factions and took over its treasury."[8] An English gold piece relinquished by an Irish slavey to her ravisher, a member of the Garrison, England's later Protestant–

Catholic instrument of the nineteenth century, brightly embodies that assertion.

II

The pilgrimage of the two seedy gallants, attached respectively to racing and the police—associations reminiscent of the sporting and military pursuits of the Ascendancy—begins with mention of Rutland Square. The day is Sunday, more specifically a Sunday evening in August when most of Dublin is to be found on parade. Joyce not only noted the relevance of this Sunday crowd to his panoramic "Irish landscape,"[9] but also in another letter hinted an unnamed work of Guiglielmo Ferrero—especially "the chapters wherein Ferrero examines the moral code of the soldier and (incidentally) of the gallant"[10]—as the inspiration for his story. Joyce probably had in mind, as Richard Ellmann suggests in his note, Ferrero's *L'Europa giovane*. If so, the reference underlines the decadent commingling of greed, peremptory self-righteousness, and sexual intrigue apparent virtually from the story's exceedingly balmy beginning. Sauntering down from Rutland Square the two gallants are imaginatively in a "memory of summer"—Joyce's phrase again—in that their antics, however diminished, are a memory of the heyday of a more bumptious crew. For, in taking their way toward St Stephen's Green, they repeat the footsteps of such unloved eighteenth-century gallants as the fire-eaters, Tiger Roche and Pat Power of Dargle; Burnchapel Whaley, the priest-hunter, his son, the famous Buck, whose winning a wager by playing handball against the walls of Jerusalem has partly obscured memory of his more unsavory activities; and then a third denizen of the Green, Copper-Faced Jack, the Earl of Clonmel, a Chief Justice of the King's Bench who bilked Catholics that entrusted their lands to him, and a gentleman no less obese or licentious than the orotund Corley of the story. Accordingly, to proceed from Rutland Square, named in 1791 after Charles Manners, fourth Duke of Rutland, an altogether too convivial lord-lieutenant, is a most signal beginning.

More than once Rutland had interested himself in the

scrapes of his companions among the Bucks. In July 1784, after one particularly vicious spree involving "a noble lord, two . . . colonels in the army . . . and others of high rank and aides-de-camp to the Lord Lieutenant, the Duke of Rutland," the Duke himself interceded on their behalf and got his cronies off scot-free. Rutland Square, a base to which Lenehan will return, is, then, a prophetic departure-point for Corley and his parasite as they urge themselves down the hill into Upper Sackville Street. Rutland Square had also been the site of the highly esteemed Lord Charlemont's town house, he who though head of the Volunteers nevertheless failed to keep Ireland independent. The Square was, moreover, blessed by the presence of the brilliant chemist and geologist Richard Kerwan who, for all his intelligence, married the extravagant Anne Blake of Menlo Castle, County Galway, and was conveyed to prison for her debts on his wedding day. The earliest building in the Square was unfortunately the Grand Orange Hall at number 10. Nearby at number 8 dwelt the notorious General Henry Lawes Luttrell, Commander-in-Chief in Ireland, who wrested or connived his seat in Parliament from John Wilkes in the Middlesex election of 1769. The tenor of Luttrell's life is caught in the words of Junius characterizing the General's family history: "As far as their history has been known, the son has regularly improved upon the vices of the father, and has taken care to transmit them, pure and undiminished, into the bosom of his successor. In the Senate their abilities have been confined to those humble, sordid services in which the scavengers of the Ministry are usually employed."

Leaving behind the south side of the Square, the two gallants stroll past the Rotunda Hospital, the remainder of its gardens recalling the swirl of high fashion that gathered there at fund-raising balls, concerts, and soirees during the eighteenth century. Opened by Bartholomew Mosse in 1745, the hospital was intended as an aid to lying-in women among the poor of Dublin. Yet the air of fashionable corruption is no less attached to this intention than it is to the memory of the gardens. One of the hospital's eighteenth-century masters is still remembered for his turning apostate to the real hopes of the Dublin poor. Frederick Jebb, master from 1773 to 1780, was the turncoat. The official history of the hospital records of him:

Jebb's energies were dissipated, for he wrote, under the name of "Guatimozin," a series of six articles in the *Freeman's Journal* in the spring of 1779. His letters were vigorous and directed against the proposed Union between England and Ireland. Jebb's writings were so effective that the Lord Lieutenant officially recommended that he should be given a pension of £300 yearly, in return for which he would change his politics and write in support of the Government. Jebb did this until he died in 1782, one year after his Mastership ended.[11]

Corley and Lenehan then approach Nassau Street by way of Sackville Street, now of course O'Connell Street, and turn into Kildare Street. Nassau Street instantly recalls the Prince of Orange, who later presided over Ireland's defeat at the battle of the Boyne and the broken Treaty of Limerick. But Sackville Street might also immediately arrest any Irishman's attention, and just as much as do the other place- and street-names dropped by the two gallants as they meander along in desultory conversation.

Although the street was probably named after Lionel Cranfield Sackville, first Duke of Dorset and Lord-Lieutenant, a popular Dublin legend has it that the street was in reality named after his son, Lord George Sackville. Commander of the combined British, Hanoverian, and Hessian troops at the battle of Minden, Lord Sackville, as the story goes, refused the repeated orders of his general, Prince Ferdinand of Brunswick, to charge the French at the height of the battle, and so left the victory incomplete. Despite the furious efforts of Lord Bute and the heir apparent (afterwards George III), Sackville was court-martialed and declared unfit for future military service. Nevertheless, in keeping with this scandal, George III ultimately heaped honors upon him, made him Secretary of State for the Colonies in 1775, and finally raised him to the peerage as Viscount Sackville—all this despite a general public disgust.[12] Thus, while our latter-day gallants pass through this thoroughfare of near-treachery and royal reward, we may yet overhear the background to their own day of betrayal and sovereign reward with firm expectations.

We learn, for instance, that Lenehan has "been talking all the afternoon in a public house in Dorset Street;" that Corley had met his slavey under Waterhouse's clock in Dame Street; that she works in a house in Baggot Street; that he had had his first success with her in a field in Donnybrook; and thereafter she had rewarded him with tramfare, cigarettes, and even cigars stolen from her employer. Corley had ingratiated himself with her further by pretending to a higher class, that is, by allowing that he had worked at Pim's. We also learn that in the past he had not been so fortunate in this lie with girls off the South Circular, except for one now "on the turf" and last seen driving with two men in Earl Street. By this time our two boys are past Trinity College, have turned up Kildare Street, and are abreast of the Club.

But Lenehan's languishing in a pub in Dorset Street links him not only to the Sackville name but also to the new Hibernian Bank, to maintain the vicious commercial theme of the story. In the same vein, Dame Street, whose eighteenth-century taverns served as meeting-places for the Hell-Fire Club, is doubtless the proper modern business street on which to meet a tart, especially since Corley met her under a clock belonging to the premises at numbers 25 and 26, described for those years in *Thom's Directory* as "Waterhouse and Company, gold and silver smiths, electro-platers, jewellers, and watch-makers to His Majesty, and the Irish court." As we may come to see, the alignment of gold, an Irish slavey, a British sovereign (especially Edward VII), and Dublin Castle, while seemingly incongruent, is most germane to the story, on a par with the odd but true juxtaposition of Irish harp and Kildare Street Club.

Equally fitting is mention of Earl Street, a place-name dating from 1728 and memorializing the Earl of Meath, a member of the wealthy Brabazon family, a name still associated with the eighteenth-century Liberties, site of the internecine and bloody battles of Irish weavers and butchers in faction feuds that frequently tied up all of Dublin for a whole day. If employment at Pim's, now closed but at the turn of the century a fashionable, Quaker-owned department store, meant class distinction to a Catholic slavey girl who worked in a house in Baggot Street, then it may have been just because Corley had tried this ruse with less success on girls from the fashionable

South Circular, a road dating from 1763, forming the south boundary of Dublin and newly graced with the Grand Canal in the 1790s. In Ascendancy Dublin the South Circular became a most elegant upper-class promenade. This doubtful alliance of privilege and debauchery is further strengthened when we realize that Baggot Street, part of the noble complex of Fitzwilliam lands and buildings, nevertheless leads to Corley's final goal, Donnybrook, whose annual fair or bacchanal was finally abolished in 1855. Drunkenness, fighting, lechery, and sharp dealing are still connotations of the word. As F. Elrington Ball wrote in 1903 in his *History of the County Dublin*:

> All references in local literature indicate that the fair was the occasion of drunkness, riot, and moral degradation which were a disgrace to Ireland, and it would serve no useful purpose to enter more fully into particulars of revel, the abolition of which was a service to civilization.

However unconscious the prudery of this Victorian condemnation, Donnybrook serves Joyce well enough with its inglorious eighteenth-century annals to tempt at least one Garrison gallant and his native doxy.

III

By now we have reached the second major square, St Stephen's Green, where the shabby Bucks spy the waiting girl at Hume Street. This setting for an assignation is an apt one. For the Green was a center of gallantry after the quality moved south across the Liffey in the mid-eighteenth century. On the north side of the Green was the most fashionable Beaux's Walk, described in 1771 as "a place of public resort, especially on Sundays when the nobility and gentry take the air and parade in their carriages."[13] The Spring Gardens themselves had been patterned after Vauxhall in London. Moreover, many a fine house was erected facing the Green during the period of its surge to popularity. Both Whaleys, fire-eating father and son, are associated with numbers 85 and 86 on the south side. Hume Street, the meeting-point, running off the Green to Ely Place, was named after Gustavus Hume, who was appointed

State Surgeon in 1791 and had made a fortune speculating in land and building great houses. Hume was connected to the Loftus family by marriage—both sides were descended from gentry in County Fermanagh—and gave his family name to one street and Ely, the title taken by the Loftuses when raised to the peerage, to the other. The Marquess of Loftus also had a reputation for extravagance—he had built, for instance, a 350–foot-long folly in the Dublin Mountains. As Earl of Ely he had been one of the principal butts in the famed satirical poem *Barataria*. Needless to say, both Hume and Loftus, like so many of the aristocracy who had lavish houses in Dublin, erected their palatial residences on profits exacted from an oppressed tenantry. Of course Lord Ely and his son, Lord Loftus, accepted a £30,000 bribe to vote for the Union.

It is right, then, that Corley should assume his role as a conqueror here. John Egan, MP for Tallaght and Chairman of Sessions for County Dublin, a Buck and duellist who had given his name to one of Lenehan's pubs, had also graced Ely Place for nearly a decade, 1789–98. Just as relevant to Corley's skulduggery, this time on a national scale, is the former abode of John "Black Jack" Fitzgibbon, Earl of Clare and Lord Chancellor of Ireland, at number 6. Adjoining Lord Ely's mansion at numbers 7 and 8, Fitzgibbon's temple to splendor included a banquet-hall forty feet long and twenty-six feet wide. Also symbolizing his compulsive magnificence was a coach built in London for 3,000 guineas that included panels painted by William Hamilton for 500 guineas. At his first levee in 1789, Fitzgibbon celebrated his accession to the chancellorship by entertaining the entire Irish bar, judges included. His unrelenting role in engineering and putting down the 1798 rebellion has made his name infamous in Ireland ever since. Previous to the rebellion, when Lord Fitzwilliam with a promise of Catholic Emancipation resigned as Lord-Lieutenant, after fierce opposition from the Castle and Fitzgibbon himself, that Lord Chancellor barely escaped being stoned to death in his resplendent coach by the mob. Working prominently with Castlereagh, he effected the massive bribery that brought Union with England. Upon his death the mob again interceded with Irish vindictiveness and hatred for the betrayer by hurling filth and at least one dead cat into his grave. Corley's magisterial stride, pompous bearing, and connections with the police are seemingly the eternal Irish remnants of this monster.

Yet here I must insist again upon the even closer parallel Lenehan and Corley make with Francis Higgins, the Sham Squire, and John Scott, or "Copper-Faced Jack," Lord Chief Justice and Earl of Clonmel. If Lenehan finds himself alone in the Refreshment Bar hankering after a girl with "a little of the ready," so had the young Francis Higgins; subsequently, he swindled her and her family. We know of Lenehan's later attempt on Molly Bloom. Like Lenehan, Higgins had also written for the *Freeman's Journal* and later became the owner. As a solicitor, he practiced in a court where his friend John Scott held sway as judge. The height of the Sham's career found him at home at number 72 on the Green, not far from his friend Clonmel's house in Harcourt Street. An underground passage from there virtually joined the two houses and schemers. Nor did the Sham Squire affect wit any less than does Lenehan, if *Ulysses* is any evidence. Altogether, then, the Stranger's and the Ascendancy taint of roguery on St Stephen's Green has not entirely faded.[14] Joyce later highlights the fact when he has Stephen approach the Green and reflect on the defects of the Royal University in the *Portrait*:

> The soul of the gallant venal city which his elders had told him of had shrunk with time to a faint mortal odour rising from the earth and he knew that in a moment when he entered the sombre college he would be conscious of a corruption other than that of Buck Egan and Burnchapel Whaley.[15]

IV

Lenehan leaves Corley to his role as conqueror and betrayer after momentarily eyeing the girl, who resembles nothing so much as a mare—what with muscular figure, wide nostrils, and projecting front teeth—and is curiously enough decked out in red, white, and blue, the colors of the Union Jack. Moodily retreating to Rutland Square, Lenehan idles for a moment at the Shelbourne Hotel and then trails the couple down one side of Merrion Square till he sees them board the Donnybrook tram. Then, retracing his steps, he lingers again at the Duke's

Lawn, and continues to the Green, where he gazes at the clock of the College of Surgeons—much as he had at Trinity's clock on his way south—and then passes down Grafton Street and into the Refreshment Bar off Rutland Square. His mood is a defeated and somber one. Yet these wanderings, too, no matter how listless or seemingly aimless, are no less dense with Irish memories of national treachery and dissipation under the Georges.

For instance, to pass the Shelbourne is also to pass a former British barracks. Once the residence of Sir William Petty, whose son was created Earl of Shelbourne in 1718, the building was known as Kerry House. Ultimately, it fell into the hands of Shelbourne's wastrel son, the Hon. Thomas Fitzmaurice, who died in debt for the usual eighteenth-century reasons. The present hotel's historian, Elizabeth Bowen, has written regarding the trustees' sale of the mansion to the speculator, Luke White: "Wild parties, neglect, and dilapidation had done their work by the time the improvident Thomas Fitzmaurice died . . . when at last it came on the market, the always noble and formerly splendid house looked but a poor investment for Luke White's money."[16] He, however, found a profitable lessee for his £6,000 investment. The British government took Kerry House as a barracks for troops come to put down the 1798 rebellion, and the once splendid Ascendancy memento became a center for inquisition and torture. No less redolent of betrayal and coercion must have been Lenehan's sight of the two clocks, the one adorning Trinity College needing perhaps no reminder that it kept time for the intellectual bastion of Protestant Ireland. A university officially unrepenting in its bias, Trinity welcomed the visitation of 1798, led by Lord Clare, a vice-chancellor, bent on rooting out members of the United Irishmen, who numbered among them Wolfe Tone, Napper Tandy, Hamilton Rowan, and Robert Emmet. No less implicated was the Royal College of Surgeons, identified with the other clock. There William Deese, a professor and one of the chief founders of the schools of surgery, died mysteriously in January 1798. While at least three theories have been advanced to explain his sudden death at 46, the patriotic explanation has been perpetuated in the nineteenth-century account by Dr Madden in his *Lives of the United Irishmen* and is still popular, since Deese was a member of that secret body and, if successfully charged and convicted, would perforce have been sacked. This nationalistic legend has it that "Deese was warned by the Surgeon-General to the Forces, George Stewart (a member of the College, and President in 1792), of his imminent arrest, and that 'he went from the College, where the intelligence was given to him, opened the femoral artery and died of haemorrhage.'"[17]

Hardly less fashionable or less compromised is the third square, Merrion Square. A house there, as Barry Lyndon learned, was an almost certain entree to high society in the eighteenth century. Like Merrion Street, where Lenehan has promised to meet Corley, and Baggot Street, where the girl performs her doubtless onerous chores, Merrion Square had been part of the Fitzwilliam lands, the Fitzwilliams being a family through the centuries most loyal to the sovereigns of England. The Fitzwilliams had their seat in Merrion; the Street was named in 1723 and the Square in 1769. The fifth and sixth viscounts, who flourished in the eighteenth century, were notable absentee landlords. The seventh Viscount Fitzwilliam let Mount Merrion House to "Black Jack" Fitzgibbon, at the time Attorney-General, upon his marriage to Buck Whaley's sister, a lady whose Irish beauty had already attracted the more than patriotic glances of the Prince of Wales, later George IV. But a cursory look at the Dublin *Georgian Society Records* will show how heavily studded was the Square with peers and Members of Parliament, among whom shone Sir Jonah Barrington, the shady judge of facetious memory who was tried by *both* houses of the British Parliament for peculation of public funds.

On the west side of the Square is Leinster Lawn, the Duke's Lawn and garden of Leinster House, where Lenehan recalls the harpist's melody. Again the incongruence seems appropriate; for not only was Leinster House the most magnificent town house in Dublin, belonging as it did to the second Duke, but it was also sacred to the memory of patriots, since Lord Edward Fitzgerald, his brother, held meetings of the United Irishmen there. Here, too, came Thomas Reynolds, the government informer, to gather evidence against Lord Edward and bring him to his end at the hands of Majors Sirr and

Swann. A persistent legend, with little basis in fact but nevertheless persistent, has Lord Edward chased across the lawn only to escape by leaping the sunken fence fronting on Merrion Square, doubtless not far from the spot where Lenehan tarries and imitates the harpist's playing. The Sham Squire also had a hand in that betrayal, though Lenehan might not know it. Lenehan's further retreat down Grafton Street toward Sackville Street may also be more than a coincidence. For Grafton Street is named after Henry Fitzroy, first Duke of Grafton, illegitimate son of Charles II by the Duchess of Cleveland in 1663. Despite his gallant origins, this Duke is known in Ireland for his deserting James II for King William in 1689. This apostasy was commemorated in Dublin's most elegant commercial street for what must have seemed to Ascendancy Dublin the Duke's altogether heroic death leading his grenadiers in the attack on Cork in 1690. Thus, when we are told that Lenehan, upon returning to Rutland Square, "felt more at ease in the dark, quiet street, the sombre look of which suited his mood," we may well wonder if Joyce is capping this panorama of betrayal by recalling us to its latest entrant, the betrayed Parnell, who lived in the Square and had his name given it in 1922.

V

Despite his own ironic yearnings for a home "if he could only come across some good simple-minded girl with a little of the ready," despite these thoughts and his own misgivings, empty as they are in the restaurant, Lenehan returns to south Dublin, the far reach of the last tide of the Ascendancy before 1800, and repeats the eternal drift of Joyce's historical story. The route taken is especially grim in memorials to British plunder, national division, and social domination.

So this lone gallant, doubtless reassuming the genteel air he had abandoned in the restaurant, heads south again, this time by way of Capel Street. Named after Arthur Capel, Earl of Essex and Lord-Lieutenant from 1672 to 1677, this street was also once the site of the King James Mint-House, where was coined the brass money castigated in the infamous Orange toast. Before the appearance of Carlisle Bridge, Capel Street, hard as it may be to believe today, stood as a main resort of fashionable Dublin. City Hall, Lenehan's next turning-point, was so named in 1852; but in Augustan Dublin it was the address for the renowned Lucas's coffee-house, haunt of some of Dublin's most insolent Bucks. Later in the eighteenth century it became the Royal Exchange and during the British-promulgated 1798 rebellion was employed as a barracks and torture chamber. Maurice Craig relates of that time and place "that a gentleman who was passing during that grim period paused to look up at the Exchange . . . and was tapped on the shoulder by Major Sirr, who told him that if he did not immediately lose interest in the building he would rapidly find himself inside it."[18] Lying as it does virtually under the shadow of Dublin Castle, citadel of British rule in Ireland, the former Exchange exemplifying English power and money sets Lenehan on his course to Dame Street, scene of eighteenth-century frivolity but by then Dublin's main commercial street, where he stops to chat with friends in George's Street.

At this intersection, under the aegis of Hanoverian Dublin, they speak of another sporting friend, Mac, who had just been seen in Westmoreland Street, recalling John Fane, tenth Earl of Westmoreland, Lord-Lieutenant from 1790 to 1794. The ubiquitous Mac had also been with Lenehan the night before in Egan's, by now a familiar name of gallantry to us, probably the pub in Sackville Place. This rogue's unanimity of gallantry and commerce is repeatedly exposed here at the end of the story, for Lenehan turns into the City Markets, or the South City Markets as they are now known, and walks along the passage that was once Joseph's Lane, named thus in 1756 after Joseph Fade, another banker. Finally, his way to Grafton Street directs Lenehan down Exchequer Street, but one more monetary reminder, the east end of the street having been rechristened Wicklow Street in 1838; then he hurries up to the Green and takes his stand at the corner of Merrion Street.

Ready to give them up, Lenehan finally sights the returning couple. Yet something seems to be wrong: "They did not seem to be speaking. An intimation of the result pricked him like the point of a sharp instrument. He knew Corley would fail, he knew it was no go." Still Lenehan follows them down Baggot

Street, and then of course the girl gets the money,[19] gives it to Corley, who heads for the Green and turns up Ely Place with himself in pursuit. There, in response to Lenehan's repeated questioning, Corley gravely displays the "small gold coin" in his hand.

The coin is a sovereign or half-sovereign. Either one, beyond even its equivocating title in Ireland, is an appropriate emblem of Joyce's theme of England's bilking Ireland during Penal and Ascendancy days with Ireland's own acquiescence. For the sovereign as Corley and Lenehan would have known it was first struck in 1817 with the Prince Regent, later to reign as George IV, giving place to George III on the obverse side of the coin. The design by Benedetto Pistrucci of St George killing the dragon appears on the reverse.[20] Given the date of the story's composition, one would hope that the sovereign—or more tellingly the half-sovereign, as I would theorize—would have modeled the head of Edward VII, not unknown for his gallantries.

For in his case the seeming conflict of images—the harp and the Kildare Street Club, lords-lieutenant and Irish torture, the Irish bar and provoked rebellion, military glory and cowardly treachery, ruling aristocracy and absentee landlord, Anglo-Irish patriot and native informer—is permanently wedded in gold, especially if we contemplate Edward VII's rubicund profile somehow completing the other image of St George belaboring the dragon in the cause of virtue. And even this final struggle is not without its power to light up the significance of Joyce's conclusion in what might have appeared but a meandering tale. For the battle depicted shows the saint attacking the dragon with only a drawn sword in his hand, his lance having already been shattered in the fight. However, as the Dublin joke has it, from the appearance of the sword, St George has missed the dragon and has ostensibly buried that sharp instrument in his horse's *derrière*. If we recall Lenehan's momentary feeling of being pricked at the thought of Corley's possible failure, and if we realize that the condition of his success included the sticking of the girl, described as a mare, then we may indeed meditate on Joyce's paradoxical images: an armed horseman; a horse stabbed in the back, so to speak; and a dragon, a specter of evil, still alive. Or we might extend these images to include an Ascendancy aristocrat riding a native mare or jade, with evil looking up to them, all held together by sovereign gold.

As for Corley, Joyce saw to it that he would fall upon even more evil days by early morning, 17 June 1904. Assuming the role of Melanthius in the "Eumaeus" episode of *Ulysses*, Corley is nevertheless happy to accept Stephen's half-crown—does he remember the girl's half-sovereign? Joyce also provides him with a rumored genealogy dating from the Regency daughter of a washkitchen wench, said to be foster sister to the heir, in the castle of the Lords Talbot de Malahide. Thus his new nickname, Lord John Corley. Yet, despite such a connection by the bar sinister, after the recent death of his father, Inspector Corley of the G Division,[21] Corley's only hope this June night is for the job of crossing-sweeper. Hence Joyce again binds even tighter the knot between dissolute Garrison riffraff and the dashing Ascendancy nobility that the story strives so cunningly to expose. So far, then, as Corley and Lenehan go, our two gallants, a half-sovereignty has been the wage of gallantry for them as heirs to the eighteenth-century Bucks, but their mastery has put them between the Club and the harp, the stranger and the patriot, and, in Lenehan's case, the constabulary and his own kind.

NOTES: CHAPTER 6

1 Robert Boyle, "'Two Gallants,' and 'Ivy Day in the Committee Room,'" *James Joyce Quarterly*, vol. 1, no. 1 (Fall 1963), pp. 3–6.

2 Florence L. Walzl, "Symbolism in Joyce's 'Two Gallants,'" *James Joyce Quarterly*, vol. 2, no. 2 (Winter 1965), pp. 73–81.

3 "Ireland, Island of Saints and Sages," *The Critical Writings of James Joyce*, ed. Ellsworth Mason and Richard Ellmann (New York: Viking Press, 1959), p. 162.

4 Boyle, op. cit., p. 3.

5 J. T. Gilbert, *A History of the City of Dublin*, Vol. 3 (Dublin: McGlashan & Gill, 1859), pp. 305–6.

6 For a general survey of the Club down to the fire of 1860, see Raymond F. Brooke, *Daly's Club and Kildare Street Club* (Dublin: G. F. Healy, 1930), passim. To avoid spattering my chapter with great numbers of superscripts and endnotes, I list below generally

accessible volumes of eighteenth-century Dublin lore that Joyce might have supposed part of the historical memory of any informed Dubliner. In addition to Gilbert's three volumes, one might browse through F. Elrington Ball, *A History of the County Dublin to the Close of the XVIIIth Century*, 6 vols (Dublin: A. Thom, 1902–20); Sir Jonah Barrington, *Personal Sketches of His Own Times*, 3 vols (London: Henry Colburn, 1827–32); Dillon Cosgrave, *North Dublin—City and Environs* (Dublin: Catholic Truth Society of Ireland, 1909); *Dublin Delineated* (Dublin: G. Tyrrell [1837]); Samuel A. Ossory Fitzpatrick, *Dublin* (London: Methuen, 1907); Wilmot Harrison, *Memorable Dublin Houses* (Dublin: W. Leckie, 1899); Maurice Craig, *Dublin 1660–1860* (London: Cresset Press, 1952); William John FitzPatrick, *Curious Family History; or, Ireland before the Union* (Dublin: James Duffy, 1880), *"The Sham Squire"* (Dublin: M. H. Gill, 1895), and *Secret Service under Pitt* (London: Longmans, Green, 1892); *The Georgian Society Records of Eighteenth-Century Domestic Architecture and Decoration in Dublin*, 5 vols (Dublin: Dublin University Press, 1909–13); C. T. M'Cready, *Dublin Street Names Dated and Explained* (Dublin: Hodges, Figgis, 1892); M. J. MacManus, *Irish Cavalcade 1550–1850* (London: Macmillan, 1939); and John Edward Walsh, *Ireland Sixty Years Ago* (Dublin: James McGlashan, 1847). This is in no sense a complete list.

7   Marvin Magalaner, *Time of Apprenticeship: The Fiction of Young James Joyce* (London/New York/Toronto: Abelard-Schuman, 1959), p. 155.

8   "Ireland, Island of Saints and Sages," *Critical Writings of James Joyce*, p. 166.

9   *Letters of James Joyce*, ed. Richard Ellmann (New York: Viking, 1966), Vol. 2, p. 166.

10   ibid., p. 133.

11   T. D. O'Donel, *The Rotunda Hospital, 1745–1945* (Edinburgh: E. & S. Livingstone, 1947), pp. 24–5.

12   Newspaper cutting in the National Library of Ireland copy of M'Cready's *Dublin Street Names*, between pp. 100–1.

13   *Georgian Society Records*, Vol. 2, pp. 38–9.

14   Harrison, op. cit., pp. 43, 46–8, and FitzPatrick, *"The Sham Squire,"* passim. Richard Ellmann, *The Consciousness of Joyce* (New York: Oxford University Press, 1977), p. 108, lists this and Fitz-Patrick's *Ireland before the Union* in Joyce's Trieste library. See also Moira Lysaght, "The Sham Squire," *Dublin Historical Record*, vol. 25, no. 2 (March 1972), pp. 65–74.

15   *Stephen Hero*, ed. John J. Slocum and Herbert Cahoon (New York: New Directions, 1955), p. 184.

16 Elizabeth Bowen, *The Shelbourne* (London: Harrap, 1951), pp. 22–3.

17 J. D. H. Widdess, *A Dublin School of Medicine and Surgery, Royal College of Surgeons, Dublin, 1789–1948*, with a foreword by William Doolin (Edinburgh: E. & S. Livingstone, 1949), pp. 38–9.

18 Craig, op. cit., p. 197.

19 She probably stole it, as Samuel N. Bogorad has argued in "Saved or stolen? The gold coin in 'Two Gallants,'" *Eire-Ireland*, vol. 7, no. 2 (Summer 1972), pp. 62–8. But her coming down the front steps doesn't prove her theft since her room would have been on the top storey, not in the basement where she entered.

20 Sir Geoffrey Duveen and H. G. Stride, *The History of the Gold Sovereign* (London: Oxford University Press, 1962), pp. 76–9.

21 One mid-nineteenth-century critic of the G or Detective Division described its formation in the following terms: ". . . collect a number of men without principle, we will not name religion in such company, men utterly regardless of the sanctity of an oath, men, whom that closest of all bonds, the consciousness of a common sin, unites in a common secrecy, men whose former habits fitted them as the associates of thieves and prostitutes; place them under a chief possessing all the above amiable qualities in an eminent degree, able to keep a secret, and having sufficient tact not to embroil his employers, but to take the blame on himself in case he went too far, and you have a Detective Police such as was created and turned loose upon Dublin. . . ." (Earnan P. Blythe, "The DMP," *Dublin Historical Record*, vol. 20, nos. 3–4 (June–September 1965), pp. 118–19.)

7

"The Boarding House": The Sacrament of Marriage, the Annunciation, and The Bells of St George's

In an exceptionally penetrating article, "The crucifixion in 'The Boarding House,'" Bruce A. Rosenberg has established Bob Doran as "a diminished Jesus." The essay goes on to picture Polly as Mary Magdalene, the forced marriage as a crucifixion, and Mrs Mooney as a composite of Herod Antipas and Pontius Pilate, while her son Jack takes on an obvious resemblance to a Roman soldier. In Rosenberg's words, which begin his summary of these views, "We may read 'The Boarding House,' then, as the story of the crucifixion in a modern Dublin boarding house. Poor Bob Doran, like Jesus of Nazareth, is being crucified."[1] Rosenberg's point, developed in his understated yet highly specific way, is major. But somehow, for all of its insight, his piece fails to account for a number of troublesome events in the story. Why, we may ask, does Joyce make repeated allusion to St George's, its bells and parishioners? Why, too, the insistent reminders of the Mooney butcher background and Doran's own employment? And how does one explain the seemingly extreme imbalance of the story? Its second division, following a line of spaced periods, briefly pictures Polly's short wait until her mother calls her downstairs. In addition to interrupting a sustained point of view, this second part would also appear anticlimactic, somehow impossibly asked to balance and conclude the story in less than a page. I shall argue the contrary.

I

First of all, let us turn to what most critics along with Rosenberg have pointed out—Joyce is exposing that harrowing Irish institution, the forced marriage. To compound that fact, Doran is also being coerced by a mother, daughter, and son who are, respectively, very much a madam, whore, and bully bouncer. Yet I would be quick to add that most critics have neglected the fact that in Catholic Ireland marriage is also a sacrament, the seventh, at least since the thirteenth century. Rosenberg aptly recalls us to the Last Supper as Mrs Mooney's servant Mary collects the scraps for next week's bread pudding. Yet the ingredients for the Nuptial Mass during that holy ceremony embody the very forces that compel Bob Doran downstairs to his crucifixion—"the implacable faces of his employer and the Madam stared upon his discomfiture." In short, whatever crucifixion lies at the center of the story also lies, by way of continuation, at the center of the Mass, an unbloody version of bread and wine nevertheless representing a sacrificial Christ's body, which concludes the wedding service.

The very name Mooney, for example, is long recognized in Dublin for its association with bread and wine. The famous public houses that go under the J. G. Mooney name are one thing. Mrs Mooney's father and husband aside for the moment, the name Mooney has also been identified with baking. Early in the nineteenth century one encounters the famous and perhaps unfortunate name of Thomas Mooney, a prominent employer in the baking and milling trades; at the end of the century, John Mooney and his Clonliffe Bakery were a familiar advertisement in the Dublin papers; this century has made famous the baking concern of Johnston, Mooney & O'Brien with its distinctive bread-trucks.[2] Needless to say, Doran's employer, Mr Leonard the "great Catholic wine merchant," had contracts enough with the city churches.[3] Marriage will yoke the Doran name—meaning "stranger," "exile," "outcast" in Irish—to the bread and wine betokened by the Mooney name and the wine sales of his employer.

Still another concentration of those forces lodges in the butcher's trade and its hacking of flesh and blood. The injunction in the Nuptial Mass that a man "cleave to his wife" takes on a grim overtone—"cleave" is also one of the few words to contain their own antonym—when we remember that the separated Mr Mooney once took the cleaver to his wife, and that she herself is a butcher's daughter who handles moral issues as she might meat with a cleaver. In the same venue, the butcher shop had been (in manuscript) in Fairview, finally changed to Spring Gardens, the same locale, on the North Strand Road. As we have discovered in an earlier chapter, the spot was best known as Mud Island, a haunt of bullies, thieves, and cut-throats, with its own disreputable king, court, sheriff, and poet laureate, all somehow living largely outside the law[4]—a likely origin for the Mooney family and a boarding house that is "beginning to get a certain fame." Now, as Rosenberg claims, the Garden may well be part of the undeniable crucifixion content of the story; but from my view of the forced marriage it can also point to a very un-Edenic look at those parental beginnings that Bob Doran will marry into. After the Pater Noster of the Nuptial Mass, for instance, the priest prays:

> O God, who by Thine own mighty power, didst make all things out of nothing; who, having set in order the beginnings of the world, didst appoint Woman to be an inseparable helpmeet to Man, made like unto God, so that Thou didst give to woman's body its beginnings in man's flesh, thereby teaching that what it pleased Thee to form from one substance, might never be lawfully separated . . .

That such words will honor the marriages of a woman separated by a cleaver, so to speak, and a daughter forced to cleave makes for harsh irony.

Jumping ahead to *Ulysses* and the "Cyclops" section for a moment, we will hear Bob in later years drunkenly naming himself Manuo, in Sanscrit the great progenitor of the human race.[5] Perverse madonna that she is called, Polly has also something of the temptress in her descended from another kind of cleaving and garden. Though the church assigns the color white to the priest's stole for his mass, it must share with red the predominant coloration in the story. This butcher's red of flesh and blood is especially signaled in Jack's threat to an

111

artiste in the past "that if any fellow tried that sort of game with *his* sister he'd bloody well put his teeth down his throat, so he would." Jack, clerk to a commission agent, that is, a likely bookmaker, had been carrying two bottles of Bass ale, with their heavy red diamond marks, when Doran remembered that remark; and Joyce insisted in a letter to Grant Richards that he would excise all mention of the word "bloody" in *Dubliners* except for its use here in "The Boarding House." Since the word originates from the phrase "Christ's wounds," and helps conclude this first section of the story, the very elements themselves, bread and wine, flesh and blood, somehow enforce the continuation of the crucifixion at the center of the Nuptial Mass. The "Cyclops" section of *Ulysses* also informs us that Bob Doran as a boy had served mass at Adam and Eve's, the church on Merchant's Quay that was formerly a Mass-house disguised as a tavern in Penal days. But the tavern, the Mooney family, a marriage ceremony, his wine merchant employer, and the priest of the confessional will make up the cross Doran will bear or cleave to in the future, a crucifixion meant to atone for the sins of two generations of monied Mooneys (the name derives from "wealthy" in Irish) that fled from Spring Gardens to their present doubtful estate.

II

In that "Cyclops" episode of *Ulysses*, Bob Doran is at his slobbering worst. When not making up to the Citizen's mongrel dog Garryowen, he tearfully laments Paddy Dignam's death, while calling him Willy, and questions Christ's goodness, even branding Him "a bloody ruffian," in permitting such a loss. The nameless commentator recalls to us that Doran had married "the Bumbailiff's daughter," that her mother was known to keep "a kip in Hardwicke street," that Polly herself had since been available naked on the stairway. Of course, despite the Dublin pub exaggerations, we had already suspected a good deal of this from the story itself. But the passage I would dwell upon occurs some ten pages later after Bob Doran staggers out of Barney Kiernan's. We hear of his being

Blind to the world up in a shebeen in Bride street after closing time, fornicating with two shawls and a bully on guard, drinking porter out of teacups. And calling himself a Frenchy for the shawls, Joseph Manuo, and talking against the catholic religion and he serving mass in Adam and Eve's when he was young with his eyes shut who wrote the new testament and the old testament with hugging and smugging. And the two shawls killed with the laughing, picking his pockets the bloody fool and he spilling the porter all over the bed and the two shawls screeching laughing at one another. *How is your testament? Have you got an old testament?* . . . Then see him of a Sunday with his little concubine of a wife, and she wagging her tail up the aisle of the chapel, with her patent boots on her, no less, and her violets, nice as pie, doing the little lady. Jack Mooney's sister. And the old prostitute of a mother procuring rooms to street couples. Gob, Jack made him toe the line. Told him if he didn't patch up the pot, Jesus, he'd kick the shite out of him.[6]

Thus we learn that Jack probably did threaten Doran; that Doran now talks against Catholicism; that he asserts some twisted knowledge of the Bible yet when sober still takes himself to church on Sunday. With the prostitutes he had also tried to pass himself off as a Frenchman, calling himself Joseph Manuo. While, as I've acknowledged, Gifford and Seidman see the Sanscrit "Manuo" as a possible source for the word, I might add that Doran could well be drunkenly combining the Latin "manus" and its presence in the English word "manufacture" for the general meaning of "worker," "carpenter," "joiner." In other words, he may have thought himself as somehow like Joseph or, according to the Joyce–Gogarty parody, "The Ballad of Joking Jesus," Joseph the carpenter or joiner—in 1955, Pius XII was to declare 1 May the Feast of St Joseph the Worker.

I have begun this section with perhaps too much attention to *Ulysses* and to Joyce's most explicit, though comically exaggerated, review of Doran's miseries since "The Boarding House." Yet I think them highly relevant. In the story itself, we view his role as a Christ to be crucified for man's or Mooney's sins. If that were not enough, I would now add to this likeness

113

the other: his resemblance to Joseph, spouse of the Virgin Mary. If the sacrifice that centers in the Nuptial Mass points to the end of the sad tale as spun out in *Ulysses*, the plight of Mary and Joseph—in all their fears and hopes—might well mock the ending of the actual story before us.

On that barely single page of conclusion, following the first true page break in the story, all our attention is fixed on Polly. As all readers of the story know, Joyce had described her earlier as "a little perverse madonna." Her "wise innocence" is also a sly version of Christ's urging his disciples to be "wise as serpents and innocent as doves." On the other hand, Doran himself may resemble Joseph in his justness, his kindliness, basic celibacy, thoughtfulness when he discovers Polly's condition, even in his wish to spare her disgrace, though we must not forget his early wish like Joseph's to put her aside. Both men are known for their attention to religious duty. Both are relegated to family life. Both were sober, industrious workers, given the exception of Doran's later annual benders. To be sure, this comparison has elements of the wildest blasphemy in it. Yet so does much more in the story—even Polly's lighting her candle at his, suggesting that lighting a paschal candle might be something like Tenebrae for Doran. Still, this last page belongs to the pregnant Polly.

Having dried her eyes and refreshed them with water, she sits at the foot of the bed, contemplates the pillows, and falls into a reverie. Thereupon she is filled with "hopes and visions," this last phrase repeated: "Her hopes and visions were so intricate that she no longer saw the white pillows on which her gaze was fixed or remembered that she was waiting for anything." What were these hopes and visions? At the risk of being called an academic Christologist, I would venture that Joyce is quietly presenting a very human version of the Annunciation, feather pillows and all, in its total calming joy. Polly cannot be called full of grace. She is not blessed among women, though she *will* be married. For the moment, amazingly enough, she is transported beyond the pillows before her and beyond the exigencies of her troubling pregnancy. Her visions and hopes, transport and trance beyond seeing and remembering, may well be delusions. But Joyce delicately hints that she shares them in common with at least one other *enceinte* Mary and her supposedly celibate spouse.

The teasing unlikelihood of such a virgin birth and its veneration in Dublin faintly colors the entire story. Most particularly it mocks Mrs Mooney's haste in going about her business of reparation with Doran. At 11:17 A.M. the Madam drifts into a reverie in *her* chair, recounting her advantages in the brief exchange to ensue. At nearly 11:30 she dispatches the servant Mary to fetch Doran. Her hope is to make short twelve at Marlborough Street, that is, low mass at St Mary's Pro-Cathedral at twelve noon, celebrated at the side altar. Worth recalling also is that not only was Adam and Eve's, where Doran served, the Church of the Immaculate Conception but the Pro-Cathedral was also. That Polly, the issue of a butcher's daughter and a bumbailiff, should share in the heritage of the Immaculate Conception is astounding. She seems the very heir of original sin. Nevertheless, of the two smaller altars for low masses, one is dedicated to the Sacred Heart and the other to Our Lady—direct emphasis on home, hearth, and purity. These sanctities, then, must follow upon no more than a twenty-minute adjuration by Mrs Mooney that will seal Doran's domestic fate in holy Dublin. Given the proximity of Hardwicke Street to St George's, Mrs Mooney will need at least ten minutes to walk to 82 and 83 Marlborough Street, the Pro-Cathedral, by noon.

For this strange mixture of piety and meanness ingrained in the story, perhaps no other locale in Dublin served Joyce so well. On the one hand, the Pro-Cathedral serves the archdiocese of Dublin. Upon its completion in 1825 (the cornerstone was laid in 1816), it signaled the first Catholic public monument to an oppressed faith to be raised in some three hundred years. Typically, its site was that of a former Ascendancy residence, Annesley House in Marlborough Street.[7] It quickly became, in Stephen Gwynn's words, one of "the high places of Catholic worship in this Catholic city." He goes on to expand on that nomination:

> The Pro-Cathedral in Marlborough Street marks its provisional character by its title. Yet its opening was a triumph. Very few years after the passing of Emancipation this, the first great church built for the Catholics as a

distinct denomination in Dublin, was opened. Daniel O'Connell, the Liberator, was, as he deserved to be, conspicuous in the ceremony. But the centre of it was the Catholic Archbishop Murray . . .

Marlborough Street . . . is a landmark in the story of the resurrection of a race.[8]

Yet in 1900 the area was described in terms that might also apply today: "In no other district of the city is there such a teeming population of poor children—with such limited resources to meet their needs—as in the Pro-Cathedral parish."[9]

This topsy-turvy account of seduction, pregnancy, and forced marriage may be bitterly accented in the reversal of sequence that is part of Mrs Mooney's proposed journey to the heart of Catholic Dublin *after* settling with Doran. Her sentence will be laid upon that ineffectual savior; meanwhile, Polly will undergo something like an annunciation. The butcher's meaning of the word "cleave" and the actual facts behind the virgin birth push the upside-down nature of the story even further. Yet one more flip-flop may be possible.

In the manuscript version of the story, what I take to be its epiphany occurs imperfectly in the last sentence: "She remembered now what she had been waiting for: this was it." No longer a concluding paragraph and considerably shortened, the published sentence finally reads: "Then she remembered what she had been waiting for." I sense that the contrast between "hopes and visions" and the actual marriage-to-come has been markedly sharpened. Less certainly, I also sense that the two mocking reminders for a Catholic couple, the sacrifice in the Mass and then the Annunciation, are perhaps brought together. The flatness of that final printed sentence signals disappointment, to say the least. In fact, for a moment Polly herself appears the victim of a system, not just a conniver with her mother—and even that great florid creature had also suffered in marriage. Still, Polly's "hopes and visions" had come unbidden and would probably never be fulfilled. After all, Mary herself was relegated to something else than human motherhood by the mature Jesus, and her Joseph seems to have died long before the Crucifixion. I place, then, with some reservations, the concept of the Mystical Marriage alongside that last sentence. As described in the *Catholic Encyclopedia* (1913), this transforming vision, this moment of grace or mystical state, in a narrow sense, is presented under three headings:

> This state comprises three elements: (a) The First is an almost continual sense of the presence of God, even in the midst of external occupations. This favour does not of itself produce an alienation of the senses; ecstasies are more rare . . . (b) The second element is a transformation of the higher faculties in respect to their mode of operation: hence the name "transforming union"; it is the essential note of the state. The soul is conscious that in its supernatural acts of intellect and of will, it participates in the Divine life and in the analogous acts in God . . . Here, as in human marriage, there is a fusion of two lives. (c) The third element consists in an habitual intellectual vision of the Blessed Trinity or of some Divine attribute. This grace is sometimes accorded before the transforming union. (Vol. 9, pp. 703–4)

Doubless all these headings at most barely pertain to Polly's reverie. In any case, the "hopes and visions" attendant upon marriage and motherhood are quick to vanish at her mother's call. Any mystical marriage is at best parodied, as are the Annunciation and the later salvation implied in the Crucifixion. In other words, all those spiritual meanings attached by the Catholic religion to the exigencies of human union, birth, and maturity have but their psychological counterpart in a fleeting delusion. Otherwise, the life of the Pro-Cathedral parish— teeming poor children, disreputable parents, Sunday duty, and then the annual bender—all lie ahead.

III

But I have dwelt too long on what must seem an altogether inveterately theoretical level. The story's manuscript version is dated "Trieste, Austria, 1/17/05." Joyce lived then with the unmarried and pregnant Nora, former chambermaid in Finn's hotel—Ellmann calls it "an exalted rooming house"[10]—Nora, whose parents were separated and whose father drank. Joyce, then, may well have been reflecting on his own likely fate in Dublin. Nathan Halper, for one, has seen the obvious parallels.[11] The near-blasphemy, the cold religious irony and disdain for the conventionally pious marriage, nevertheless, might also include a touch of humor, however dour, by one who had survived. That last scene, so important despite its length, thus might also include a glimpse of the coquette in Polly, for when she rinsed her eyes she also "looked at herself in profile and readjusted a hairpin above her ear" before the mirror. This side of her, so very evident in the rest of the story, may lend whatever touch of humor the story maintains.

St George's Church, at the meeting of Eccles, Temple and Hardwicke Streets, might appear but for its bells and proximity to obtrude upon the story. After all, St George's is Church of Ireland. The fact that it was built by Francis Johnston between 1802 and 1814, and remains to this day the finest classical church in Dublin, probably meant little to Joyce.[12] In the story, moreover, mention of St George's is brief. At 11:17, Mrs Mooney realizes "that the bells of St George's had stopped ringing," and rightly so since Sunday service was at 11:30.[13] A little earlier in the story we had learned that "the belfry of George's Church sent out constant peals and worshippers, singly or in groups, traversed the little circus before the church, revealing their purpose by their self-contained demeanour no less than by the little volumes in their gloved hands." A snide glance at Protestant worship, even a hint of social condescension may be intended here, yet I cannot exclude a possibly playful look at this rather strange oasis remarkable even today in the heart of Catholic Dublin.

For in both passages the bells summon our attention and afford but one of the many legends and stories that attach to this magnificent, Wren-like church. For instance, Wellington was married there to a lady recently recovered from smallpox who may have inspired Tom Moore's "Believe Me if All Those Endearing Young Charms."[14] The large vaults beneath the church were used until 1875 as a bonded warehouse by the Revenue authorities; once the casks were tapped by a thief using a secret passage from the church into the vaults.[15] These items may reflect dimly on the events of the story, but the church bells are another thing. The eight bells given the church by Johnston and his wife included six hung in the Gothic tower of his stable at 64 Eccles Street—the stable done in Gothic to show his contempt for the style—where he rang them for his own delectation and to his neighbors' annoyance. Moreover, the first peal of bells in the church is said to have marked the death of Johnston himself. Although allowed to stand silent for many years, the bells began to peal again during the incumbency of Canon Peacocke beginning in 1876.[16] Shortly after that time, a parody of Father Prout's (Francis Mahony's) "The Bells of Shandon," itself a parody of Moore's "Evening Bells, a Petersburg Air," came to light.[17] What, we might ask, has all this to do with Polly at the looking-glass?

Now, the inscription on the font of the church reads: "Wash thy sins away and not thy face only." Whether they apply to Polly while adjusting herself, I cannot say. But the parody of Father Prout's parody seems strangely appropos:

> Thim bells of George's, they sound so gorgeous
>   Upon my conscience as I sit at tay,
> On a Sunday evenin' I fall a dreamin',
>   And git transplanted to Sweet Arran Quay.
>
> And there I wander, and in fancy ponder,
>   Till odours fragrant as the Liffey sweet,
> And roughs a screamin' disturb my dreamin'
>   And bring me back again to Temple Street.
>
> For it's there the car-boys, the roughs and Wrenn [sic] boys,
>   Around Saint George's now take their stand,
> And tho' you're hustled the Vestry's muzzled,
>   Bould Canon Peacocke says: "Thim bells is grand."[18]

Joyce most certainly knew of Father Prout, the nineteenth-century multilingual punster, at one time associated with Clongowes Wood.[19] Likewise, living as close to St George's as he did in the nineties, Joyce probably knew these lines as well as he knew the bells. In any case, the bells have just stopped ringing when Polly finds herself alone. Though the time is noon, not evening, she nevertheless falls to dreaming. Joyce, good Dublin man that he was, not only knew the extremely distinctive smell of the Liffey; he rather enjoyed it. In its praise, he once told Arthur Power that it was "not always a very sweet smell perhaps, but distinctive all the same."[20] A smell of like redolence is probably compounded of the warm breeze coming through the boarding-house windows along with the odor of breakfast remains and Jack's Bass ale. Marlborough Street itself begins on the quays. The poor I have referred to doubtless contain many a visible car-boy, rough and Wren boy (at Christmas time). Disestablished in 1869, the Church of Ireland perhaps might have done very little about such rowdiness. So, indeed, the church seems to stand aloof from the boarding house and all its stink, scandal, and sin yet, like its self-possessed parishioners, with Canon Peacocke proclaims: "Thim bells is grand."[21]

Polly, then, will not change. Other bells will ring for her wedding. Yet the realities of St George's circus and its environs are momentarily banished from her mind. Certainly, the likes of the Protestant parishioners Joyce has pointed out would be of no more help to her. And the very mention of St George, patron saint of England, would probably be anathema to her. His also being patron of the Order of the Garter might again force her to cast her gray-green eyes on the ceiling. The legend of his saving a king's daughter, his slaying her tormenting dragon, and then his enduring torture and suffering execution might, did she even contemplate such ironies, reflect oddly on Polly's own plight, the evil of her mother and Doran's sure fate.[22] The real power of Catholic Dublin, church and city, makes such improbable ironies almost humorous. Mary, Polly, and the nameless mob will settle according to the bells of the Pro-Cathedral.

IV

Perhaps my conclusion ought to continue from that mention of St George's. For, just as I hesitate to claim any powerful relevance for the saint himself, so I also hedge on any truly patriotic significance in the names surrounding his church.

Hardwicke Street, for instance, derives from Philip Yorke, third Earl of Hardwicke (1757–1834),[23] Lord-Lieutenant under Wellington and Pitt. Despite his position, however, he seems to have been genuinely sympathetic to Ireland, pushing hard for Catholic emancipation, and doing what he could to mollify the popular rage at the legislative union. But for his early efforts on behalf of William of Orange, Marlborough also is little more than a Whig name in Ireland. The fact that the amateur architect from Paris, John Sweetman who designed the Pro-Cathedral, had been exiled for his part in the 1798 rebellion; the despised Irish association of bumbailiffs with evictions; and the green in Polly's eyes, not to say the West of Ireland touch in her visions, might all seem to portend some national reflection on Joyce's part—yet the likelihood seems faint indeed. Much more likely is the fact that Hardwicke Street is known as the place "where Talbot the informer was murdered."[24] Even closer, I think, is the analogy of "The Villanelle of the Temptress" written by Stephen in the *Portrait*. As Robert Scholes has pointed out, the poem brings together a composite of female types: Eve, the Virgin, and the muse of Ireland herself. I might except the role of Irish muse for Polly, however, since the unholy combination of Magdalene and Madonna appears powerful enough. Her song "I'm a Naughty Girl" tells us far more about her than she realizes, though Zack Bowen may be doing her less than justice in marking her down as but "impish."[25] She is actually of a deeper dye, though also deserving of some sympathy. This is certainly not the simple story that most critics have called it.

The title itself, like the rest in the volume, may be outright proof enough. As others have seen, a bawdy house or bordello is the next step for such an establishment and its madam. In the early phrase "bed and board" that eventual likelihood peeks out. The figure of "board" as a table or being above board or placing one's cards on the table may also lead us to the statement that Mrs Mooney "counted all her cards before sending Mary up to Mr Doran's room to say that she wished to speak with him. She felt sure she would win." The *Oxford Dictionary* also cites "board" as a table where a council is held or, in fact, the very meeting itself—this also lies ahead for Doran. The even more hostile note may reside in the nautical connotations of boarding or overboard. "To board" can also mean to place in a coffin. I might also add that the words "board" or "boarder" may do more than signify restriction. They may also be virtually synonymous with carpentry and, stretched a bit, insinuate an altogether grim pun on a crucifixion. And that's where this chapter began. At the end Mrs Mooney's "Come down, dear, Mr. Doran wants to speak to you" brings together annunciation and crucifixion. But Joyce's last sentence underlines Polly's visions and their reality: "Then she remembered what she had been waiting for," just as the verses on the bells of St George's told us.

NOTES: CHAPTER 7

1 Bruce A. Rosenberg, "The crucifixion in 'The Boarding House,'" *Studies in Short Fiction*, vol. 5, no. 4 (Fall 1967), p. 50.

2 G. L. Barrow, "Justice for Thomas Mooney," *Dublin Historical Record*, vol. 24, no. 1 (December 1970), pp. 173–88. For a typical advertisement for John Mooney and his bakery, see *Irish Times*, 21 March 1889, p. 4. A leader in the *Irish Times*, 9 June 1890, p. 5, cites Bolands; Johnston, Mooney & O'Brien; and Herron, Connolly & Company as Dublin's three great bread companies.

3 An advertisement for Kelly Brothers, wine merchants, at 39 Upper O'Connell Street, suggests the fierce church connection of Doran's employer. Testimony by John Campbell, MD, Fellow of the Royal University, Ireland, Professor of Chemistry, Catholic University of Ireland, for the purity of their altar wine begins, "Gentlemen, I have analyzed the sample of Malaga for altar-use sent lately . . .," and follows upon the notice

Pure Altar Wine

We beg respectfully to direct the attention of the CATHOLIC HIERARCHY AND CLERGY to the following CERTIFICATE OF ANALYSIS, CU SCHOOL OF MEDICINE

See *Freeman's Journal*, 12 February 1890, p. 4.

4 "Memorials of Mud Island," *Irish Builder*, vol. 12, no. 254 (15 July 1870), pp. 163–4.

5 Don Gifford and Robert J. Seidman, *Notes for Joyce* (New York:

Dutton, 1974), p. 279.

6 *Ulysses*, Modern Library Edition (New York: Random House, 1946), pp. 308–9.

7 Rev. N. Donnelly, *Short History of Dublin Parishes* (Dublin: Catholic Truth Society, 1913), Vol. 3, pp. 96–100.

8 Stephen Gwynn, *Dublin Old and New* (New York: Macmillan, 1938), p. 159.

9 "The poor schools of the Pro-Cathedral parish," *Freeman's Journal*, 10 February 1900, p. 4.

10 Richard Ellman, *James Joyce*, rev. edn (New York/Oxford/Toronto: Oxford University Press, 1982), p. 162.

11 Nathan Halper, "'The Boarding House,'" in *James Joyce's Dubliners: Critical Essays*, ed. Clive Hart (New York: Viking Press, 1969), p. 77.

12 C. P. Curran, *James Joyce Remembered* (London: Oxford University Press, 1968), p. 40. For the beauty of this Francis Johnston church, see Edward McParland, "Francis Johnston, architect, 1760–1829," *Quarterly Bulletin of the Irish Georgian Society*, vol. 12, nos 3–4 (July–December 1969), pp. 112–18.

13 *Thom's Official Directory of Ireland for the Year 1895* (Dublin: A. Thom, 1895), p. 1305.

14 R. J. Kerr, *A Short History of the Parish and Church of St George, Dublin* (Dublin: Corrigan & Wilson, 1962), pp. 7–8.

15 D. A. Chart, *Dublin* (London: Dent, 1907), p. 325.

16 For more on Johnston, his bells and their inscription, along with the amateur society of bell-ringers, see "The bells of St George's," *Irish Times*, 31 October 1889, p. 6; H. A. Wheeler and M. J. Craig, *The Dublin City Churches of the Church of Ireland* (Dublin: APCK, 1948), pp. 18–20; and A. M. Fraser, "Old bells of Dublin," *Dublin Historical Record*, vol. 6, no. 2 (March–May 1944), pp. 57–9.

17 [Rev. Francis Mahony], *The Relics of Father Prout* (London: George Bell, 1881), pp. 56–62, 159–60. See also Edward C. McAleer, "Understanding 'The Shandon Bells,'" *Modern Language Notes*, vol. 66, no. 7 (November 1951), pp. 474–5.

18 Kerr, op. cit., p. 9. Precisely why the "Vestry's muzzled" escapes both me and the present incumbent of St George's, the Rev. C. A. Faull: letters to the author, 11 February and 14 March 1977. The question is why were the bells "allowed to stand silent for many years" before the incumbency of Canon Peacocke? It could be that before 1876 the local Vestry shared the low-church prejudice against the Italian (Popish) predilection for campanology and that their view was overruled by the new canon, who thought that "thim bells is grand." The result

would have been the "muzzling" of the Vestry on this subject. See also various references to evangelicalism in Donald H. Akenson, *The Church of Ireland: Ecclesiastical Reform and Revolution, 1800–1885* (New Haven, Conn.: Yale University Press, 1971). In particular note the strength of evangelicalism among the laity and lower clergy as opposed to the bishops and other dignitaries (pp. 132 ff. and pp. 302 ff.). See, too, the prohibition on ringing of bells during divine service (p. 306). As regards Canon Peacocke and the Vestry, see p. 276: "Hence they [the laity] demanded greater power not only because it was now paying for the religious tune, but because the tune played by the clergy often offended the more evangelical laity." I am indebted to Desmond Kennedy for this information.

19 Vivian Mercier, *The Irish Comic Tradition* (Oxford: Clarendon Press, 1962), pp. 222–5.
20 Arthur Power, *Conversations with James Joyce* (New York: Harper, Row, 1974), p. 93.
21 For more on the anti-Irish association of St George's, see J. T. Gilbert's *A History of the City of Dublin*, Vol. 3 (Dublin: McGlashan & Gill, 1859), pp. 180–4.
22 Alban Butler, *The Lives of the Saints*, ed. Herbert Thurston and Norah Leeson (London: Burns, Oates & Washbourne, n.d.), Vol. 4, pp. 264–6.
23 C. T. M'Cready, *Dublin Street Names, Dated and Explained* (Dublin: Hodges, Figgis, 1892), p. 48.
24 *Dignam's Dublin Guide* (Dublin/Belfast: Eason & Son, [1891]), p. 106. Hardwicke Street was also the first location of the Jesuits after the restoration of the Society. See Dillon Cosgrave, *North Dublin—City and Environs* (Dublin: Catholic Truth Society of Ireland, 1909), p. 49.
25 Zack Bowen, *Musical Allusions in the Works of James Joyce* (Albany, NY: State University of New York Press, 1974), p. 17.

8

"A Little Cloud": the Prisoner of Love

Several critics have made a reading of "A Little Cloud" easier for at least one perplexed reader. Two especially, Clarice Short and Maurice Harmon, have proved the importance of Byron to the story, since the poems "On the Death of a Young Lady" and *The Prisoner of Chillon* go a long way to providing the usual ironic contexts that Joyce so frequently uses to gain his lingering effects.[1] James Ruoff has also helped by pointing to Little Chandler as but another of Joyce's would-be artists.[2] Many another critic has fixed a Christological lens on the story, with varying results at best.[3] Finally, Richard Ellmann, both in his biography and in his edition of Joyce's letters, has demonstrated how figures like Gogarty and Fred Gallaher served Joyce for his composite character Ignatius Gallaher. What, then, remains to be said? Perhaps that both Little Chandler and Ignatius Gallaher may represent much more finely than hitherto recognized attitudes toward life and letters that Joyce would have us eschew. And these attitudes derive, I shall argue, from Fred Gallaher, Gogarty, and Ignatius Loyola on one side, and just as pitiably from George Roberts, one of the *New Songs* poets, on the other. The first side might be thought of as projecting a decayed tradition of eighteenth-century life and letters, as did Buck Gogarty to Joyce, while the other exemplified the timidity and sentimental effusions of a decayed Romanticism caught in the Twilight songs of AE's anthology. And then, at the end of this chapter, I shall try mightily to show how both parties, in life and in letters, while seemingly so opposed, are very much the same.

125

I

Their apparent contrast, yet actual likeness, subtly marks the very beginning of the story that sets Little Chandler on his way to meet Gallaher. Not a law student but a clerk, probably in the Registry of Deeds (his writing is "tiresome"), Little Chandler picks his way from the King's Inns and Henrietta Street to Corless's on Church Lane near the Hibernian Bank, a restaurant once described as "the centre of fashionable life, and one of the most perfect and best kept dining rooms in the city."[4] Its official name was the Burlington Restaurant and it became Jammet's in 1905. But the King's Inns and its surroundings ought to halt us for the moment.

Aside from closely resembling a prison—and others have seen the beginning of the *Prisoner of Chillon* theme here—especially as one passes through its arch facing Henrietta Street, the King's Inns, built by Gandon, does face on a street in whose mansions "the old nobility of Dublin had roistered," to repeat Joyce's words. The cornerstone of the present building was laid on 1 August 1800.[5] But the fading elegance of the building was still recognized a year after the story was written:

> The building was designed by James Gandon, and the stone carving was entrusted to Edward Smyth. Though the entrance is in Henrietta Street, the building really faces Constitution Hill, and consists of two wings, each of two storeys in height, surmounted by a pediment, and connected by a central building above which is a graceful octangular cupola. The central building is entered by a lofty arched gateway communicating to Henrietta Street. Over the latter are the Royal Arms carved in Portland Stone by Edward Smyth. The doorways in the wings are flanked by fine allegorical Caryatides. Over the windows of the second storey of the north wing is an alto-relievo representing Bacchus and Ceres, attended by the Seasons, sacrificing on an antique tripod; and over the front of the north wing are Wisdom, Justice, and Prudence similarly employed, and attended by Truth, Time, and History. The finest apartment is the dining-hall, measuring 81 feet by 42

feet, ornamented by fluted Ionic columns, and having a handsome ceiling with figures in alto-relievo, representing the four Cardinal Virtues. The hall is adorned with portraits of legal celebrities. The Library occupies the site of Primate Robinson's dwelling-house, and was built in 1827, at a cost of £20,000, from the designs of Frederick Darley.[6]

Within a hundred years, however, all had changed and the neighborhood had decayed into the fallen splendor and inelegant tenements that greet Little Chandler at every turn. As one Dublin wit put it in his *Adversaria Hibernica*:

Subsequent events proved that the site on Constitution Hill, Primate Robinson's garden, was not so cheap nor so free of difficulties as was imagined. After compensation being paid to minor claimants, it was found so difficult to adjust the matter of title, that we believe a special act of Parliament had to be procured. However pleasing the site of the Inns of Court might have appeared nearly a century ago, time has since worked great changes in its surroundings. The glory of the fine old mansions in Henrietta-street has long since departed, and dilapidation is fast setting in out and about here. Constitution Hill, which "backs" the Inns, has a rotten constitution, and the place has for many years been more unsavoury than sanitary. The old branch canal that towered over the Temple grounds has lost its fly-boats and picturesque character years ago. The railway station and its belongings are more business-like than picturesque, and give forth more frantic noise than law students studying Blackstone or Coke upon Littleton care to hear . . .[7]

On the other hand, Joyce regales us with the stately eighteenth-century names—Grattan, Henrietta, wife to Charles Fitzroy, second Duke of Grafton, Lord-Lieutenant from 1721 to 1724, and Capel, another lord-lieutenant. On the other hand, one senses the merging of this landscape with the fashionable and romantic melancholy, sadness, autumnal sunshine, and sense of futility that hover about, so to speak, Little Chandler. The very motto of the King's Inns, *Nolumus Mutari*—"We do not wish to change"[8]—signals the inherent apathy of Little Chandler's life and literary daydreams. Yet, although he is aware of the drabness of Capel Street, Little Chandler, as Joyce assures us, has no memory of that glorious past. Nevertheless, it will accost him in what may well be a personification of the worst parts of that century, Ignatius Gallaher himself.

II

Gallaher, for instance, lives by his wits, revels in being a rake among rakes, remains an unreconstructed gent who gambles, drinks, whores, scribbles, has an heiress in mind, and desperately borrows money. He is in other words a striking instance of a modern eighteenth-century buck. Though he has charm and talent enough, his exterior is gaudy, he affects a fearless accent, sometimes called a Protestant shout, flaunts an orange tie, and by his occasional French words would be thought most cosmopolitan. In truth, as Little Chandler comes to realize, Gallaher is vulgar, patronizing, and articulate only in his mastery of the cliché. For all his bravado, he is obviously burned out. His appearance may, then, come close to Gogarty's, but his stilted language is that of a considerably decayed eighteenth-century buck, the language of Fred Gallaher, one-time editor of *Sport* and then a successful demon journalist appointed to a high position on the English *Sportsman* in February 1890.[9] First, then, we might listen to a few passages of Gallaher's prose from his little book *Our Irish Jockeys*. In this instance his subject is the famous jockey, Thomas Ryan:

> In selecting Thomas Ryan as the subject of my first sketch, I think the public will agree with me that the right man is in the right place; for though early this year this popular jockey has been unfavoured by Dame Fortune, his performances have long since marked him out as the premier of Irish professionals . . .

> His parents, at the time of his birth, were in humble circumstances . . . his father attempted to direct his

attention to farming pursuits, but the spirit of roving strongly prevailed . . .

Ryan gamely won his spurs . . . Delighted with his success he built vast castles in the air . . .

Through the kindness of Mr. Moneypenny, Lord Drogheda's trainer, Ryan secured an engagement to ride, both on the flat and over the country, for the noble Marquis. The Fates, however, seemed to have decreed against him, and he rode with little or no success. His lordship's favorite mare, Lady Bird, was entrusted more than once to Ryan, but he seemed doomed to carry the black and silver jacket ever in the ruck.[10]

Yet the resemblance is, as many have insisted, also to Gogarty or, better, to Buck Mulligan. Gogarty, too, was a pub wit, whether at the Ship, the Pearl or the Bailey in later life. Yeats and Gogarty's idolizing biographer, Ulick O'Connor, saw him uppermost as the last of the eighteenth-century bucks. For all of his vociferous anticlericalism, Gogarty somehow also usually found himself on the proper side, once even blessed by the Pope alongside his highly pious friend, the first president of the Executive Council of the Irish Free State, William Cosgrave. Like Ignatius Gallaher, Gogarty also loved a lord, overdressed, made up to the English, and was full of gossip. Even the physical likeness is startling: the close-cropped hair, the pale face, the blue eyes, if not the gaudy tie. If Ignatius Gallaher's talk seems close to Fred Gallaher's prose, how very distant is that talk from Gogarty's own prose? True enough, Gogarty had a certain memorable and malicious Dublin wit, as did Joyce himself. But Gogarty's later writing tended more and more to journalism, at best toward that Irish staple of weakly strung together anecdotes, seen at its best in *As I Was Going Down Sackville Street*. Otherwise, for all his enthusiasm for the classics, and despite his reputation as a minor poet, Gogarty as early as 1903 was writing for Dublin papers and magazines. What's more, Ulick O'Connor discovers him at the end of his life very much at home in New York, making his living by writing for popular magazines, giving lectures, and reminiscing among the wealthy and important. Ignatius Gallaher, then, is a cheap edition of the eighteenth-century rake with all the obvious vulgarity of Fred Gallaher, with perhaps just as much of the successful, English-aping aplomb that sits so askew on Buck Mulligan, and with no small amount of the aggressive worldliness caught in his Christian name, Ignatius.

We might linger on that name for the moment. Perhaps we have heard enough of Ignatius Loyola's dramatic conversion from cavalier, soldier, and vain glorious pursuer of women to militant for Christ, organizer of the Jesuits, and writer of the bad prose of the *Spiritual Exercises*. Yet from a curious point of view Loyola's career has a strange pertinence for Ignatius Gallaher's own checkered existence. Where Loyola was virtually forced out of Spain to carry on his mission in Paris, Gallaher after some financial difficulties in Ireland has succeeded well enough in London. Loyola took his final vows in a chapel in Montmartre. Gallaher has much to say about Bohemian Paris and its *cocottes*. He, too, is something of a womanizer and has been associated, if not with the military, at least with sports. If his writing has not included spiritual exercises, we nevertheless learn in the newspaper office of *Ulysses* that he had been quick enough to get out the story, not entirely accurate, of the Phoenix Park murders by something like a clever sleight-of-hand. I may exaggerate in sensing a likeness between the two men, but my point is that the seemingly incongruous name Ignatius when appended to Gallaher may not entirely ill-accord with Gallaher's real character, and may in any case jolt an alert reader into at least a dim recognition that Christian names in Ireland often have a way of mocking the piety of their bearers. In condemning the evil ways of the world, Gallaher, in what I take to be Joyce's careful selection of words, makes "a catholic gesture with his right arm." Perhaps that's enough. Harking back to the importance of Byron to the story, however, one must say that Fred Gallaher, Gogarty (though not at his best), and Loyola together were a long way from the Regency buck who could write *The Prisoner of Chillon*. Still, one might expect the flat language of Byron's juvenilia, "On the Death of a Young Lady," from either of the three—and from Little Chandler, too.

III

Yet Little Chandler admires Byron, though for the wrong poem. This I take to be Joyce's way of discovering not the aftermath of Georgian Dublin in his day but rather the namby-pamby, cloying, sentimental imitation of Yeats's worn-out coat, one of the last dilutions of Romanticism in literature, the Celtic Twilight. I refer specifically to those poets, George Roberts among them, whom Joyce bemoaned on their appearance in the 1904 *A Celtic Christmas* edited by AE, some of those whom Yeats designated as his fleas when asked by AE to praise them. As Joyce wrote to his brother Stanislaus in January 1905:

> *What* is wrong with all these Irish writers—what the blazes are they always snivelling about? Isn't it funny to read Roberts' poems about a mother pressing a baby to her breast? O, blind, snivelling, nose-dropping calumniated Christ wherefore were these young men begotten?[11]

At least one offending poem in *A Celtic Christmas* was doubtless Roberts's "Maternal Night." A mere glance at it will show that Joyce's judgment was not harsh:

> Warm, odorous summer night,
> As a mother to her breasts,
> You press the Earth's sun-wearied face;
> While a babe in her arms she rests.
> With loosened robe you lie,
> Till your baby's breath in sleep
> Brings the peace long sought through starry ways,
> Up from the inmost deep.[12]

The ending of "A Little Cloud" stands in sharp contrast. On a fall evening, a sobbing child finally finds peace in his mother's arms, yet the scene is ugly. Man and wife hate each other, and the man, Little Chandler, breaks into childish tears. I shall go on to suggest, then, that the Roberts who wrote the above poem and the Little Chandler of the gentle melancholy amid crumbling eighteenth-century Dublin are both much closer to the mawkish, maudlin, snivelling Romantic spirit that Joyce detected in those lesser imitators of the Twilight than most critics have noted.

Amazingly, a number of strong likenesses hold between Roberts and Little Chandler. Both, for instance, were much the same physically. Roberts was approximately five feet three inches tall, and even in old age appeared to be, for all his portliness, a fragile little man, if newspaper pictures may be trusted. When, from 1918 to 1919, Edward MacLysaght knew him at Maunsel's, where Roberts had been a managing director since 1903, Roberts had two boys and had been married for nearly ten years to a woman described as savage but decent. He had a familiar means to escape trouble by inevitably pleading family difficulties. MacLysaght and his friends would repeat of Roberts: "Don't hit me now, I've a baby in my arms."[13] Joyce may also be glancing at his determined legality by having Little Chandler copy legal documents in the King's Inns. Though Roberts's early associations were with Belfast, and after 1926 he lived in London until his death in 1953,[14] his memoirs clearly show him to have been attracted from Belfast to Dublin at the beginning of this century largely because of the literary revival ferment and his introduction to the AE circle.[15] As "Gas from a Burner" insinuates, Joyce knew that Roberts had for a time traveled for a woman's underwear concern—and thus made Little Chandler skittish about buying women's blouses. Amazingly enough, as secretary of the National Theatre Society he also acted such roles as Timmy the Smith in *The Well of the Saints*—did Joyce also glance at that incongruence? In any case, Roberts was much taken by the Celtic note. He had, to a degree, no little aesthetic sensibility. His book designs, for example, were highly praised. So were the printing and typography of his Maunsel volumes.[16] But, as in his treatment of Joyce later on, Roberts as businessman was notoriously "inept, capricious, and scheming."[17] Perhaps not quite the same charge can be leveled at Little Chandler. Yet his surname itself can mean "dealer," and he, too, had his schemes—to become known in London as a minor poet of the revival. His ineptness in handling his child is transparent. No less, his capriciousness is part of that ineptness, especially when he suddenly shouts at his child and just as unexpectedly breaks into tears. Even forty years after publication, Roberts could still whine his innocence after clashing with Gogarty over the rejection of *Dubliners*.[18]

IV

The distance between Roberts's poetic view of maternity, love, and children, on one hand, and the grim facts of these three subjects, on the other, are most apparent in the story's last scene. Aside from the poem on mother and child that Joyce abhorred, other poems, this time from *New Songs*, are equally apropos. For example, "The Prisoner of Love" almost demands to be read against that scene if the full irony is to be caught:

> Still, although I know our ways
> Are divergent through all time,
> Following love will shed its rays
> On the path you choose to climb.
>
> And your eyes my thought will meet
> Shining in your guiding star;
> Flowers shall spring before your feet
> From my brooding love afar.
>
> But your voice I hear that cries,
> "Oh! the brambles trip my feet—
> Oh! the lights that blind my eyes.
> When shall love and freedom meet?"

Moods, infantile hopes, melancholy, sadness, perhaps echoes from Yeats and Synge in Little Chandler's imagining tenements as tramps who will "arise"—all these easy counters have come to express the personality of Little Chandler from the time we saw him leaving the King's Inns for Corless's. But Roberts's poem "The Prisoner of Love" reverses the eyes Little Chandler focuses on in that last scene. Annie's photograph offers eyes set in a prim, pretty, mean face, eyes too composed, eyes that "repelled him [Little Chandler] and defied him; there was no passion in them, no rapture." The actual eyes that he meets upon her return are filled with a glare of hatred. The voice he hears is hardly a prisoner of love. *He* is the prisoner of love, and his prison is what has passed for love in his altogether loveless life. Only for him will freedom and love never meet. He, not his child, is the real subject, however unwittingly, of Annie's words at the end:

—My little man! My little mannie! Was 'ou frightened
love? . . . There now, love! There now! . . . Lambabaun!
Mamma's little lamb of the world! . . . There now!

Of course Little Chandler is "Mamma's little lamb of the
world" and, as the Irish word would have it, a white lamb. He
also is in the keeping of women with the names of two very
famous mothers, as Robert Boyle has pointed out: Anne, the
mother of Mary, and Annie's sister, Monica, the mother of St
Augustine.[19] Given the howling brat, virginal wife in blue
blouse, and husband out of the lamplight, some have seen
Little Chandler as a comic Joseph. Perhaps so.

But a few more poems by Roberts from *New Songs* may lead
to the conclusion of this chapter. As Little Chandler retreats
from the lamplight before Annie's baleful glare, we may be
witnessing the end of a day that parodies one more tootling
Celtic tone. This poem is entitled "Earth and the Infinite":

> By day the Dagda hunts afar,
> While silent is each unseen star.
> And Dana busied in her house,
> Heeds not the absence of her spouse.
> Till with the twilight he comes back,
> Leaving a sunset in his track.
> The mother's voice speaks through her woods,
> Her heart's thought is her solitudes.
> The purple mist on vale and hill
> Is her face leaning over the window sill.
> By night, the rushlight moon is lit,
> Together Dagda and Dana sit.
> And then beyond where joy subsides,
> Peace welleth up on rippling tides.
> In dreamy rivers flowing—Sleep
> Unveils the vast mysterious deep.

One need only say that the Registry of Deeds has not been a
very happy hunting-ground for Little Chandler. Nor has his
(for a long time) unseen star, Ignatius Gallaher, been silent.
Dana, Annie, may have been busy about the house but has
certainly not left her spouse's absence unheeded. He has
returned past twilight and has heard a mother's voice offering
him short answers. Her face may have been at the window sill,

but now it has disappeared around the corner to get sugar and tea. The face in the photograph that remains behind is anything but misty. When she returns, joy remains subsided, but peace has yet to well up. What sleep will bring is any reader's guess. Whatever rivers flow are the tears of man and child. In short, a very real wife and a mawkish poet are at the breaking-point after a most trying day. Neither is very earthy, nor is the infinite attached to their anger and melancholy. Moreover, he has all too easily resisted the call to poetry. Or, to put the point in Roberts's own words, this time in his fourth and last poem from *New Songs*, "The Call":

> From the fireside of your heart
> Where love blew the peats aglow,
> I arise, I will depart,
> I must go.
>
> Peace was dwelling in your eyes,
> But across my soft content,
> Gleams like rays in midnight skies
> Quivered and went.
>
> I arise though blind with tears
> To fare forth on the long way.
> When the beckoning gleam appears
> I must obey.

Little Chandler may well be called to poetry and London, but we know he won't go, even though he must go. No peace of course is in Annie's eyes. He is hardly contented—yet to no avail. Blinded with tears all right, he will nevertheless refuse the long way. He disobeys any beam of the Celtic Twilight. Something has blown the peats aglow in Annie's heart, but hardly love. As Gallaher said of an attachment to one woman, "Must get a bit stale." For Little Chandler it has. The remorse that overtakes him is defined by Skeat's *Etymological Dictionary* (1882), a favorite word-quarry for Joyce, as "pain or anguish for guilt." This meaning may certainly suffice. Yet the word derives from the Latin *remordere*, "to bite again." Now, while the exact meaning of that remorse has been a moot point of the story, I see it here as not so much for his failed literary career, mean marriage, or even crying child who would not be stopped. Rather, I regard the word as a "biting again," an "in-biting," where Little Chandler may have once more bitterly rejected any thought of a literary career and, full of shame, more than acquiesced to being a prisoner for life.

V

How, then, must we finally judge this story, broken by Joyce with a line of periods into two parts, not three? Perhaps the best way to start is for me to pay tribute to James Ruoff's essay, "'A Little Cloud': Joyce's portrait of the would-be artist," for at the end of that essay Ruoff insists of Gallaher and Little Chandler that "in the important things, they are similar." He goes on to enumerate these likenesses: both are disappointed writers; with varying disguises each finds the world somewhat hopeless; each senses the passing years; both have in fact fled from life, though in opposite directions; and each is capable of bullying and insinuating intimidation.[20] This is well said and helps me to add my own point by way of corollary.

I would start by looking at a typical review of *New Songs*, this one from the *Freeman's Journal*, and at the same time reminding ourselves of Joyce's and Yeats's scornful reaction to such poets. The full opening paragraph is the more relevant of the two, coming as it does at the end of an omnibus review:

We have kept the best wine till last. In almost every poetic virtue this volume is the freshest and most striking of the three. It consists of lyrics selected by A.E. from the work of the young poets who have clustered about "The Celtic Christmas" and "The United Irishman," eight writers in all being represented. Some of the names are already fairly well known, such as Alice Milligan and Padraic Colum; the other six—Eva Gore-Booth, Thomas Keohler, Susan Mitchell, Seumas O'Sullivan, George Roberts, and Ella Young—come before the general public practically for the first time. . . . They all agree . . . in breaking away completely from "The Nation" tradition. We find no longer the stock metres, somewhat threadbare with long use, nor the clear rhetoric and daylight ethics of that famous school. On the contrary, we find, as to method, a general preference for measures, more delicate and less emphatic, and, as to matter, a cultivation of that rare and more mysterious colour of emotion which nourished best in the twilight. Artistically, there is a very great advance. Not one of these eight "New Singers" writes badly; and if the experience of life of many of them is somewhat thin and borrowed, that was only to be expected. The influence most clearly traceable in the book . . . is that of A.E. himself, numerous pieces recalling not only the passionate glow of his verse, but also his Indian metaphysics and somewhat baffling symbolism. We do not mean, however, to suggest that, as a whole, the book is merely derivative. Nothing of the kind . . . but in due time they will honour their master by ceasing to imitate him. An imitation of A.E. to the uninitiated reader wears often the appearance of parody.[21]

Oddly enough, Gogarty's review of the same volume approximates the same qualified praise—although his major literary defender denies it.[22] If Gogarty laments the thinness of matter, the lack of inspiration, and the artificiality inherent in these poems—as the above review does—he nevertheless finds much to praise. Here are some instances: "The impressions derived from a reading of 'New Songs' are indefinite, variegated, confused and beautiful, as if one gazed at a great figured window in an unknown cathedral. Perhaps a sense of the skill and faultlessness of the verse is most present . . ." Then, after quoting the first stanza of Seumas O'Sullivan's "The Twilight People," Gogarty comments: "This is beautiful and rare music. . . ." Gogarty goes on to misquote the last two lines of the second stanza of the same poem and adds: "I do not call such poetry weak. Evasive and retreating as its music is, it inspires one with strength as a silent vale among mountains." Colum's "Drover" also gets patted on the head for "its great lurching movement."[23] Remarking the success of *New Songs* in a letter to G. K. A. Bell in early September 1904, Gogarty broached his intention of issuing a like volume—with the help of Seumas O'Sullivan.[24] To be sure, the poems would be satirical and critical, hence anonymous, but the recognition of AE's gathering and its success is clear. By the way, Gogarty's volume finally did appear, anonymously, as *Secret Springs of Dublin Song* in 1918.

One may, then, believe that Ignatius Gallaher and Little Chandler, one working for the English press, the other dreaming of that press's recognition of his poetic talents, might well have combined in admiration of *New Songs* and Byron's juvenilia. Chandler might have written Roberts's drivel, and Gallaher applauded it—with reservations—in both the English and Irish presses. After all, the name Gallaher derives from the Irish term signifying "foreign help."[25] On the other hand, his mother's name, Malone, which Little Chandler hopes will Irish out his own, derives, so help me, from the Irish word for "servant of St John," Gogarty's middle name. The English name Chandler, with its commercial associations, may be bad enough, but Malone took on equally English connotations very early in Ireland. As Father Woulfe goes on to elaborate in tracing the rise to prominence of the Malone family: "In the 17th century they rose to power and influence as landed proprietors, and after 1691 seem to have thrown in their lot with the English."[26]

No less, if Little Chandler admires Byron's "On the Death of a Young Lady," written when he was 14, so, too, might any decayed and ignorant Regency buck resembling Gallaher. The poem demands a childish view of women as one staple for its admiration. I have mentioned Ruoff's list of likenesses in the two men. Still, Little Chandler saw only their differences at the end of the first part of the story. But in the second he begins to envy Gallaher again. The rich, passionate, and desirable Jewesses Gallaher bragged of as possibilities for his bride allow Little Chandler to see Annie as cold, mean, and raptureless. No less fatuously, Gallaher's life now strikes him as a brave one. Where he had remembered some financial shenanigans said to have forced Gallaher's departure from Dublin, now Little Chandler envies him that departure. But the mean and pretty furniture that Annie had bought remains to be paid for. Thus, in addition to the equivalence of their literature, their appreciation of that literature, and the emptiness of their lives that would evade the real life of Dublin and London, the two men also unite in Byron's early poem. Remnants of a decayed eighteenth century and an outgrown nineteenth century, Gallaher and Little Chandler really contrast with the Byron of *The Prisoner of Chillon* and the Joyce who wrote "A Little Cloud," for Joyce and Byron expose the worst of their characters, while writing in the best of both literary traditions.

NOTES: CHAPTER 8

1   Clarice Short, "Joyce's 'A Little Cloud,'" *Modern Language Notes*, vol. 72, no. 4 (April 1957), pp. 275–8, and Maurice Harmon, "Little Chandler and Byron's 'First Poem,'" *Threshold*, no. 17 [1962], pp. 59–61.
2   James Ruoff, "'A Little Cloud': Joyce's portrait of the would-be artist," *Research Studies of Washington State College*, vol. 25, no. 3 (September 1957), pp. 256–71. See also A. J. Solomon, "'The Celtic note' in 'A Little Cloud,'" *Studies in Short Fiction*, vol. 9, no. 3 (Summer 1972), pp. 269–70.
3   See, for instance, Harold Brodbar, "A religious allegory: Joyce's 'A Little Cloud,'" *Midwest Quarterly*, vol. 2, no. 3 (Spring 1961), pp. 221–7. Much more germane is the possible Ignatian structure of the story pointed out by David Weir in his "Meditative structure in 'A Little Cloud,'" *James Joyce Quarterly*, vol. 14, no. 1 (Fall 1976), pp. 84–7.
4   *Dignam's Dublin Guide* (Dublin/Belfast: Eason & Son, [1891]), p. 19. For more on Corless's, see Stephen Gwynn, *Dublin Old and New* (New York: Macmillan, 1938), pp. 236–9.
5   Liam Cosgrave, "The King's Inns," *Dublin Historical Record*, vol. 21, no. 2 (March 1967), p. 51.
6   Samuel A. Ossory FitzPatrick, *Dublin* (London: Methuen, 1907), pp. 173–4. For but one list of the distinguished names—Graftons, Blessingtons, Montjoys, and Gardiners—that graced Henrietta Street, see Dillon Cosgrave, *North Dublin—City and Environs* (Dublin: Catholic Truth Society of Ireland, 1909), p. 40.
7   *Irish Builder*, vol. 34, no. 769 (1 January 1892), p. 1 and "The tenement system in Dublin," *Irish Times*, 2 December 1889, p. 6. See also E. MacDowell and Leonard R. Strangways, *Dictionary of Dublin* (Dublin: Sealy, Bryers & Walker [1907]), p. 117.
8   Liam Cosgrave, op. cit., p. 52.
9   "Mr Fred Gallaher," *Irish Times*, 13 February 1890, p. 5.
10 Fred Gallaher, *Our Irish Jockeys* (Dublin: Christopher Smyth, [1874?]), pp. 9–11.

11 *Letters*, Vol. 2, p. 78.
12 *A Celtic Christmas* [*The Irish Homestead*, Christmas Number], vol. 10 (3 December 1904), p. 22.
13 Interview with Edward MacLysaght, Dublin, 1970.
14 The best short account of Roberts is in Alan Denson's edition of *Letters from AE* (London: Abelard-Schuman, 1961), p. 269.
15 "Memoirs of George Roberts. I: A Meeting with AE," *Irish Times*, 13 July 1955, p. 5.
16 Richard Burnham, "Poor George Roberts, Dublin publisher," *Eire-Ireland*, vol. 10, no. 3 (Autumn 1975), p. 145.
17 ibid., 146.
18 W. R. Rodgers (ed.), *Irish Literary Portraits* (New York: Taplinger, 1973), p. 42.
19 Robert Boyle, "'A Little Cloud,'" *James Joyce's Dubliners: Critical Essays*, ed. Clive Hart (New York: Viking Press, 1969), p. 91.
20 Ruoff, op. cit., p. 269.
21 "Literature: three volumes of verse," *Freeman's Journal*, 18 March 1904, p. 7.
22 James E. Carens, *Surpassing Wit* (New York: Columbia University Press, 1979), p. 22.
23 O. Gogarty, "Literary notice. *New Songs*," *Dana*, vol. 1 (May 1904), p. 32.
24 Oliver St John Gogarty, *Many Lines to Thee: Letters to G. K. A. Bell*, ed. James F. Carens (Dublin: Dolmen Press, 1971), pp. 38–9.
25 Patrick Woulfe, *Irish Names and Surnames* (Dublin: M. H. Gill, 1923), p. 538.
26 ibid., p. 599.

9

"Counterparts":
Hell and the Road to
Beggar's Bush

"Counterparts" has puzzled commentators, who often see it as little more than a panorama of Dear, Dirty Dublin, and discover in Farrington the bestial wrath of a supremely frustrated average man, ultimately a hog of a man, so that the story finally becomes an extended "swine song."[1] Almost all writers on the story have sensed the virulence of the Irish–English, Catholic–Protestant conflict as Joyce moves through his apparent tripartite structure of paralysis in work, play, and love. All have also speculated on what precise counterparts Joyce had in mind. Most helpful has been Professor Stein's reading that finds Farrington committing all seven of the Deadly Sins, though the implication of these sins may have escaped Stein as may have the date of the story.[2] For, rather than consigning Farrington to the future pangs of hellfire, I believe that Joyce is portraying the typical hellish day of all too many Dubliners who have no choice of jobs. Even Farrington's name, along with his bulk, points to a country or a farming life that should be his as farrier, farmer, or pig-breeder.

I shall contend that the hell he endures is also something of an inverted thing: at home he is at his most hellish, yet his home ought to be the haven or heaven from his unrewarding work. On the other hand, the rank hell of the pubs is for a time heaven enough for him. His purgatorial labors in a law office, on the other hand, keep him shuttling from ground floor (and nearby pub) to the grinding pressures of his first-storey desk to the awful heaven of the God of the office, the abode of Mr Alleyne on the third level, a sheer hell for Farrington. What's more, few among his universal detractors recall Joyce's distinct if muted sympathy for Farrington. One example may lie in the oft-reiterated "the man" in the first section where we watch, as Joyce must have supposed, something like everyman at his daily Sisyphean labors. A well-known passage in a Joyce letter also speaks of Farrington as an example of the Dublin fact that "few wives and homes can satisfy the desire for happiness."[3] Let me turn, then, to that hell Joyce discovers in Dublin office, pub, and home on what I take to be Wednesday, 17 February 1904, Ash Wednesday.[4]

I

After his two encounters with Mr Alleyne, Farrington tells himself that "his life would be a hell to him." It already is. For I take this entire first section to be no less than a parody of the Crucifixion, recalling the companion story, "The Boarding House," and at the same time an equally direct experience of hell. Almost immediately we learn that Farrington had a "hanging face," a pun on its length and likely future. Before that a bell and a voice, both described as furious, summon the man—Ecce Homo—upstairs. The bell may take off on the consecration of the Host as a sacrifice, yet the voice of heaven is an all-too-piercing North of Ireland voice summoning the slothful man to a chastisement for slowness in copying a contract and for taking too much time for lunch. Quite literally, Farrington's elevation has taken him to the place of a skull, Golgotha, for Mr Alleyne's bald skull thoroughly dominates this heaven. So far, on this visit Farrington has already blasphemed his god-like employer—"Blast him!" Before being dismissed again to his work he is threatened with Mr Crosbie, a possible parodic reference to the Cross. Thoroughly tormented, Farrington returns to his copying, that is, to making a counterpart, a copy of a legal document, the original meaning of the word "counterpart." We may also speculate that Miss Parker and her typewriter portend an actual threat to his job.

After doffing his shepherd's cap—another crazy reminder of Christ?—the man has a glass of plain and a caraway seed in

O'Neill's snug. If these are also a take-off on the hyssop and vinegar given Christ, so be it. In any case, though confused by drink, Farrington maintains the impenitence of the damned while returning the Delacour correspondence to Mr Alleyne. But by the end of the day, hopelessly behind in his work, his mind filled with the heaven of the public house come nightfall and with fourteen pages—Stations of the Cross?—to go, he looks up to find Mr Alleyne addressing him again. Two letters are missing and Farrington knows it. Hell and crucifixion proceed apace. So now, after undergoing the fiery pain of sense—the need for a drink—he undergoes a so-called pain of loss—the letters. His final impertinence to Alleyne accents his continued impenitence. The incomplete phrase, "In no case shall the said Bernard Bodley be," now applies to him. He had already focused on those three last words. At best, while denied the presence of a weeping Mary, he has nevertheless gained the smile of a woman, possibly Jewish, with the name Miss Delacour, on whom Mr Alleyne is said to be sweet. I cannot help seeing her as a slightly comic Virgin Mary, the final touch in this first parody and, to expand the scene of torment, the only sympathizer with a Dublin Prometheus beset by the fires of a Northern God.

II

Next Farrington will visit what he takes to be the heaven of three Dublin pubs—Davy Byrne's, the Scotch House, and Mulligan's of Poolbeg Street. Yet the almost constant rounds of hot whiskeys give the impression of hell wherein he will again suffer its principal pains, those of sense and loss. Yet I think something of the same counter-parody continues, that is, Farrington repeats grotesquely and generally something of Christ's experience after three o'clock on Good Friday. With money in his hand and joy in his heart, after leaving the pawn office in Fleet Street, Farrington masterfully takes his way down Westmoreland Street among children and the young, something like Christ's descending into limbo to assure the innocent of their access to heaven. In other words, the Dublin counterpart, not legal copy now but ironic contrast, of a man out for a good night of drinking (the office staff "could all go to hell") might be Christ's descent into limbo and then purgatory—the streets and pubs where "curling fumes of punch" await Farrington. Like the heaven of the office, however, the purgatory of the pubs, with their "whining match-sellers at the door," will turn out to be no less hellish, even though drinks are hot all around.

By the end of his pub crawl, Farrington has thoroughly enmeshed himself in yet more pride, lust, anger, covetousness, and envy to accompany his predominant sloth and gluttony. At Mulligan's he encounters yet one more fantastic take-off on the Virgin, the London lady of attractions with a huge blue scarf adorning her hat and chin. Brushing against him, she asks his pardon. She addresses predictably yet amazingly enough another rakehell. Christ had proclaimed on his visit to those in purgatory: "I will penetrate to all the lower parts of the earth, and will behold all that sleep, and will enlighten all that hope in the Lord." Granting or granted pardon—it matters not—Farrington full of anger and cursing his lack of money moves on to his second loss of the day, his trial of strength with the Englishman Weathers. The loss is compounded when a red-headed curate exclaims stupidly to Weathers, "Ah! that's the knack!"—the last word suggesting intelligence and not the least of taunts. Waiting for his tram at O'Connell Bridge, Farrington curses his entire day—the disaster at the office, his watch in hock, the squandered money, not to mention the departed London female. Half-sober, he still feels the thirst upon him, a sense of pain like the rich man's in hell who asked for a smahan of water to cool his tongue.

To maintain the thread of this discourse or parody, Farrington, the counterpart of Christ (now the meaning of "counterpart" is clearly opposite in connotation), will be resurrected to his heaven on earth, his home, perhaps Mount Olivet, that Joyce chooses to establish in Sandymount. And so he boards the little tram.

III

But let me pause for a moment. On the question of Joyce's parody of the Crucifixion, Hell, the Resurrection and ultimately the Ascension, I have been following generally the *Maynooth Catechism* (Dublin: M. H. Gill, n.d.) and a typical school text based on the catechism, Charles Hart's *The Student's Catholic Doctrine* (London: Burns, Oates & Washbourne, 1916). The parodic movement of the story, both comic and sad, so far would be recognized by any Catholic Dubliner who knew these texts and imagined that Joyce might use them to make a secular point. I pause also for another reason.

So far we have found Farrington in two hells of his own making, but may we not also justify, at least in part, his so-called sins or, better, character defects? As I have also suggested, Joyce seemed to ask that some sympathy be extended to Farrington by showing him to be a Dubliner distinctly in the wrong job and not altogether singular in succumbing to the national failing, drink, when we place him among his cronies. I shall go on to claim that he may be even more sinned against than sinning, for if we consider for a moment his tormentors much ill might also be laid at their doorsteps. We might even spy out among them—Alleyne, Weathers, and later Farrington's wife—a concatenation of sins even more deadly than his, though all three tormentors gain the highest approval from office, pub, and home in the story. While all three plainly lack much real faith, hope or charity—the three theological virtues, as far as the hulking Farrington goes—they also aren't blessed with many of the virtues contrary to the Seven Deadly Sins: humility, liberality, chastity, meekness, temperance, brotherly love, and diligence. But even more telling than this lack in them is their holding to the Six Sins against the Holy Ghost. Father Hart puts the matter this way:

> More malicious than the Capital Sins, and more dangerous to salvation, are the Six Sins against the Holy Ghost. These do not arise from mere frailty or ignorance, but are generally accompanied with so much malice and such wilful obstinacy to the Spirit of God and the known truth that they who are guilty of them are seldom converted. . . .[5]

No doubt a not-too-strained reading could also put the onus of these sins on Farrington himself: Presumption, Despair of

God's mercy, Resisting the known truth, Envy of another's spiritual good, Obstinacy in sin, and Final impenitence. Yet Mr Alleyne, for instance, is no less culpable. He is presumptuous in his threat of Mr Crosbie. He despairs in his remarks about Farrington's sloth. When he puts the question about his being a fool, he might well resist the truth when he forces Farrington to apologize for his answer. Nor are we sympathetic to Weathers. His equally unpleasant nature parodies a few more of these six sins. Sponge and braggart that he is, Weathers comically drapes himself with the fourth and fifth, envy of another's spiritual good and, given his failure to buy his share of rounds, a resounding obstinacy in sin. Farrington's wife's nagging him when he's sober we might even call a final impenitence.

To close this section, then, I repeat that Joyce is not leveling Catholic doctrine at his characters. Rather, I think, he uses it to expose real defects, miseries, and hypocrisies in a world where religion is at once all and nothing.

IV

All comedy ceases on Farrington's return. Perhaps enough has been written on the series of counterparts that finds him victim and tyrant in the story, victim of Alleyne and Weathers, tyrant over his own son. But the locale of his home is more important here if we are to understand the shift in the story. He alights at Shelbourne Road, we are told, "and he steered his great body along in the shadow of the wall of the barracks." Apparently, he lives in Haddington Road or Shelbourne Road, both streets bordering the noted Beggar's Bush Barracks. The name derives from a famous bush used as shelter and loitering-place in the eighteenth century by sturdy beggars—in fact highwaymen and desperadoes, robbers and smugglers. Until 1820, a ruinous building known as Le Febre's Folly, at the northeast corner of the later barracks, was the center of such criminal affairs.[6] If we add to this heritage Farrington's wife's name, Ada, which he bawls out twice, then his hellish behavior is now more a counterpart to a criminal, and a criminal Cain at that, since Ada was reputedly Cain's wife.[7] If Farrington now may be likened to one of the thieves crucified with Christ, I neverthe-less won't speculate on his final salvation, as St Luke's Gospel would have it. Nor can I think that Joyce is through with his original counterpart, the crucifixion and resurrection of Christ, if we keep in mind the dark and empty kitchen, like a tomb, the presence of soldiers in the barracks, and the appearance of a Thomas, though hardly a doubting one after his beating.

Yet the epiphany is his, "I'll say a Hail Mary," repeated three times. The reference is doubtless to the petition at the end of the prayer, "Holy Mary, Mother of God, pray for us sinners now and at the hour of our death. Amen." So the boy would gain Mary's intercession and thus reconcile God and a sinful father. But for a man in hell no intercession is possible. In the end we are left in a dark place, but for one lamp with the fire out. I speculate, moreover, that Mrs Farrington is at the chapel, probably St Mary's in Haddington Road, to experience the service for Ash Wednesday, opening the liturgical season of Lent, and has already heard the words "Remember, man, that thou art dust, and unto dust thou shall return." His earthly life a hell and his treatment of his son hellish, Farrington may have some such thoughts while gazing at the ashes in the fireplace, but one cannot tell.

How, then, to conclude? The figure of the frightened boy on his knees pleading with his father demands our sympathy. It rouses our sense of injustice thoroughly. Yet Farrington the tyrant still has our attention if but little of our sympathy. In tramping from an office in Eustace Street—the name derives from Sir Maurice Eustace, who made a reputation for himself by fighting the Irish and overcharging Dublin for the lands of Phoenix Park—in returning to his loathed home in Beggar's Bush, the afterthought of Lord Lansdowne, great-grandson to Sir William Petty, the political economist who had even less time for the Irish,[8] Farrington remains unremittingly in hell and ends by beating his own child and mimicking his flat accent, sign of the family's social decline. To confront his son Thomas may, then, be the final and most painful counterpart. The discipline Thomas had doubted Christ's return, but Farrington's son Tom has no doubts. Yet, should he say a Hail Mary, no change will follow in his father, who will return to his eternal round of frustration the next day, and the next, and the next. And his son may never believe again. Meanwhile, Ada will return and, if I've theorized rightly, with ashes on her forehead in the form of a cross for all to contemplate. Then she will begin to bully a man crucified in his office, left thirsty after a night of drinking, and reduced to a beggared rogue in his own home with no watch to pawn for his cure the next day.

NOTES: CHAPTER 9

1 See such representative comments as Florence L. Walzl, "Patterns of paralysis in Joyce's *Dubliners*," *College English*, vol. 22, no. 4 (January 1961), p. 226; John V. Hagopian, "'Counterparts,'" in *Insight II: Analyses of Modern British Literature*, ed. John V. Hagopian and Martin Dolch (Frankfurt a.M.: Hirschgraben-Verlag, 1964), pp. 201–6; William Bysshe Stein, "'Counterparts': a swine song," *James Joyce Quarterly*, vol. 1, no. 2 (Winter 1964), pp. 30–2; and R. Bruce Kibodeaux, "'Counterparts'—*Dubliners* without end," *James Joyce Quarterly*, vol. 14, no. 1 (Fall 1976), pp. 87–92.

2 Stein, op. cit., p. 31.

3 *Letters of James Joyce*, ed. Richard Ellmann (New York: Viking, 1966), Vol. 2, p. 194.

4 Because of the low bridge by Beggar's Bush Barracks, the Sandymount tram is described in the story as "little." It corresponds to the "funny little single-decker electric tram" that replaced the last horse-tram on 13 January 1901. See Denis Johnston, "The Dublin trams," *Dublin Historical Record*, vol. 12, no. 4 (November 1951), p. 102, and Samuel A. Ossory FitzPatrick, *Dublin* (London: Methuen, 1907), p. 349. Joyce completed the story on 12 July 1905, a little after "The Boarding House;" hence it takes place between those dates. *Thom's Directory* records 17 February as the date for Ash Wednesday 1904, and we know that the month is February and "the middle of the month was passed." According to the perpetual calendar, only 1901 would be the other possibility in those years, since Ash Wednesday also fell on 21 February in 1901.

5 Charles Hart, *The Student's Catholic Doctrine* (London: Burnes, Oates & Washbourne, 1916), pp. 370–1.

6 See Weston St John Joyce, *The Neighbourhood of Dublin* (Dublin: H. M. Gill, 1939), pp. 21–2, and *Rambles near Dublin* (Dublin: Evening Telegraph Office, 1890), pp. 35–6. Consult also P. D. O'Connell, "Dublin Military Barracks," *Dublin Historical Record*, vol. 25, no. 4 (September 1972), p. 152.

7 Helena Swan, *Girls' Christian Names: Their History, Meaning and Association* (London: Swan Sonnenschein, 1900), p. 153. As a contraction of Edith, Ada can mean "rich-gift, blessing, or happiness." It is often also identified with the Hebrew Adah, "ornament," the name of Cain's wife. Both possibilities seem heavily ironic to me.

8 C. T. M'Cready, *Dublin Street Names Dated and Explained* (Dublin: Hodges, Figgis, 1892), p. 117.

10

"Clay":
Maria, Samhain,
and the Girls Next Door
in Drumcondra

More than ever, the story "Clay" remains the center of a swirl of critical commentary, perhaps because of the four stories treating the theme of maturity it appears the simplest. Maria provides many perspectives for her admiring and pitying and doubting critics. Since anyone reading this chapter will be familiar with most of them, I shall only mention the general categories fixed upon her. As we all know, Maria has been likened to the Virgin Mary or to a witch, sometimes to both at the same time. Some critics find her highly conscious of her spinsterhood and ingrown virginity. Others discover the Shan Van Vocht, the banshee, or even Mr Punch himself shadowed in her situation at the laundry and perambulations during her evening out. Her lost plumcake has raised questions of Freudian slips and sexual repression, as has her repeating the first verse of Balfe's song. The many meanings implied in the title "Clay" itself are now familiar counters in discussions of the story. Halloween games, the mass to be said on All Saints Day, marriage divination, plant lore, and a host of other relevant topics stand witness to the ingenuity expended on this story. Yet the fullest accounts of the tale tend to be the sympathetic ones, almost always written from a Catholic if not always an Irish point of view.[1] If they tend to slight Joyce's animus against the Catholic church in Ireland, they nevertheless realize that Maria commands our respect—despite her "ferreting," her witchlike exterior, her shy compromises with the world about her, and infrequent bumblings. All of these studies, those that I favor and those unnamed, cannot but help us understand some part of this deceptively mild story. Yet other sides of the story remain to be puzzled over, and that's what this chapter will do.

For instance, while Halloween and All Saints Eve coincide in focusing the appearance and a good deal of the quiet reality of Maria, we ought to recall that the night is also Samhain eve, the prologue to the death of the Celtic year and the beginning of winter. If Maria is toothless, as more than one critic has demonstrated, then she approaches what Joyce will in *Ulysses* denominate Gummy Grammy in appearance, a rather grim version of the Shan Van Vocht first noticed by William Tindall.[2] I maintain, as does Warren Beck most delicately, that we are meant to discover her beauty in the end, the beauty that drives the maudlin Joe to tears.[3] But, while the tone of the story persists in remaining a moot point after so many readings, I shall also claim that Joyce's attitude is very close to that of Jonathan Swift's toward Ireland in *The Story of the Injured Lady* and in his subsequent reply. The culmination of this tone impresses me as resounding from the trick of the neighbor girls that gives the title to the story. Thus I shall also look at the party again before concluding with a parting glance at Maria's passage from Ballsbridge to the Pillar to Drumcondra during her evening out.

I

But let me start with a consideration of Samhain, background to the interpretation I shall make of the story and the topic to which I'll recur in my conclusion. Maria by name and appearance seems to be the expected confluence of Christian and pagan that makes up the modern Halloween. Yet the word Samhain, "end of summer," suits her just as well, being the Feast of the Dead, the beginning of winter. In ancient Tara it was the signal for a three-day feast. Prognostications and divinations were made for the year ahead. The faerie hills were said to be thrown open and the Sidhe set loose. The eve, as might be expected, was also a celebration of the memorable dead, though wanton faeries and sprites often attached themselves to mere human beings. More mischievous harpies like copper-red birds of war, the *Babdh* or *Morrigan*—words now used to mean a scold, a hag and war goddess, now often identified with the fearsome Washer at the Ford—hounded men only slightly less dreadfully than did the impish, horse-shaped pooka. In any event, to commemorate the first half of the Irish year—winter ending on Beltane, 1 May—Samhain was the occasion of warning fires, starting with the warning beacon at Da Derga's Hostel, fires in defiance of the victory of the Formorians who heralded the hosts of the dead and the onset of cold and darkness. To sum up: fire, divination, mischievous spirits, and the triumph of death and darkness are the mingled elements of Samhain eve.[4] But let me return to the beginning of the story, for nearly all these elements are there. As we have come to expect, Joyce once again insinuates his more remote effects into the very tissue of his story's beginning.

Samhain obviously shares with Halloween the usual pranks and prevalence of spirits abroad in the night. Yet I would insist that the onset of death and winter, contrasted with defiant fires, points to something in the story older, even more Irish than Halloween. The first paragraph accents that fire and those festivities that attend it. Maria, as the cook reminds her, probably can see herself in the copper boilers. The rest of the story, I speculate, treats how she reflects herself to others, though Maria never, as I shall argue, catches that image. In any case, for the moment at least, the cold and darkness seem to be banished. All are joyous; the former prostitutes regale Maria with a noisy toast. The women are monstrous: huge, restive, and volatile. Yet they like Maria, while Ginger Mooney constantly complains of another member of the help, the dummy, who is otherwise regarded. If Ginger could only get her hands on the dummy! Ginger, *Morrigan*, war goddess enough. The Protestant matron has, none the less, given Maria leave for the night out. Yet the reward for the fortunate former prostitute who endured the spiritual renewal of Dublin by Lamplight for two years was usually emigration to America to make a new start.[5] That will not be Maria's option—one of the many subtle hints that winter, darkness, and death are Maria's certain fate.

On the first part of her trip to Drumcondra, that is, from Ballsbridge to the Pillar, we hear only that Maria had her "old brown rain cloak." Then she is forced to take a stool at the end of the tram where she must face all the other riders. Once at the Pillar, she "ferrets" her way through the crowds, waits a long time in Downes's cake shop, and then takes her way to Henry Street for a plumcake where she is mocked by the salesgirl. Joyce's touch is light, but he has prepared us for Maria's subsequent misadventure on the Drumcondra tram, for brown, as we all know, is the color of decay and death in *Dubliners*; Maria's smallness is exhibited to the other riders on the tram since her feet can hardly touch the floor; in a crowd her appearance is that of a ferret, not just a witch; she must wait, and then she is scorned for her spinsterhood.

On the Drumcondra tram, however, she appears to have better luck. A gentleman makes room for her. Yet Joyce's description of him bodes ill: "He was a stout gentleman and he wore a brown hard hat; he had a square red face and a greyish moustache. Maria thought he was a colonel-looking gentleman and she reflected how much more polite he was than the young men who simply stared straight before them." She also recognizes that he had a drop taken—a typical Irish understatement for his being drunk. Nevertheless, he speaks cordially to her of the evening and the rain. Each bows to the other when she alights. He even raises his hat. She later discovers she has lost her plumcake. Doubtless she had been flustered and left it on the tram. At the party, she nearly weeps over her loss.

What are we to make of that? I'm not certain, yet Joyce has left a baffling note on the story in the Buffalo notebooks for *Finnegans Wake*:

> gentleman horse (stallion)
> sie studiert immer etwas
> murders child[6]

However relevant this afterthought may be—"gentleman horse (stallion)"—the picture Joyce projects in this polite old gentleman is the Irish portrait of a member of the declining Protestant Ascendancy—"the colonel-looking gentleman." One recalls Brendan Behan's definition of the Anglo-Irish: a

Protestant with a horse. The custom of identifying a Protestant house by the white horse behind the fanlight—the image is of King Billy's horse at the Boyne—may also pertain here. The gentleman horse's unintentional mischief, with the aid of a bit of drink, may nevertheless put us in mind of the Irish pooka, especially if we keep in mind a note by Yeats to some of his early poems:

> November, the old beginning of winter, or of the victory of the Fomor [sic] or powers of death, and dismay, and cold, and darkness, is associated by the Irish people with the horse-shaped *Pucas*, who are now mischievous spirits but once were Fomorian divinities.[7]

Among his other misdeeds, the pooka, according to one recorder of Irish folklore, "befouls unpicked fruit,"[8] to which rude behavior I am tempted to attribute, however far-fetched, the lost plumcake. Thus, Halloween aside for the moment, along with the equally important Allhallows Eve, already the shadows of winter, Formorians and death have begun to fall on Maria before she has even arrived at a party where she will be served clay.

II

But let me pause to consider Swift as an aid in discovering Joyce's presentation of Maria so far. Whether Joyce had read Swift's first Irish tract, *The Story of the Injured Lady. In a Letter to Her Friend, with His Answer*, is not important, for Swift never departed from that text, even in his essential Irish pamphlets from 1720 on. The point is that Swift like Joyce always held Ireland responsible for her plight, although both recognized the depressing hand of England. Again like Swift, Joyce in the "Cyclops" episode of *Ulysses* could be equally sardonic at the expense of the patriotic pomposities of both countries. In *The Story of the Injured Lady*, Swift, for instance, casts Ireland in the role of the cast-off mistress to England, while her unworthy rival, Scotland, managed to effect a marriage or union with that bullying nation. But the fault, as *The Answer to the Injured Lady* elaborates, nevertheless rests with Ireland herself. Now, one sees at once the distance between Joyce's account of the Catholic spinster Maria and Swift's lady, doubtless a personification of Protestant Ireland. Yet they both hold to that national failing, irresponsibility, winning though each lady may be. Swift, after all, points out that all those to whom Ireland has been kind were in fact rascals. On that head, the lady's yielding to her master, England, has also emptied her coffers, not to say ruined her house, depressed her trade, and reduced her to something like slavery. If we may think, then, of her successful rival, Presbyterian Scotland, as something like the extreme Protestant spirit that surrounds Maria, then she is as much the victim of those she serves—former Dublin prostitutes—as she is of those of an alien faith to whom she is nevertheless beholden for a job. Swift's characteristic retort to Ireland's complaint—come to a crescendo in *A Modest Proposal*— does more than approach Joyce's:

First.　　That your Family and Tenants have no Dependence upon the said Gentleman, further than by the old Agreement, which obliges you to have the same Steward, and to regulate your Household by such methods as you shall both agree to.

Secondly.　That you will not carry your Goods to the Market of his Town, unless you please, nor be hindered from carrying them any where else.

Thirdly.　That the servants you pay Wages to shall live at home, or forfeit their Places.

Fourthly.　That whatever Lease you make to a Tenant, it shall not be in his Power to break it.[9]

Joyce's admonitions are more a matter of tone, vocabulary, even outright parody in presenting Maria. Words like "nice" and "genteel" are constantly in her mouth in decribing those, Protestant or Catholic, who push her about or even openly mock her. Her job, for all her content, must be that of a kitchen manageress to Irish washerwomen, former prostitutes. She has her health drunk somewhat condescendingly by their leader, Ginger Mooney—a common woman at best, as Maria notes. Yet she can imagine herself an independent and fortunate woman, though nodding and hemming to the colonel-looking gentleman. Again, she dresses in that old brown cloak, must ferret her way through a crowd, and later will give way to Joe when he cries his brother down and forces stout on her.

So it is not just England or Protestant Ireland that molds her—everyone does. On the Protestant side, we remark notably the drunken member of the disappearing Ascendancy, the Whit present from Belfast, the Protestant tracts on the wall of the laundry, its matron, board, even the touch of Empire and adultery at the center of Dublin, Nelson's Pillar, that might offend Maria did she think about it, and finally even the song Maria sings by the Protestant Michael William Balfe. In the twenty-fifth year of Dublin by Lamplight, the institution operated on land leased from the Protestant Pembroke Estate had admitted representatives of other religions to its board (apparently unbeknownst to Joyce), yet its aims remained resolutely the same as ever. Here is an example in that year, 1879. The tone is unmistakable:

> The Dublin by Lamplight Institution has now been in existence for a quarter of a century. What good it has, by God's blessing, effected—what lives it has saved—how many fallen sisters it has rescued—to how many desolate hearts it has brought hope and peace—to how many perishing souls salvation—the great day alone will reveal.
>
> The founders of this valuable Institution are—many of them—long since before the Throne. Many also of those who were the objects of their anxious solicitude are gathered home, their souls being washed in the blood of the Lamb; and thus, by God's grace, they who laboured, and those for whom they laboured, are now alike, "safe in the arms of Jesus."[10]

Even more succinctly, the motto that accompanied that annual report of the institution remained unalterably Protestant: "That they may recover themselves out of the snare of the devil, who are taken captive by him at his will" (2 Timothy 2:26).

Still, on the Catholic side, Maria also suffers disregard, patronizing, indifference. Discourteous men fill the first tram; the bantering laundresses had set the tone for the evening. The snide shopgirl follows. The peremptory Mrs Donnelly, the soured children, and the angered Joe are yet to come but make Maria's life no easier. Nor need Joyce be very subtle in placing her in the role of the Shan Van Vocht, as so many critics have agreed, for she is patronized or disregarded on all sides. To most she resembles a witch; her motives are those of a saint. Despite her four green fields, her plants, her four barmbracks with their four slices, she does not foment conflict; rather as we all know, she's a peacemaker. Yet her real future is that heralded by Samhain. She will no more understand this than did her forlorn sister heed Swift's advice from 1707 till the end of his life.

III

Yet there is one piece of cruelty at the Donnelly party that maintains even more powerfully this Samhain theme. I of course refer to the action that underlies Joyce's title, the nasty trick by the two neighbor girls. Their consigning Maria to a symbolic death is made even more poignant in Maria's likely failure to understand the import. Just about all critics of the story have sensed the irony in Mrs Donnelly's rectifying matters by seeing that Maria gets the prayer-book. A convent life, and death as a spinster are about the same. Thomas Connolly's essay, "Marriage divination in Joyce's 'Clay,'" already mentioned, has made clear what kind of traditional game Maria has joined. Nevertheless, with Swift's *Story of the Injured Lady* in mind, we might take another look at the game. After all, the two neighbor girls have arranged it, have led the four blindfolded Donnelly children one by one to the saucers on the table; then one of the neighbor girls gets the ring; and only after that is Maria led to the table, the saucer of dirt, and her fate.

The total process may be a telling one, for this allotment of futures—Maria's fateful encounter with earth and the neighbor girl's prize of the ring—strikes me as altogether telling. Marriage divination aside for the moment, that four children of the same family should receive prayer-book and water strongly suggests the narrowed options in Irish life since the Famine— the church, the marriageless state, and emigration. Of the seven participants in the game, we know that one will die a spinster, one will go into the church, three will emigrate, while a neighbor girl will marry. The luck of the second neighbor girl we are not told. I may be descending into speculation again, but these neighbor girls, what with their arrangements, reward, and spite, may not be such distant personfications of Caledonia and Britannia in their relation to their sister Hibernia and her children.[11] While in no sense trotting out statistics to match the results of a game to be played again the next year, I must view this jape as not only a grim joke on Ireland lured into wintery night by something like wicked spirits that portend her loveless death but also a stab at the children of him who calls Maria mother, now promised by such neighbors the church or emigration. One of those girls—England?—will wed, will fulfill herself, and will indeed look after her neighbor's children. If this rough scheme has any plausibility, we might go on to ask how Maria's singing twice the first verse of "I Dreamt" imaginatively follows on this game.

IV

The usual explanation of Maria's repetition is that she finally sees her dismal position, especially in regard to the unlikelihood of marriage. Thus, the account goes, she refuses the more amatory second verse where suitors seek her hand and bend their knees. Her hand has already been sought for something else. To be sure, the story is understandable by this reading. But I'm not sure that Maria is—not that she lacks native intelligence. We have seen how she gauges the character of those about her, when she chooses to do so, fairly shrewdly, including Joe's likely unpleasantness when drinking. I would submit, then, that she simply doesn't know the second verse. Maybe Joe does, along with his assembled family and guests. Moreover, if she has been the victim of taunts because of her marriageless state, she has nevertheless sung a first verse that ends with a dream of love. If she omits the suitors of the second verse, she has still admitted a dream of love despite what she calls throughout the story her good fortune.

Customarily in Ireland, when one is called upon to sing or

recite at birthday, banquet, or holiday celebrations, one may well repeat the part of a song or poem that he remembers to fill out the performance. A classic and farcical instance of this practice is Joxer's attempt at song in the second act of *Juno and the Paycock*. But even the context of the opera, *The Bohemian Girl*, from which Maria's song is taken may offer some excuse for Maria's repeated verse. Arline had been dreaming and, now awake, sings to Thaddeus of her dream. She is in fact noble, though unaware of her birth, as Thaddeus himself, also noble, knows. Not suspecting her identity, Arline dreams of rank and glory yet delights in the hope that Thaddeus, whom she takes to be a commoner, might love her still. The irony of Maria's singing this verse to the assembled family and guests is powerful enough even without the second verse. Her halls are a laundry. She is identified with clay, not with marble; she is in charge of feeding reformed prostitutes; and she is hardly their hope and pride, much less that of the Donnellys and their guests. She has no riches; she must count every penny. Instead of a "high ancestral name," Joyce chooses to omit her surname altogether or at least the other characters in the story do. Who loves her "still the same"? No one in the story, although I'm sure we readers are meant to. To sing that first verse twice is really to accent these ironies and reverse the actual scene in the opera, even to mock that opera's joyful conclusion.

Perhaps Joe's eyes are also opened at least for a moment to Maria's real fate that contrasts so strongly with Arline's. Many critics have said so. Yet I wonder if his tears might not also result from a sharper look at himself. For all his rebellious nature, Joe is not Thaddeus. For that matter, he is not much more fortunate than Maria. He lives in the past, he has sentimental illusions of the present, he is dominated by a boss, he drinks too much, is hardly a peacemaker, and can't even control, as we've seen, the likely futures of his children. And where was the nutcracker? And now the corkscrew?

What a contrast, then, Joe, head of a household, and Maria, a tiny singer, make as compared with legendary Irish kings sung to by their *file* or poets at such a season and night. A turn-of-the-century authority on the subject has this to say:

During the long winter evenings the epic pieces or tales . . . were recited by the *file* before the kings as they sat in the great halls of their *duns* or palaces, surrounded by their vassals. They also recited them to the great crowds gathered together at the great periodical assemblies of *Beltene* on the 1st of May, *Lugnasad* on the 1st of August and *Samain* on the 1st of November. . . .[12]

So far the story seems to be Maria's, but partly understood by Joe, who speaks last, and perhaps most fully understood by the alert reader. Before, however, we leave her silent in the wake of Joe's tears, we might finally ask what it really means to leave Dublin by Lamplight, then shop near the Pillar, and complete an evening out in Drumcondra, specifically on Samhain eve when the sun-god supposedly succumbed to the powers of darkness.[13]

V

Drumcondra is located in the parish of Clonturk, that is, the Meadow of the Swine—a point I shall return to. But the locale in its variegated nature also sums up the two by now commonplace descriptions of Maria that I have called her real self and the self others behold. As the finest historian of County Dublin declares, Drumcondra was most famous for All Hallows' College, St Patrick's College, St Mary's College, and St Joseph's Asylum for the Blind that "had their prototypes in the Priories of All Saints and Holy Trinity and the Abbey of St Mary amongst which the lands were divided."[14] The area contained so many religious institutions that it came to be called, *mirabile dictu*, the Holy Land.[15] We may be recalled to the story's embracing Allhallows Eve, Maria's seeming blindness, and even the day to come, All Saints—but I would insist on none of these. To keep up the theme of marital disappointment or its opposite, the joyous romantic twaddle that *The Bohemian Girl* celebrates, as a former citizen of Drumcondra, Joyce may want us to know that the Priory of All Saints was founded by Dermot MacMurrough; that the rebel Earl of Tyrone, Hugh O'Neill, married the Helen, as she is called, of the Elizabethan wars, Mabel Bagenal, in Drumcondra Castle; while Lord Charlemont seems to have designed the Casino at

160

Marino expressly for reading and equally pleasant solitude. But by the nineteenth century Drumcondra had dwindled in precisely a worse direction—by becoming notorious for much strong drink, many taverns, and finally for a haunt of highwaymen who made the road to Santry one of the most dangerous in Ireland.[16]

To observe this downturn allows us to return to the Meadow of the Swine. Just as I shall try to insist that a final vision of the West of Ireland enhances the ending of "The Dead," and that Dun Laoghaire harbor and the confluence of the Dodder and the Liffey embody the final meaning of "After the Race" and "An Encounter," to name but three stories, so I find Drumcondra lending its own conclusive weight to the ending of "Clay," most significantly to the motif of Samhain eve. That Maria should sing a song by a Protestant Irishman, Michael William Balfe, generally regarded as English, a man who retired to Hertfordshire and was buried in Westminster Abbey, all this is beside the point.[17] His popularity in Ireland then and now makes him insipid and Irish enough for the occasion.

No, this Samhain eve in Drumcondra is appropriate enough, first by virtue of the nearness of neighboring Puckstown, the name itself recalling not only Puck but also our familiar pooka. Next because, after describing Drumcondra as the "Holy Land," Dillon Cosgrave went on to qualify that holiness by adding: "But the townland of Puckstown, where it is connected with the highroad by the short turn called the Yellow Lane, takes its name from an ancient Irish spirit who has scarcely the note of sanctity."[18] One creature remains, nevertheless, even more fearsome, darker, and more thoroughly identified with this Formorian pooka. He is the famous Black Pig, to be found, among other places, in Yeats's well-known poem "The Valley of the Black Pig." Some of Yeats's pseudo-scholarly scattering of notes on the poem deserve rereading, inaccurate as they may be, though generally believed:

> The pig seems to have been originally a genius of the corn, and, seemingly because the too great power of their divinity makes divine things dangerous to mortals, its flesh was forbidden to many eastern nations; but as the meaning of the prohibition was forgotten, abhorrence took

the place of reverence, pigs and boars grew into types of evil, and were described as the enemies of the very gods they once typified. . . . The Pig would, therefore, become the Black Pig, a type of cold and of winter that awake in November, the old beginning of winter, to do battle with the summer, and with the fruit and leaves, and finally, as I suggest; and as I believe, for the purposes of poetry; and of the darkness that will at last destroy the gods and the world.[19]

Unfairly, perhaps, I take Joe Donnelly and family and guests to be the final version of Samhain eve's tumultuous triumph of darkness.

Likeable enough, Joe is probably known as a good bloke and is in some respects, if only in keeping his temper, at his best this evening. Yet he is also something of a pig. His eldest child is named after his brother, yet Joe asks that God strike him down should he, Joe, mention that brother's name—Alphy is no brother of his. He insists on Maria's drinking stout; he is a bit tiddly himself. His children are at best indifferent, if not downright hostile, to Maria. We know what the bigger neighbor girls did. Then, too, Mrs Donnelly strongly urges the timid Maria to sing. Joe Donnelly's "pleasant talk and reminiscences," like his tale of the smart answer made to his manager, are no doubt self-centered. He may, indeed, be moved in the end by Maria and her pitiful song. He probably also realizes that she knows but refuses to recognize what she has touched. But his increased drunkenness and tears, praise of old times, and general helplessness, while predictable, leave Maria silent and at the mercy of a polite—"no one tried to show her her mistake"—but unheeding audience. And she is left in the kind hands of a woman who of necessity must rule such a home. Donnelly does indeed stem from the Irish word meaning "brown valour"[20]—and why not? Without pushing my point too far, then, I shall claim that the light and gaiety of the party, like that of the tea at the beginning of the story, have really impressed on us—if not on Maria—the defeat of any real light that she might have to offer. She dare not face this fact. That's the crux of the story. The actual dark that the war goddesses, the pooka, and the Black Pig all too naturally, pleasantly, sentimentally, and mortally have to offer her on this Samhain eve, her life or night out, has settled in.

NOTES: CHAPTER 10

1   I have in mind especially William T. Noon, "Joyce's 'Clay': an interpretation," *College English*, vol. 17, no. 2 (November 1955), pp. 93–5; Thomas E. Connolly, "Marriage divinations in Joyce's 'Clay,'" *Studies in Short Fiction*, vol. 3, no. 3 (Spring 1966), pp. 293–9; and H. E. Nebeker, "James Joyce's 'Clay': the well-wrought urn," *Renascence*, vol. 28, no. 3 (Spring 1976), pp. 123–38.
2   William Tindall, *A Reader's Guide to James Joyce* (New York: Noonday Press, 1959), p. 30.
3   Warren Beck, *Joyce's Dubliners* (Durham, NC: Duke University Press, 1969), pp. 213–18.
4   See P. W. Joyce, *The Social History of Ancient Ireland* (London/New York/Bombay: Longmans, Green, 1903), Vol. 1, pp. 229–33, 264–76, 288–93, 608–10, and Vol. 2, pp. 387–92. See also E. Estyn Evans, *Irish Folk Ways* (London: Routledge & Kegan Paul, 1961), pp. 276–7. For an essay stressing something of the same link, this time between Maria and the *banshee, glaistig,* and *bean-mighe,* see S. A. Cowan, "Celtic folklore in 'Clay': Maria and the Irish washerwoman," *Studies in Short Fiction*, vol. 6, no. 2 (Winter 1969), pp. 213–15.
5   *Thirteenth Annual Report of Dublin by Lamplight* (Dublin: Samuel G. Downes, 1868), pp. 6–8.
6   "Buffalo Notebooks VIA, Ser. 7," *The James Joyce Archive*, ed. Michael Groden (New York/London: Garland Publishing, 1978), Vol. 16, p. 69.
7   *Variorum Edition of the Poems of W. B. Yeats*, ed. Peter Allt and Russell K. Alspach (London: Macmillan, 1957), p. 808.
8   Evans, op. cit., p. 277.
9   Jonathan Swift, *Irish Tracts 1720–23*, ed. Herbert Davis, and *Sermons*, ed. Louis Landa (Oxford: Basil Blackwell, 1963), p. 11.
10 *Twenty-fifth Annual Report of Dublin by Lamplight* (Dublin: Steam Printing Company, 1880), p. 3.
11 See, for instance, the cartoon in the *Irish Times*, 13 April 1900, p. 6, taken from *Punch*, after Queen Victoria had visited Wales and talked of going to Ireland. The caption is "Come back to Erin." The cartoon features a barefoot colleen pleading with Victoria in these words: "If ye plaise, yure Majesty, as ye've seen me sisters at home, shure won't ye come an' see me? Ye'll be

very welcome!!"

12   H. D'Arbois de Jubainville, *The Irish Mythological Cycle and Celtic Mythology*, trans. Richard Irvine Best (Dublin: Hodges, Figgis, 1903), p. 3.

13   John Rhys, *Lectures on the Origin and Growth of Religion as Illustrated by Celtic Heathendom* (London: Williams & Norgate, 1888), pp. 516–17.

14   Francis Elrington Ball, *Southern Fingall, being the Sixth Part of "A History of County Dublin"* (Dublin: The University Press, 1920), p. 156.

15   Dillon Cosgrave, *North Dublin—City and Environs* (Dublin: Catholic Truth Society of Ireland, 1909), p. 64.

16   M. J. Tutty, "Drumcondra," *Dublin Historical Record*, vol. 15, no. 3 (September 1959 [January 1957]), pp. 86–96. See also Ball's *Southern Fingall*, p. 182.

17   William Alexander Barrett, *Balfe: His Life and Work* (London: William Reeves, n.d.), pp. 293–4. Also H. O. Brunskill, "Michael William Balfe," *Dublin Historical Record*, vol. 16, no. 2 (October 1960), pp. 58–64.

18   Cosgrave, op. cit., p. 64.

19   *Variorum Yeats*, p. 809.

20   Patrick Woulfe, *Irish Names and Surnames* (Dublin: M. H. Gill, 1923), p. 505.

11

"A Painful Case": the View from Isolde's Chapel, Tower, and Fort

Most intelligent accounts of "A Painful Case" at least mention that Mr Duffy's residence in Chapelizod suggests the relevance of the Tristan and Isolde legend. But, since writing an early draft of my own essay, the most extended discussion I've discovered runs as follows:

> During the years that Joyce was first hearing the operas of Wagner in Italy, he was also writing *Dubliners*; the first product of his interest in Wagner appears in that work. "A Painful Case," finished in 1905, employs a pattern of references to *Tristan and Isolde*. While it is impossible to establish that Joyce used only Wagner's version of the myth, the times and his current interest in the composer suggest that Wagner is the most probable source. Mr. Duffy, the story's stuffy, middle-aged Tristan, lives in Chapelizod. The town is, according to legend, the home of Isolde, and the word itself is an Anglicization of the French *Chapel d'Iseult*. The pathetic death of Mrs. Sinico is life-giving, for it forces Mr. Duffy finally to realize his responsibility in causing it. She had offered him love, albeit adulterous love, as in the Tristan myth; but Mr. Duffy, a respectable Dubliner, is horrified when she takes his hand and refuses to have anything more to do with her. The setting in Chapelizod and the situation of adulterous love parallel the Tristan myth. Wagner's lovers are heroic creatures who surrender themselves completely to their passion and are finally destroyed by it. Joyce's Tristan is a bourgeois, Dublin recluse who rejects his

Isolde and drives her to alcoholism. The Wagernian pattern in the story provides an ironic contrast to its characters and situations, but the final effect is a Joycean combination of ridicule and pathos.[1]

Although one may demur over minor points in this statement—Duffy the respectable Dubliner, for instance—the gist seems right. Joyce probably knew the Malory and Bédier treatments of the legend also,[2] but I would join in plumping for Wagner's rendition, especially the larger events like the love potion, Tristan's daring, the predicament of King Mark, perhaps the *liebestod* that gives the story its ironic framework.

Of course a great deal else has been written about "A Painful Case." Its relationship to Stanislaus and even James himself, the puritanical religious overtones, the make-up of Mr Duffy's library, the mention of Hauptmann and Nietzsche, Freudian interpretation and, not to be outdone, the application of humor psychology, all these studies have helped students of the story. But I would stress that all such insights may also describe a modern Tristan equally melancholy in name—Duffy in Irish means "black." If he is hardly the gallant, fated lover who died for his love, he nevertheless achieves some knowledge that he has been "mean, modern and pretentious."

But before spelling out that biting contrast we should remember that we have more than Chapelizod alone to guide us. For Iseult or Isolde is associated with at least four places, not one, around Dublin, and Joyce appears to make good use of all of them. Izod's Chapel, as we might call it, was probably the site of the present Protestant church, a chapel having existed there since 1228. As one historian explains, "The present church was built in 1832, but the square tower is obviously much older and has been constructed round an earlier tower which seems to have been round in shape." She adds that "there is a granite font on a well carved pedestal in the porch. This was probably taken from the old church."[3] Next, in nearby Phoenix Park, the Magazine Fort rests on the site of what was once Isolde's Fort, and close to it lay a spring or well, now vanished, called Isolde's font. In Dublin itself, near George's Street where Mr Duffy takes his frugal lunch, Isolde's tower formed part of the old Dublin city wall and may have been demolished in 1675. In its place Essex Gate appears, although a recent study of Dublin's Wood Quay maintains that the tower remains as part of the buildings at the southwest corner of Capel Street Bridge. The name Isolde is still used in the area; the former Isolde's Lane is now Exchange Street Upper. In the old Exchange, now City Hall, a fresco depicts Tristan requesting her father, King Anguish or Aengus, for Isolde's hand in marriage to King Mark.[4]

The force of these four locales lies in their strategic placement at each of the important junctures of the story. We begin in Chapelizod, learn of Mrs Sinico's death near Isolde's tower, return to Chapelizod, and finally accompany the slowly comprehending modern Tristan to Magazine Hill where Isolde's fort and font once flourished. With an eye on Wagner's opera, I shall then trace the importance of these legendary reminders of a passionate Irish tragedy by taking yet one more measure of Mr Duffy's surroundings in Chapelizod, his affair with Mrs Sinico and the written account of her death. The implications of her ghostly presence at Isolde's Fort I shall hold till last.

I

After offering what will be two ironic reasons for Mr Duffy's living in Chapelizod, Joyce turns to the gaunt old house Duffy occupies with its view across the Liffey—"he could look into the disused distillery." This was the Phoenix Park Distillery on the north side of the river. Joyce's father had worked there earlier, as we know. Yet that is hardly the point. After going bankrupt during his tenure, the distillery was partly reconstructed in 1900 only to suffer a serious fire on 17 January 1901, but the damage was repaired and the plant left in working order by 12 September of the same year. The fire had been confined to the mill; the loss had been restricted to roof, walls and grain.[5] Aside from dating the beginning of the story, the disused distillery also gives us the proper overtones of lassitude of spirits, even burned-out seed, that can stand as mirror metaphors for Mr Duffy's own spiritual desuetude and sexual lack. Mrs Sinico will try to redress this lack by seeking out other spirits.

But there is more in that opening paragraph. Mr Duffy's writing materials and library, especially Hauptmann's play and the *Maynooth Catechism*, have received full attention. In a thoughtful essay on the story, Thomas Connolly, however, directs his gaze as other critics have to Mr Duffy's room itself. He sees it as a "monk's cell," but one side of what Connolly will later call Duffy's "bifurcated personality."[6] This is well and good, far better than claiming that "Duffy is a man without any inherent identity, as the description of his room and effects suggests."[7] Yet strong identity there surely is, and perhaps something more formidable than a monk's. In keeping with the knighthood of Tristan, turned modern, mean and laborious, the room strikes us with its overwhelming hues of white, black and red, its pronounced presence of iron, its lofty walls and general hardness. But let me quote the passage in full:

> The *lofty* walls of his uncarpeted room were free from pictures. *He had himself bought every article of furniture in the room*: a *black iron* bedstead, an *iron* washstand, four *cane* chairs, a clothes-*rack*, a *coal-scuttle*, a *fender* and *irons* and a *square* table on which lay a double desk. A bookcase had been made in an alcove by means of shelves of *white* wood. The bed was covered with *white* bed-clothes and a *black* and *scarlet* rug covered the foot. A little *hand-mirror* hung above the washstand and during the day a *white-shaded lamp* stood as the sole ornament of the mantelpiece. (My italics)

I submit that Joyce has already established Mr Duffy's identification with a railway engine, an identification that many critics have made at the story's end, after the accident and the final sight of the goods train moving out of Kingsbridge Station toward Cork. The iron, the black and red colors, the white resembling puffing smoke, the engineer's mirror, the lamp and fender, however, make the image important, coming at first and unmistakable as a clue to his character. From this spiritless, orderly, cell-like abode, Mr Duffy sets forth daily, a rather determined, one-track, iron-purposed knight, for his adventureless life in a private bank.

But like Tristan he is susceptible to music. At the former scene of frivolity, flirtation, and extravagance in the eighteenth century, the Rotunda, he first meets his Isolde with daughter, not Brangaena, in tow. Yet both Mrs Sinico and Mr Duffy become, after a series of meetings, and despite Mr Duffy's skittishness about women, somewhat intoxicated with each other. While they don't swoon in each other's arms, Joyce does tell us twice that their thoughts became entangled. Their increased intimacy begins to insinuate the mood of the second act of Wagner's opera. Walks in Phoenix Park, lent books, rendezvous in the Sinico cottage, often with darkness descending upon them alone, faintly approximate the frenzied lovers meeting in a darkened garden, Isolde avidly waving her scarf, both under the sway of Venus, both finding night holy and ecstatic, day but dreary and dead. At this point, Tristan is badly wounded by his treacherous friend Melot. But, in Leoville, Mr Duffy wounds Mrs Sinico by repulsing her fervent gesture—he had hoped to "ascend to angelical stature." She had sought human love.

Their last meeting also strangely parallels the beginning of Wagner's last act. That act opened in a castle garden. Mr Duffy and Mrs Sinico meet for the last time in what might be called the garden to Castleknock, Phoenix Park, where they walk the roads for three hours. Just before parting, she is beside herself and shakes with emotion. By contrast, Wagner's Tristan had assumed that role, staggering with fatigue and excitement before dying in Isolde's arms at the beginning of the second scene. These two reversals deeply underline the irony of repulsion and parting in "A Painful Case." Little did Mrs Sinico realize the import of her early plaint to Mr Duffy: "It's so hard on people to have to sing to empty benches."

II

In the story, four years pass. Our Dublin Tristan has not languished; his Isolde has. No shepherd's strains have promised Isolde's return. Rather, a cliché-ridden newspaper account reports *her* demise, in the third person—an accident that was no accident. During these intervening years no change has ruffled Mr Duffy. His love of music and errant if not chivalrous pride of intellect have been abetted by new pieces of music on his music-stand. Two volumes of Nietzsche now also grace his library. Still, he writes little and avoids concerts. Then in George's Street, meaning South George's Street, he reads of her death. Returning home in the November evening (*Ulysses* places the death at 14 October 1903), he rereads the account as might a priest. I venture to say that the two readings, both at places identified with the legendary Isolde, make the otherwise dreary and banal newspaper report the center of the story.

But, first, why must Mrs Sinico die at Sidney Parade? The manuscript at Yale has Mrs Sinico living in Merrion, and in fact a dwelling named "Leoville" is listed there in *Thom's Directory*. Now, both Merrion and Sidney Parade are adjacent to Sandymount, but Joyce probably chose Sidney Parade Station because at that time it was the station with a level crossing closest to Dublin (it has recently been reopened and provided with an overhead crossing). In other words, on part of the old Pembroke estate, which lent such names as Fitzwilliam, Herbert, and Sidney to the district, a person is killed by a slow train from Kingstown. It had happened before, and no blame was attached to the railway officials for the victim who had "crossed the lines."[8] But the station also recalls the chivalrous, charitable, and noble Sidney Herbert of the nineteenth century and, even more pertinently, the very mirror of chivalry, Sir Philip Sidney, the second Earl of Pembroke's brother-in-law.[9] But, instead of finding a cloak before her feet, the modern Isolde is greeted by the buffer, or rebuff, of a slow train.

Let me turn, however, to that seemingly straightforward newspaper account that I have made such high claims for. First of all, we learn that Mrs Sinico was "attempting to cross the line," thus repeating, if the metaphor holds, her action and the rebuff she had received four years earlier. In raising Mr Duffy's hand to her cheek, and despite his reading of Wordsworth, she had clearly crossed the line of propriety, at least in his eyes. Her injuries to head and right side are in some way reminiscent of Christ's own injuries. Yet Mrs Sinico had fallen in Mr Duffy's view. And so literally reported P. Dunne, the railway porter. On the other hand, the engine-driver had stopped when he heard "loud cries," something like Mr Duffy's leaving Mrs Sinico trembling and greatly agitated at their last meeting. Yet her death had actually been a result of "shock and sudden failure of the heart's action," another way of stating what happened to her after being repulsed by Mr Duffy. The company had sought to have people cross lines by bridges only. One wonders if Mr Duffy remembers that Nietzsche had seen the free spirits of the world—and Mr Duffy would count himself as one—as bridges for the superman. But no matter; no *liebestod* occurs here, yet one senses that her death of the heart has been a lingering one. Her nightly crossing the lines probably came as she walked westward toward shops and pubs through the narrow passageway, since the large gates closed off the road and pavements, but the small gates on either side of the pavement would let her through. The social system, a Roman Catholic culture as straight and narrow as the railway line, would attempt to keep her from crossing marital lines by the usual checks and proscriptions for marriage. In the absence of a love potion, she had sought real, liquid spirits during the last two years. Of course she was left alone most of the time, including the night of her death. She had sought the font while King Mark and her daughter were away. But the blame attaches to Mr Duffy and, of course, he is the more painful of the cases. I cannot help but think that Mr Duffy is also ambiguously included in the Deputy Coroner's urging "the railway company to take strong measures to prevent the possibility of similar accidents in the future." Catechism or no catechism, he has been partly responsible for a suicide over his dead body or fender. Thus Tristan and Isolde in Sandymount.

III

Yet, as every reader has sensed, blame is attached. Tristan and Isolde were fated lovers. Her two powerful drafts for love and death nevertheless combine in the final ectasy of the lovers' death union. In Wagner's opera, King Mark, after Brangaena's confession, casts no blame and blesses both Tristan and Isolde. At the inquest, Captain Sinico merely admitted he had been happily married for twenty years! But Mr Duffy, gazing at the Liffey and empty distillery through his window, revolts at the newspaper account of Mrs Sinico's death and easily condones his own action in abandoning her. Then night begins to fall and, with the night, the holy time for the legendary lovers, Mr Duffy feels the touch of her hand on his.

Separated from Isolde at the beginning of Act III, Tristan had nevertheless felt Isolde with him. Just so, Mrs Sinico's ghostly presence persists; for, after leaving and drinking hot punch at a public house, Mr Duffy continues in the dark to Phoenix Park where he not only feels her hand again but also hears her voice at his ear. Full of self-accusation by then, he achieves Magazine Hill, where the Magazine Fort had been since 1801. With this site of Isolde's Fort behind him, he has one of the best views of Dublin before him, commemorated in one of Malton's famous picturesque and descriptive views, this one dedicated to Henry Grattan. While Mr Duffy is made uneasy by the presence of a couple lying by a wall below him—they ought to be a direct reminder of Tristan and Isolde embraced in what seemed the endless night of the second act—he also views the final tableau of his misadventure: the Liffey flowing toward Dublin and, moving in an opposite but parallel direction, "a goods train winding out of Kingsbridge Station, like a worm with a fiery head winding through the darkness, obstinately and laboriously." How many critics, like Marvin Magalaner, have detected the male and female principles in these two—Mr Duffy and Mrs Sinico never able to consummate their love.[10]

Doubtless, Joyce is indeed hinting the buried sexuality beneath Mr Duffy's mechanical drive, as we have come to see from the beginning in his room, his life, readings, and writings. But foremost, I speculate, we are also meant to see that no crossing of the line will be allowed *him* here, for when the rhythm of the engine repeating the syllables of her name dies in his ears her hand and her voice also vanish. The Liffey, lovely and gleaming, named after the beautiful wife of an early Irish cup-bearer, has also been with us from the beginning, flowing beneath Mr Duffy's window and now taking its lonely way to the sea that washes Sandymount. On the other hand, the goods train, probably headed for Cork, is an image not just of Mr Duffy but also of the middle-class, male, Irish Catholic suburbanite—"a worm with a fiery head"—persistent in his "modern, mean and pretentious" life. When he stops under a tree until the sound of the train ceases, Mr Duffy ought to be reminded that in Chapelizod opposite the Protestant church, St Laurence's, the place of Isolde's chapel, stands another tree where funeral processions traditionally circle.[11]

IV

We are left with Mr Duffy absolutely alone. The night is silent. Ghost, train, and syllables are gone. He turns back to Chapelizod and that other tree. His music and Nietzsche await him among his other effects. I hope the music is not Wagner's opera. If Mr Duffy has read *The Case of Wagner*, he might agree with Nietzsche that the decadent Wagner could only present the perfect husband, King Mark, was in any case no dramatist in that opera, and was generally no thinker, no musician, and so on. But, then Nietzsche's life was also notoriously lonely. Even his sister's biography of him was titled *The Lonely Nietzsche*. Might Mr Duffy also remember that all accidents at Sidney Parade Station were taken to the City of Dublin Hospital on Upper Baggot Street? Oddly enough, the hospital and the station in 1903 were both outside the city boundary. Perhaps that is why Lord Pembroke contributed £6,000 for its expansion and renovation in 1894.[12] Whereas Mr Duffy and Nietzsche are finally thoroughly alone, at least Mrs Sinico was taken not only to an accident hospital for all cases but also to a nonsectarian charity one. Yet Mr Duffy may well deserve our own charity when we contemplate his utter loneliness at the end of the story and then listen to the opening of Isolde's *liebestod* sung over the dead Tristan and imagine the counterpoint in him:

> Mild und leise
> Wie er lächelt,
> Wie das Auge
> hold er öffnet:
> seh't ihr, Freunde,
> seh't ihr, Freunde,
> Immer lichter
> wie er leuchtet,
> wie er minnig

immer mächt'ger,
Stern-umstrahlet
Hoch sich hebt:
Seh't ihr Freunde
seh't ihr's nicht?
Wie das Herz ihm
muthig schwillt,
voll und hehr
im Busen quillt:
wie den Lippen
wonnig mild,
süsser Athem
sanft entweht:—
Freunde, seh't—
fühlt und seh't ihr's nicht!—

The irony is strong even though the names Tristan and Duffy both have the underlying suggestion of melancholy in them. Still, the first sentence of "A Painful Case" informed us that Mr Duffy had chosen Chapelizod because it took him as far as possible from the other citizens of Dublin. Little did he realize how chapel, tower, and fort enshrined a love that mocked that distance.

NOTES: CHAPTER 11

1 John Louis Di Gaetani, *Richard Wagner and the Modern British Novel* (Rutherford/Madison/Teaneck, NJ: Fairleigh Dickinson Press, 1978), pp. 135–6.
2 See James S. Atherton, *The Books at the Wake* (London: Faber, 1959), pp. 265–6, and Richard Ellmann, *The Consciousness of Joyce* (Toronto/New York: Oxford University Press, 1977), pp. 101, 132.
3 This is part of the general information on Chapelizod summed up by Carmel McAsey, "Chapelizod, Co. Dublin," *Dublin Historical Record*, vol. 17, no. 2 (March 1962), pp. 35–53. A fuller account down to the close of the eighteenth century is that of F. Elrington Ball, *A History of the County Dublin* (Dublin: A. Thom, 1906), Pt 4, pp. 163–78.
4 John T. Gilbert, *A History of the City of Dublin*, Vol. 2 (Dublin: James Duffy, 1861), pp. 114–20, and *History of the Viceroys of Ireland* (Dublin: James Duffy, 1865), pp. 2–4. I am also heavily

indebted to a recent, splendidly lucid and popular review of these materials by Vincent Caprani and Frank McCartney, "Tristan and Isolde—the Irish connection," *Ireland of the Welcomes*, vol. 28, no. 4 (July–August 1979), pp. 10–15.

5   See "Special extra. Great fire at Chapelizod. Distillery ablaze. Serious damage," *Irish Times*, 17 January 1901, p. 5; "Destructive fire at Chapelizod," *Irish Times*, 18 January 1901, p. 6; and "Works executed at the Phoenix Park Distillery, Chapelizod, Dublin," *Irish Builder*, 12 September 1901, pp. 860–1. See also James O'Driscoll, *Cnucha: A History of Castleknock and District* (Dublin: no publisher, 1977), p. 91.

6   Thomas E. Connolly, "'A Painful Case,'" in *James Joyce's Dubliners: Critical Essays*, ed. Clive Hart (New York: Viking Press, 1969), pp. 108–9.

7   John William Corrington, "Isolation as motif in 'A Painful Case,'" in *James Joyce's Dubliners: A Critical Handbook*, ed. James R. Baker and Thomas F. Staley (Belmont, Calif.: Wadsworth, 1969), p. 134.

8   For a 1904 example, see Robert M. Adams, *Surface and Symbol: The Consistency of James Joyce's "Ulysses"* (New York: Oxford University Press, 1962), pp. 52–3. For an earlier instance, see "Serious accident on the Kingstown line," *Irish Times*, 13 May 1889, p. 5, and "The accident at Sidney Parade," *Irish Times*, 15 May 1889, p. 5.

9   M. O. Hussey, "Sandymount and the Herberts," *Dublin Historical Record*, vol. 24, no. 3 (June 1971), pp. 78–9.

10 Marvin Magalaner, *Time of Apprentice: The Fiction of Young James Joyce* (London/New York/Toronto: Abelard-Schuman, 1959), p. 96.

11 McAsey, op. cit., p. 53.

12 See "The City of Dublin Hospital, Upper Baggot-Street," *Irish Builder*, 15 December 1892, p. 262; E. MacDowell Cosgrave and Leonard R. Strangways, *Visitors' Guide to Dublin and Neighbourhood together with Supplemental Guide to the Irish International Exhibition of 1907 Giving a Complete Dictionary of Dublin* (Dublin: Sealy, Bryers & Walker/London: Simkin, Marshall, Hamilton, Kent, n.d.), p. 67; E. MacDowell Cosgrave, *Dublin and Co. Dublin* (Brighton/London: W. T. Pike, 1908), p. 43; and *Royal City of Dublin Hospital Reports* (Dublin: Royal City of Dublin Hospital, n.d.), passim.

12

"Ivy Day in the Committee Room": Fanning the Phoenix Flame, or the Lament of the Fianna

From his earliest poems, through his essays, short fiction, and novels, we know very well Joyce's admiration for Parnell, nay, even his self-identification with the man. Like Yeats, Joyce also saw in Parnell's destruction a sacrifice that might well go unheeded in Irish life. Historians, to be sure, like F. S. L. Lyons, have shown Parnell's fall to be as much a failure on his part as it was the result of any betrayal. And Lyons, like Conor Cruise O'Brien before him, is right. Yet failure is in Ireland likely to propel a dead leader into the golden realm of myth. Thus, Joseph Blotner, one of the more able critics of "Ivy Day in the Committee Room," has demonstrated how the large implications of the story stand in ironic parallel to the betrayal, martyrdom, and resurrection of Christ. Blotner makes good use of Joyce's essay "Home Rule Comes of Age" that renders explicit the analogy of Christ's crucifixion to Parnell's end with both men hounded by a Judas and hostile clergy.[1] Those critics who have noted the added parallels with Moses and his seeking the Promised Land have also been well served by Joyce in the essay "The Shade of Parnell" and in *Ulysses*.[2] How well these analogies stand up in fact is another question. But, in keeping with the historical gist of my own pages, I shall nevertheless try to point to some more immediate Irish determinants in this sleazy reminder of Parnell's death.

I have in mind specifically not just the immediate political background, touched on rather gingerly by Frederick C. Stern,[3]

176

but also the meaning of the Phoenix Flame in Hynes's doggerel poem, and then the Fenian tradition that lies behind it and contrasts with the utterances of the assembled stout-drinkers, and finally the large pattern of Irish myth that stands behind them. I shall also try to look a little more closely at that poem, "The Death of Parnell," since it powerfully unites so many elements of the story.

I

The story opens with old Jack maintaining a fire in necessitous Irish fashion by rekindling what is left of the cinders. This action introduces and finally summarizes the story. When he fans the dome of cinder-covered coals into flame again, his face emerges from the darkness, and his shadow grows on the wall. The hint here and later is that the mixture of shadow and light continues as old Jack the caretaker returns to fanning the flame until he lights the two candles. Meanwhile, his companion Mat O'Connor, a young man but already a gray-haired and ugly one, lights a cigarette from the fire with the aid of an electioneering card. He wears the ivy, reminiscent of Parnell's estate, Avondale, in Wicklow, the ivy that memorializes his death-date. The conversation is curious, largely one-sided. Old Jack is drawn out on the subject of his family. His son drinks, won't work, has the mother on his side, refuses respect to his father, especially when old Jack is in liquor himself. And this despite a primary education with the Christian Brothers and added beatings from old Jack. Already 19, the son sponges off old Jack and is little more than a bowsy. At this point Joe Hynes enters, asks if this is a Freemason's meeting—why are they in the dark?—and the candles are lit. After no matter how many readings of the story, one still asks *what* has Joyce introduced?

I suspect that we are witnessing a travesty of the famous Phoenix Flame. Neither its caretaker nor its user shows any signs of regeneration about him. The subject broached, indeed, is the degeneration from Parnell's time to the present, from father to son, from respect to impudence, from a hoped-for "union of hearts" to a divided family. The flame itself, while traditionally identified with Ireland's resurgence, was also the emblem of the Fenian movement as Desmond Ryan has reminded us.[4] More on that in a moment. But, when Hynes enters, the darkness and supposed secrecy lead him to call out, as we have seen, "Is this a Freemason's meeting?" Quite possibly, Joyce may also be pointing to the alleged Arabian origins of Freemasonry, with its emphasis on the renewal of the spirit, as also identified with the Phoenix, the famous bird of renewal in Egyptian mythology. If so, it is hard to avoid the irony of old Jack's using the fire to light two candlesticks, usually set by the dead in their coffins as we saw in "The Sisters." Moreover, the Phoenix Flame itself is also identified with Parnell. It burns atop his monument at the north end of O'Connell Street, and, perhaps just as pertinently, had been identified since 1745 with the Phoenix Pillar of the Phoenix Park.

So far, then, the meager flame must be nourished by the worn-out cinders of men. It has served to light up Parnell's memory, with the aid of a Tierney election card, by showing for a brief moment the ivy in O'Connor's lapel. That flame has also magnified the shadow of its caretaker, who remains but dimly aware of the Fenian tradition of violence and active resistance. Thus, the opening of the story has also illuminated the continued darkness in the death-room of any longed-for revival of Irish political life.

II

As far as Parnell's promise of that renewal goes, Joyce and his brother felt that in the final struggle in Committee Room 15 only eight men stood with Parnell.[5] Precisely how they arrived at that figure, given the fact that the final division was 45 to 27 (excluding the chairman, Parnell), remains a puzzle. Nevertheless, Joyce, to maintain the irony of his story of memory and the ghost of a dead man, has given the new chief, Tierney, eight supporters. If we view old Jack solely as a caretaker, and Father Keon as about some mysterious but pertinent business with Fanning, then we have the canvassers O'Connor, Henchy, Crofton, and Lyons, then Father Keon, the guarantor

Father Burke, Fanning the registration agent, and the ally, Alderman Cowley. All are on Tierney's side, though some may not secure votes. In either case, we ask what, aside from their support of Tierney, the group have in common.

Most are down on their luck. Some are suspicious. All drink. In fact, their leader may be a Poor Law Guardian but he is also a publican. His father, the secondhand dealer in Mary's Lane, also made his way selling illicit drink on Sunday. Tierney's pub is the Black Eagle. Despite the day, the eleventh anniversary of Parnell's death, the place in Wicklow Street, recalling again the Avondale residence, the real business in Tierney's campaign for city councillor is done with the aid of Fanning the agent and Alderman Cowley—and Father Keon, who is off to see Fanning—in the Black Eagle.

If we pick up the story again at Hynes's departure and Henchy's arrival, we learn more about the Tierney background, the money demanded by Fanning, the inanity of life in the Mansion House, and the doubts that Henchy harbors about Hynes's true loyalties—but since Hynes derives from the Irish for "ivy"[6] I suspect that we are not meant to take Henchy seriously. In any case, instead of the intoxication of national politics, all present are devoted to drink, even the 17-year-old delivery boy from the Black Eagle. The very gas in the stout-bottles is employed, after being heated by the substitute Phoenix Flame, to pop the corks. Money, drink, gas are the forces in the new nationalism where once selflessness, clear water, and something like truth had served. In fact the Phoenix Park and its memorial are a corruption of the Irish *Fionn Uisge*, Feenisk, meaning "clear water," named after the original well and its reputed curative powers.[7] Moreover, the phoenix on the thirty-foot monument erected by Lord Chesterfield is still often called the Eagle or, in north Dublin parlance, Da Eagle. The Black Eagle pub, then, has its appropriate political commentary embedded in its name. And this is the real election headquarters where the mayor-maker Fanning fans the real Phoenix Flame.

In keeping, however, with the story's beginning, old Jack opens the first four bottles of stout, for he had heated up the fire, which had then received Mr Henchy's spittle, and then the fire did its real job—opened the rest of the gaseous bottles.

But this heavy insistence on drink has already been prepared for in the appearance of Father Keon. He has business with Fanning—they are termed "thick"—and is on his way to the Black Eagle when we last see him. He may be a defrocked priest, he may also be a pederast if earlier manuscript readings can count, but he is most certainly an alcoholic. In Ireland the yellow cheese complexion, the red cheekbones, and the description of Keon as an "unfortunate man" are tell-tale signs. When Mr Henchy admits that he had thought Keon the "dozen of stout," the fact is clinched. This subject of drink, more or less with us from the beginning of the story, for a moment gives way to Edward VII's coming visit, another compromise in the offing. Whatever the moral objections might be, most present agree with Henchy that such a visit will attract capital to Ireland, and objections to Edward are brushed aside. In like manner, a Conservative voter, Ward of Dawson Street, may have been persuaded to vote for the Nationalist Tierney. And Crofton the Orangeman has also put his Conservative bias aside to work for the Nationalist candidate, though he dully insults his Catholic comrades by calling Parnell a gentleman, which they could not be. Then Crofton's bottle opens, Hynes rejoins the company, and old Jack hands Henchy a bottle to be placed on the hob for Hynes. We are ready for the poem that keeps one man from his bottle and derides all compromise.

III

Every stanza points to these stated compromises—alcoholic, religious, political, and moral. Consider the first:

> He is dead. Our Uncrowned King is dead.
>   O, Erin, mourn with grief and woe
> For he lies dead whom the fell gang
>   Of modern hypocrites laid low.

As many critics have discovered, the fact that Parnell is indeed dead lies at the very center of the story. And now talk has just concluded on the crowned king of Ireland, Edward VII. Those like Henchy who approve of him, and those others like Crofton and O'Connor who refuse to stir up feelings over Parnell's and Edward's like failings, sustain the hypocrite gang right into the year 1902. We are in the Royal Exchange ward, and the Royal Exchange had been the City Hall since 1852, before that Ireland's treasury when not used as a barracks and torture chamber in 1798. Thus, the very locale suggests compromise and hypocrisy.

The next stanza asks us to contemplate the continued mire of Irish politics:

> He lies slain by the coward hounds
> He raised to glory from the mire;
> And Erin's hopes and Erin's dreams
> Perish upon her monarch's pyre.

None has been raised to glory. What hopes and dreams exist reside in the likelihood of Edward's visit. What memory of a pyre remains has been employed to light cigarettes and open bottles of stout. While the next stanza speaks of the woe that burdens the Irish heart, little real woe accompanies this day except perhaps in the heart of Joe Hynes. The green flag unfurled in the fourth stanza can be viewed only in the brief glimpse we get of ivy in a few lapels. The statesmen, bards, and warriors that might bring Ireland fame among the nations of the world are considerably diminished in the actual presence of a candidate like Tierney, a poet like Hynes, and the half-hearted canvassers out hunting votes. The next stanza dwells on Parnell's dream of liberty for Ireland. But the continued treachery and talk of treachery in the Committee Room, no less the likely machinations of Fanning, Cowley, and Tierney in the Black Eagle, assure us that liberty is but a name. And the next stanza goes on to reflect on the likes of Father Burke and Father Keon, fawning priests that they appear to be. Then the pride insisted upon in the seventh stanza is no more, yet Parnell may well be said to unite "with Erin's heroes of the past" in the eighth stanza when we realize how most of them were betrayed or rejected all too often by their erstwhile followers. And so we come to the last three stanzas that relate most strongly to this 6 October 1902:

> No sound of strife disturb his sleep!
>   Calmly he rests: no human pain
> Or high ambition spurs him now
>   The peaks of glory to attain.
>
> They had their way: they laid him low.
>   But Erin, list, his spirit may
> Rise, like the Phoenix from the flames,
>   When breaks the dawning of the day,
>
> The day that brings us Freedom's reign.
>   And on that day may Erin well
> Pledge in the cup she lifts to Joy
>   One grief—the memory of Parnell.

Well, plenty of strife remains. One cannot imagine Parnell resting calmly. High ambition is not a mark of this crowd. Rather, low ambition appears to reside all too fully in Tierney. The only spirit that rises from the feeble fire is the gas to open a bottle. The men hardly drink to Joy; in fact no cups are available. Though Freedom is not likely to reign, for a moment the grief for Parnell is genuine in more than one sentimental heart in the Committee Room.

IV

But the poem may have also insinuated a more or less invisible grief that hangs like a pall over the story. I speak of the sad state of Irish leadership. We had started with an old man, old Jack, talking with another youthful but aged creature, Mat O'Connor, about Parnell. Passing references were subsequently made to the time of the Fenians—defiant men like James Stephens, Thomas Luby, John O'Leary, Jeremiah O'Donovan Rossa, Charles Kickham, John O'Mahony, and the like. Even Major Sirr, the *bête noire* of the 1798 rising, is dragged in. All these times—1891, 1867, even 1848, and 1798—had seen nationalism go a-glimmering. They were, as Yeats used to call them, slack periods in the national life. And he came to feel that September 1913 was another one, as his poem testifies. As we listen, then, to this melancholy conversation between old

Jack and his prematurely aged friend, we not only remember the Phoenix Flame, symbol for the Fenians, but, as we watch old Jack's shadow suddenly grow larger on the wall, we may also ponder Joyce's translating us back to the original Finn and his Fianna, to the days of another chief, another aftermath of defeat, the battle of Gabhra, also an all-Irish struggle where Finn's grandson Oscar died. We may even include the survivor Oisin in the person of Joe Hynes, finally returned from the intoxication of the Tir-na-nOg, become a bent old man, so to speak, full of memories, and now doomed to argue with St Patrick, herald of the new Christian Ireland.[8] All in Ireland, including Parnell, recognized the Fianna–Fenian connection. And, though no Fenian himself, Parnell insisted from his very beginning in politics "that Fenianism was the key of Irish nationality."[9] His first notice in Parliament came after his speech defending the so-called Fenian murderers in Manchester. Despite his bias for constitutional means in combatting England, he always supported the Fenians and was rewarded by their loyalty during his last days.[10]

Most important for my argument, Joyce also acknowledged the link between the nineteenth-century Fenians and their heroic predecessors. As he wrote in the first sentence of his essay "Fenianism": "With the recent death of John O'Leary in Dublin on St. Patrick's Day, the Irish national holiday, went perhaps the last actor in the turbid drama of Fenianism, a time-honoured name derived from the old Irish language (in which the word 'fenians' means the King's bodyguard) which came to designate the Irish insurrectionist movement."[11] When later in his essay Joyce contrasts the Fenian movement with the ineffectual insurrection of 1803 and the Young Irelanders of 1845, I cannot help but catch the real, not the ironic, ancestors of this dreary committee room and its short-lived flame on a cold and wet 6 October: "Unlike Robert Emmet's foolish uprising or the impassioned movement of Young Ireland in '45, the Fenianism of '67 was not one of the usual flashes of Celtic temperament that lighten the shadows for a moment and leave behind a darkness blacker than before."[12] Of course my extensive identifications may be too arbitrary between characters in the story and heroes of the Fianna. But surely a dead king, Finn MacCool, killed in a later fratricidal battle after Gabhra, between fellow-Fianna, could well recall a like fratricidal division in 1890 and Parnell's subsequent death in 1891. Beyond that likeness, if we might agree that Joe Hynes faintly resembles Oisin, the poet and loyal son of Finn, the rest of the canvassers and hangers-on cast an ironic light on Joyce's definition of "King's bodyguard." For the likes of Caoilte, the dead Oscar, and the rest, I can make no reasonable claim for historic parallels. Yet the dead king, his bodyguard, and protesting poet-son seem stamped on the story from beginning to end. Let me, then, conclude.

V

We have witnessed a miserable remnant, not only of Parnell and his party but also of that fierce, illegal organization that took the Phoenix Flame as its symbol, a miserable remnant that finally pales before the ultimate band of heroic warriors who lost their lives and their leader Finn by drinking-horn taboo in a third-century murderous brawl between Irish clans. As far as the memory of Parnell goes, Joyce claimed, as I have mentioned, that of eighty-three Irish members, only eight remained loyal to Parnell in Committee Room 15.[13] In the story, we witness four canvassers in the Wicklow Street Committee Room loyal in their grudging way to Tierney, while four others—Cowley, Fanning, Father Burke, and Father Keon—are elsewhere. These eight, but for Hynes, who probably backs Colgan, lack all those traits that Joyce felt characteristic of Parnell's genius: "melancholy serenity," "the light of his sovereign bearing, mild and proud, silent and disconsolate."[14]

As I have argued, the contrast of these eight (and now I am going to add old Jack) with the original Fianna is even more shocking. The Fianna gave themselves principally to hunting and fighting, not to bickering and canvassing. The ten conditions demanded of a candidate for this band of warriors—and the smallest unit consisted of nine men and their leader—reads fabulously yet none the less pointedly:

> The following are the other conditions which Fionn son of Cumhall attached to the degrees in bravery which each

184

one was bound to obtain before being received into the Fian. The first condition: no man was received into the Fian or the great Assembly of Uisneach, or the Fair of Taillte, or the Feis of Tara, until his father and mother and clan and relatives gave guarantees that they would never demand any retribution from anyone for his death, so that he might look to no one to avenge him but to himself; and that if he should inflict great injuries, retribution should not be visited on his kinsmen. The second condition: no one was admitted into the Fian until he had become a file, and had made up the twelve books of Filidheacht. The third condition: no one was admitted into the Fian until a large pit reaching above his knees had been made for him, and he was placed in it with his shield and a hazel staff as long as a warrior's arm in his hand; and nine warriors, with nine spears, were to approach him, leaving the space of nine furrows between him and them; and they hurled nine spears together at him, and if he were wounded in spite of his shield and his hazel staff, he would not be received into the Fian. The fourth condition: no man was admitted into the Fian until, having his hair plaited, he was sent through several woods with all the Fian in pursuit of him with a view to wounding him, while he got but the odds of a single tree over them, and if they overtook him, they would wound him. The fifth condition: no man was admitted into the Fian whose weapons trembled in his hand. The sixth condition: no man was admitted among them if a branch of a tree in the woods unloosed from its plait a single braid of his hair. The seventh condition: no man was admitted among them if he broke a withered bough beneath his feet. The eighth condition: no man was admitted among them unless he leaped over a tree as high as his forehead, and unless he stooped beneath a tree as low as his knee, through the great agility of his body. The ninth condition: no man was received into the Fian unless he could pluck a thorn from his foot with his hand without stopping in his race for the purpose. The tenth condition: no man was admitted among them unless he had sworn to the Ri Feinnidh that he would be faithful and submissive to him.[15]

Now, if Tierney may be called the leader, the tenth member or decurion of the group, Hynes again excluded, none would have avenged Parnell or, for that matter, Tierney; not one is a *file* or poet; none seems especially brave or particularly agile. The canvassers are a-tremble over pay. Hardly any is truly faithful to Tierney. While I may be insisting on a too close series of ironic parallels, these modern, diminished Fianna are certainly an undistinguished, ambiguous lot, with a younger generation—old Jack's son and the errand boy—like Oscar clearly dead to life. Oisin, away with Niamh during most of the *Colloquy of the Old Men*, seems like an earlier mirror for Hynes. Yet he probably ought to see himself as closer to old Jack. In some versions of the *Colloquy*, St Patrick condemns the Fianna to hell, as Yeats has him do in his poem *The Wanderings of Oisin*. This troop of latter-day Fianna is certainly condemned to the hell of a seedy committee room or an equally doubtful pub, the Black Eagle. The real flame is a dismal hell-fire fanned by the mayor-maker, Fanning. Any resemblance to the Phoenix Flame must promise no resurrection, only the assured visit of an English king. The last word is given appropriately to the Orangemen Crofton. What he calls "a fine piece of writing" is not writing at all. The poem has been a recital, a lament and elegy, a truly ancient Irish oral performance in praise of a dead chief, a performance quite foreign to the English tradition of fine writing. For all of the mediocrity of the poem as a piece of writing, as a recital—no matter how the name Parnell is pronounced—it is stirring enough to fire even those least worthy of Parnell's memory.[16] The shabbiness of the poem and the grandeur of the recital bring together one dismal present and many isolated, lost splendors of the past.

NOTES: CHAPTER 12

1   Joseph L. Blotner, "'Ivy Day in the Committee Room': death without resurrection," *Perspective*, vol. 9, no. 4 (Summer 1957), pp. 210–17.
2   For a splendid summary of these points, along with a treatment of the political and personal background of the story, see M. J. C. Hodgart, " 'Ivy Day in the Committee Room,' " in *James Joyce's*

Dubliners: Critical Essays, ed. Clive Hart (New York: Viking Press, 1969), pp. 115–21.

3 Frederick C. Stern, "'Parnell is dead': 'Ivy Day in the Committee Room,'" *James Joyce Quarterly*, vol. 10, no. 2 (Winter 1973), pp. 228–39.

4 Desmond Ryan, *The Phoenix Flame* (London: Arthur Barker, 1937), passim. So far as I can tell, the only critics of the story who even mention the Fenians and the Fianna are Gifford and Seidman in their *Notes for Joyce*, p. 61.

5 *The Critical Writings of James Joyce*, ed. Ellsworth Mason and Richard Ellmann (New York: Viking Press, 1959), p. 227.

6 Patrick Woulfe, *Irish Names and Surnames* (Dublin: M. H. Gill, 1923), p. 564.

7 Kenneth MacGowan, *The Phoenix Park* (Dublin: Kamc Publications, n.d.), p. 26. I cite this pamphlet as a convenient repository of information on the Park that Joyce might have read in any of the accounts by Chart, Falkiner or D'Alton. The confused meaning of Phoenix in the name of the Park has been common knowledge in Dublin for at least two centuries.

8 See, for instance, the connection that John O'Mahony makes between the heroic life of the original Fianna and the ideals of the Fenians of his own day: Geoffrey Keating, *The History of Ireland*, trans. John O'Mahony (New York: P. M. Haverty, 1857), pp. 7, 10–11, 345 n. 64. Ryan, op. cit., p. 58, cites O'Mahony's notes to Keating and discusses further the connections the Fenians established between themselves and Finn and his Fianna.

9 R. Barry O'Brien, *The Life of Charles Stewart Parnell*, 3rd edn (London: Smith, Elder, 1899), Vol. 1, p. 87.

10 ibid., Vol. 1, pp. 95–6, 98; Vol. 2, p. 340.

11 *Critical Writings of James Joyce*, p. 188.

12 ibid., p. 189.

13 ibid., p. 227.

14 ibid., pp. 225–6.

15 Geoffrey Keating, *The History of Ireland*, trans. S. Dinneen (London: David Nutt, 1908), Vol. 2, pp. 333, 335; and *Silva Gadelica*, ed. Standish H. O'Grady (London/Edinburgh: Williams & Norgate, 1892), Vol. 2, pp. 99–100.

16 cf. C. F. Burgess, "A note on 'The death of Parnell' in Joyce's 'Ivy Day in the Committee Room'", *James Joyce Quarterly*, vol. 9, no. 1 (Fall 1971), pp. 123–5.

13

"A Mother":
Ourselves Alone

"A Mother," perhaps the simplest-appearing story in *Dubliners*, as most critics agree, has nevertheless been the most difficult for me to understand. In a word, too many references, as I shall try to show, hint of something more than the usual Irish betrayal and paralysis. Even with the self-evident spoof of the Irish Revival on nearly every page, some larger issue has long seemed to me to lie very close to the surface of the story. The difficulty is not that we lack sensitive readings of "A Mother." Warren Beck's discerning paraphrase in his chapter is an exemplary one, although I can't wholly agree with his conclusion on Mrs Kearney's defeat. Nor do we lack knowledge of the original facts behind the story. Beyond Stanislaus's mention that the story was one of two derived from Joyce's actual experience, Richard Ellmann has identified Olive Kennedy as the model for Kathleen Kearney and summarized Holloway's account of the Grand Concert. Mary Power has reminded us that Kearney in Irish means "victorious." Ben Collins, in a rather diffuse essay, explains the likely parody of Yeats's *Cathleen Ni Houlihan* and reminds us that "Ni" can also mean "not" in Irish. Gifford and Seidman in their notes on the story point to the added relevance of *The Countess Cathleen*. John Scarry has added to the Stanislaus and Holloway remembrances the importance of John McCormack's presence. Eugene Sheehy has provided us with the programme for the evening. And the *Freeman's Journal*, from Monday, 22 August, to Monday, 29 August 1904, divulges the week's details of the several concerts. Yet the most intelligent handling of fact and story might well be the short essay by Michael J. O'Neill, "Joyce's use of memory in 'A Mother'". With the aid of

Holloway's pages, O'Neill reconstructs the series of concerts at the end of Horse Show Week, 1904. He then concentrates on the Grand Concert on Saturday, the 27th, by focusing on the performers, counterparts to those named in the story, and even identifies "the Freeman Man" and O'Madden Burke. Perhaps most important, O'Neill points to the fact that Joyce transferred the time of the story to almost a year later, 22 July 1905, the end of the week after Mrs Patrick Campbell and Sarah Bernhardt acted on Monday, the 17th, the matinee and evening performances of *Pélléas and Mélisande* in Dublin.[1]

Yet difficulties remain. Why should Holohan be lame? Beyond establishing the time of the story, what does mention of Mrs Patrick Campbell contribute? The song "Killarney," talk of the Wallace opera *Maritana*, the education in French and music repeated in mother and daughter, these also beg for explanation. And why should Mr Kearney turn out to be a bootmaker? At the end, strangely enough in such a comic story, Mrs Kearney is said to resemble "an angry stone image" in her frozen fury, while Hoppy Holohan feels "his skin on fire." David Hayman's bizarre claim for an ironic parallel to the Lot story aside,[2] what do these peculiar images point to?

I shall try, then, to make sense of these lingering references, since something appears inherent in them, just as Miss Healy's betraying Kathleen seems inherent in her name. In the first place, most critics see "A Mother" among the last three original stories that treated politics, art, and religion respectively in public life. Yet I see in "A Mother" sentimentalized history as a greater obsession for the average Dubliner than was art, or at least history artfully presented. For the story is really something more than a mere spoof on the Revival. Irish history diluted, twisted, or sentimentalized is the substance of the concerts. Even the first paragraph of the story in citing the Eire Abu Society places us in that dreamy ethos heralded by the slogan "Ireland to Victory." For me that paragraph sets the real drift of the story: Eire's, a mother's, triumph over a family, an audience, a society, their artists, and not least herself. Mother Ireland, Mrs Kearney, "in the end . . . arranged everything," as the paragraph concludes. Mother Ireland, as I hope to show, has many more characteristics beyond those usually fixed on Eire, including spite. Thus, I see the story as offering the awful reality—off-stage, so to speak—behind the unconscious parody of Irish historical ideals. After all, the year was 1905, a year after Griffith write *The Resurrection of Hungary*, and the year Sinn Fein—"Ourselves Alone"—was founded. To understand ourselves together, as Joyce mocks them, I shall first glance at the many minor characters who swell out Joyce's theme of Revival paralysis (if I may call it that) and then contemplate more thoroughly the mother and family at the center of something less than an indomitable Irishry.

I

We might begin with the principals of the Society—Holohan, Fitzpatrick, and Beirne. Miss Beirne is indeed a little old woman, something like the Shan Van Vocht in ordinary appearance. Her marked characteristic is a twisted face. On first sight, Mrs Kearney scrutinizes an "oldish face which was screwed into an expression of trustfulness and enthusiasm." But the rainy night and then the likelihood of an only partly filled hall remove that expression. We are left with the twisted face, suggesting, as the term "twister" implies in Dublin, a deceitful person, hardly the traditional Shan Van Vocht. Her name, Beirne, according to the Rev. Patrick Woulfe, was also that of "stewards to the O'Connors, Kings of Connacht and sometimes of all Ireland." Woulfe adds another possibility: families of some respectability near Ballinrobe in Mayo.[3] Both locales are associated with the Shan Van Vocht of Yeats's play. But, as we later learn, it is Miss Beirne's idea that Mrs Kearney, after the interval, must give the Society all the scheduled time or be paid nothing more—this last information from O'Madden Burke, another descendant of the West of Ireland. Miss Beirne is the Little Old Woman with a vengeance.

But Fitzpatrick, the secretary of the Society, has also something of the same ironic inheritance. As Edward MacLysaght records of the name, "this is the only surname with the prefix Fitz which is of native Irish origin, the others being Norman. The Fitzpatricks are Macgilpatricks . . . meaning son of the servant or devotee of St. Patrick."[4] But this Fitzpatrick has a flat accent, wears his hat on the side of his head, has paper-chewing habits, all adding up to a craven, ill-mannered lower-class Dubliner given to horseplay with friends in the audience. His most damning characteristic is his vacant expression, a fact Joyce repeats three times. When pinned down by Mrs Kearney about payment to Kathleen, he retreats into the usual formalities of an Irish honorary secretary and refers her to the committee. Initially, on the night of the last performance, he is not to be found. If we can believe Holohan, Fitzpatrick was nevertheless the man in charge of payments all along. In fact, at the last moment, he bursts into the dressing-room to make partial payment. Thus the secretary to Eire Abu and his vacant dedication to the patron saint of Ireland.

But Hoppy Holohan deserves most of our attention. Aside from his limp, the word that best describes his ways is "devious." His name fittingly derives from the diminutive of the Irish word "proud."[5] In *Ulysses* something of his financial slipperiness may be added to his game leg when he is nicknamed "hop and carry one." Despite his managing the concerts celebrating an Irish Revival, his presence cannot be the one attached to his daughter of legend. Yet, in the context of Joyce's story, his cooperation and then contention fasten on Mrs Kearney. From the first we also identify him with the dirty pieces of paper he uses for notes. As an assistant secretary to the Society, he nevertheless appears to take Mrs Kearney's expert advice, is made to feel at home, and helps himself to the decanter at her urging. At the same time, he, too, falls back on the committee to explain the change in plans—first, reserving the best talent for the last night, then canceling Friday night's concert. And, though he signed the contract, he passes off payment to Fitzpatrick. To ensure a favorable account of the evening, he leads the *Freeman* man, Hendrick, to the predictable room where bottles of stout are being opened. On his return, discovering the delay, Holohan explodes into violent behavior: he becomes red, excited, speaks volubly, points desperately before haling Fitzpatrick in with the money. During the interval, however, he retreats again into the priggish formalities of Irish politeness: Mrs Kearney has treated him badly; the committee will consider the matter on Tuesday; Mrs Kearney lacks a sense of decency. She is not a lady. He is done with her. At the end, he paces up and down the room "in order to cool himself for he felt his skin on fire," exclaiming, "That's a nice lady . . . O she's a nice lady."

What are we to make of him? I can't equate him, literally or ironically, with any one heroic figure, human or divine. Yet he does seem to assemble in his person a parody of many heroic traits that the Revival liked to recall. If he has a limp, he is still not the Goban who dispensed beer to the gods, notably in Yeats's poem "The Gray Rock." His devious ways, dirty papers, and submission to a woman may well parody moments in battle, heroic recitals, and triumphs in love among Finn and his companions. Nor, despite his rages and skin on fire, does he much resemble Caoilte or, more likely, Cuchulain for whom it took seventy bare-breasted women to cool his rage and bring his temperature down to normal. His reliance on the committee and then his priggishness at the end are hardly the proper thing (O'Madden Burke's term) for a heroic spirit. Whatever other names might pertain, the popular Revival tales of the Tuatha De Danaan, Finn and his companions, Cuchulain with Emer or Maeve, all make Holohan pale before them. Yet Holohan, along with his secretary and committeewoman, have abettors. We should glance at them next.

II

Before all present turn against Mrs Kearney—after she blurts out, "I'm a great fol-the-diddle-I-do"—the contention against her had included the three above members of the Society plus two stewards, the unnamed baritone, Mr Duggan the bass, and Mr O'Madden Burke.

The baritone starts the second portion of the program and in doing so thoroughly scotches Mrs Kearney's hopes. Like the first tenor (based on John McCormack), he is described as "well dressed, stout and complacent." At first he refuses to comment on Mrs Kearney's demands since he has been paid, but he does express polite concern for the other artistes. He seems, however, more closely associated with Miss Healy. In reply to her question, he rejoins that he had heard that Mrs Patrick Campbell had performed well. With Miss Healy as his new accompanist, he forces Mrs Kearney to step aside after the interval. His unctuousness also forces her decision to leave and gains him her countenance of "an angry stone image," hardly Ireland's applause for one of her singing celebrants. He also openly contrasts with Duggan the bass, yet Duggan's opposition might have been even more galling. He who drinks milk for his voice, says "yous," speaks little, wipes his nose with a gloved hand, and once played the foolish King Carlos in *Maritana* strikes one as probably an uninspiring as his "scattered black moustache" and name in Irish, the diminutive of "black." Both baritone and bass, therefore, also appear to me as preparations for our acquaintance with O'Madden Burke, he of the "magniloquent western name," troubled finances, and wide respect.

We first confront him with the *Freeman* man, Mr Hendrick, to whom Miss Healy pays something like bodily tribute. He is off to the Mansion House to cover a more important national event, a lecture by an American priest, for "concerts and *artistes* bored him considerably." Though in top-coats, Hendrick and O'Madden Burke, both gentlemen of the press, claim the fireplace—"take possession" is Joyce's phrase. And O'Madden Burke will write the notice. By instinct he has already found the room with the bottles of stout. Described as "a suave, elderly man who balanced his imposing body, when at rest, upon a large silk umbrella," O'Madden Burke affects the role of social and artistic arbiter. Appropriately, for him at least, he makes the final judgment on Mrs Kearney's derelictions: "You did the proper thing, Holohan." This I take to be Joyce's epiphany in the story, and the crux is the word "proper."

Part of such pretension resides in O'Madden Burke's very name. Usually termed a pompous device in Ireland, the grandiose double surname—that "magniloquent western name"—nevertheless joins two of the greatest surnames from Galway, specifically from Ir Connacht and Hy Maine. The O'Maddens were an ancient, noble Irish family, and the Burkes, descended from the Norman De Burgos, later the earls of Clanrickard, were one of the most powerful families in Europe. In some sense O'Madden Burke's poise balances the claims of both names, though in the end they may seem to cancel each other out. But let me set down some descriptions of each name to catch the illustrious veneer with which Joyce has embellished this pompous master of deportment. O'Madden was

. . . the name of a distinguished branch of the Ui Maine in Co. Galway, who derive their descent from MADAVAN (slain 1008), [the name is a diminutive of *madav*, a dog] who was the son of Gadhra Mór, chief of Ui Maine from 1014 to 1027, and are of the same stock as the O'Kellys, with whom they originally formed one clan—the Ui Maine. About the middle of the 11th century . . . to the middle of the 17th century the chieftaincy of Siol nAnmchadha continued in almost unbroken succession in the family of O'Madden. The clan-lands, which in accordance with Irish usage were named from the clan, comprised the barony of Longford, in the south-east of Co. Galway, and the parish of Lusnagh, on the other side of the Shannon, in the present Offaly. Many distinguished chiefs of the name are mentioned in the Irish annals.[6]

The same author concludes of the Burkes on an earlier page:

This family ranks with the Fitzgeralds and Butlers as among the most illustrious of the Anglo-Norman settlers in Ireland. They derive their descent from William Fitz Adelm de Burgo who, in 1171, accompanied Henry II to Ireland, was made governor of Wexford, and in 1178 succeeded Strongbow as chief governor of Ireland. In 1179, Fitz Adelm obtained a grant of a great portion of Connacht. By marriage with an heiress of the de Lacys, Walter de Burgo acquired, in addition to his other possessions, the earldom of Ulster; and the Burkes became the greatest Anglo-Norman family in Ireland.[7]

Needless to say, the distinguished native Irish family and the proud Norman intruders warred with each other—and married. Yeats's Thoor Ballylee was a De Burgo castle, and a Burke had tenants there down to its purchase by the Gregorys in 1783. If Yeats fabled right in his poem "The Tower," the Burkes had brought their share of extravagance to that locale.

But the O'Maddens were scarcely outdone as fire-eaters. A description of Eoghan O'Madden, who died in 1347, will give a sharply worded hint of the family reputation for honor, predatory violence, and self-satisfaction:

There is a tranquil, benign, great, hardy, sweet-voiced, generous, vehement, regal king over the Siol nAnmachadha, and this king is the noble Eoghan, son of the loud-voiced Murchadh, son of the lively-preying Cathal, son of the expertly-wounding Diarmid, son of the affluent Madudan, son of the bright-faced Diarmid, son of the munificent Madden, son of the fettering Gadhra; and this rapid-routing was the last of his tribe . . . [8]

Needless to say, the annalist goes on to show how Eoghan regained that dominion, defeated the De Burgos in 1306, and had a son slain by them in 1340. As might also be expected, Eoghan also fought many battles on the English side. Other O'Maddens are trotted out, right down to the end of the nineteenth century, with more than a fair portion given to duelling, gaming, heavy drinking, and the singing of bawdy songs. A Malachy Fallon who became part of the family by marriage had a favorite song that began with the words "My Wife she is the Queen of all sluts."[9]

To return to O'Madden Burke. We ought to add to the buried suggestion of "son of a dog" and one who "burkes" (murders by suffocation, gets rid of quietly), both less than noble hints in the name, some details elaborated in *Ulysses*. I submit that in *Ulysses* our man is proved to be much the same as he will be a year later in July 1905. For instance, he is called "that minstrel boy of the wild wet west." Ned Lambert professes that O'Madden Burke will someday write something on "St Mary's Abbey, where Silken Thomas Fitzgerald proclaimed himself a rebel in 1534."[10] Whatever elephantine roguery may inhere in these subjects, in the meanings embedded in his name, and in the exploits of his forebears, we find him no less sartorially impressive in the newspaper office than he is in our story—and no less inflated in pronouncement. There we discover O'Madden Burke "tall in copious grey of Donegal tweed" as he announced his and Stephen's entrance, "Youth led by Experience visits Notoriety." He is either given to clichés—"the divine afflatus" or "Lay on, Macduff"—or filled with the catchphrases of the town—"Help! I feel a strong weakness." Typical is his observation on Molly Bloom: "The vocal muse. Dublin's prime favourite." Nevertheless, his umbrella is there to support him with grace; he affects the loose tie of the Latin quarter; his face is called sphinx-like. Already he is the friend of Holohan. In his colossal effrontery, he is in the van of the retreat to Mooney's allied with that other sponge, Lenehan. This habit of not standing his round may be echoed in his plea to Bloom in "Circe": "Free fox in a free hen roost." In short he is another one of the humorous, literary, writing, drinking crowd of what might appear to outsiders as no more than ne'er-do-wells, but in Dublin he and they retain the mixed blessings of talented failure. In "A Mother" we see the worst side of him: the self-imposed moral adjudicator, he who will write up the event, the affectedly exasperated man who pronounces the demise of Kathleen Kearney's musical career. Plainly he's the self-appointed judge of decorum. Thus, all the hardihood, the wiliness, the gallantry, the spectacular waste by nobles and gentry in the West of Ireland are reduced to a stance, a pose, a certain reputation, a basic insolvency summed up in a silk umbrella and a double surname that maintains a shaky stance from that past.

III

What, then, must we think of the counter-force, the Kearney family and, for the moment, its supporters? These last include the lady of the patriotic recitation, Mr Bell the bronze medalist, and for a time Miss Healy. True to her name, of course, she deserts Kathleen and takes her place as accompanist. Beforehand she had made up to Hendrick the *Freeman* man: "her laughter and fragrance and wilful glances were his tribute." With such an ally—a Healy—no mother or Ireland needs an enemy. Doubtless the recital, patriotic or not, was bogus enough. We also know that Mr Bell—small, nervous, fair-haired, and egregiously friendly—is nevertheless a determined seeker after Feis Ceoil prizes and is beset by jealousy. Those who take sides with the Kearneys do not inspire so much as insinuate misplaced trust.

A little of the same reversal or, better, questionable appearance may also invest Mr Kearney. Bootmaker, thrifty father with dowry for two girls, pious observer of the Sacred

Heart, bearded mumbler, and solid, substantial man (likened to the Post Office), Mr Kearney seems another parody, perhaps the most comic in the story. "Large, secure, and fixed"—so Joyce describes him. He contrasts wildly with the puckish, pixie, sly, elusive leprechaun, the imaginary bane of Irish commercialism, yet a figure thoroughly exploited by the commercial and tourist trade. With beard, crock of gold, hideout, boot- and shoe-making, and impish ways the leprechaun directly reflects on the reserved, quiet, and solicitous bachelor married old in Ireland.

W. B. Yeats's famous explanation in *Irish Fairy and Folk Tales* could well be the source of Joyce's ragging description:

> "The name *Lepracaun*," Mr. Douglas Hyde writes to me, "is from the Irish *leith brog—i.e.*, the One-shoemaker, since he is generally seen working at a single shoe. . . ." [Yeats goes on to mention O'Kearney's rare book, the *Feis Tigh Chonain*, as a source of information. Did Joyce get the Kearney name from here?]

> The *Lepracaun, Cluricaun*, and *Far Darrig*. Are these one spirit in different moods and shapes? Hardly two Irish writers are agreed. In many things these three fairies, if three, resemble each other. They are withered, old, and solitary, in every way unlike the sociable spirits. . . . They dress with all unfairy homeliness, and are, indeed, most sluttish, slouching, jeering, mischievous phantoms. They are the great practical jokers among the good people.[11]

On the same page, Yeats goes on to describe the wealth and crocks of gold belonging to the leprechauns, the drunkenness of the cluricauns, and the hideous joking and red clothes of the far darrig. For all his superficial resemblance, Mr Kearney can hardly be a member of this troop. Yet even his place of business, Ormond Quay, may reflect something of this facetious opposition. Named after the great seventeenth-century viceroy, Ormond Quay is nevertheless best known for the faction-fighting on its bridges between north and south Dublin. The butchers, for generations associated with the locale, were the fiercest combatants of all, taking on all and sundry—weavers, Trinity students, soldiers, the constabulary and the like. But Mr Kearney, none of these, is part of a grimmer Irish folklore of January–May marriage, though his bootmaking and gold make him a laughable patron of the Revival. But he also has a daughter.

Kathleen Kearney—whom Molly Bloom thinks a chit, at worst a sparrow-fart—is a lesser edition of her mother. She readily falls in with her mother's plans. She, too, is convent-bred, had endured French instruction, graduated from the Royal Academy of Music, and receives an Irish teacher sent by her mother to their home. Now she has musical *and* Nationalist friends. After mass they gossip and say goodby in Irish. Yet she is also vulgar like her mother and already has a touch of her mother's high-handedness. For instance, witness her crude remarks at the expense of Madame Glynn—"I wonder where did they dig her up. . . . I'm sure I never heard of her." While I see in her no resemblance to the flirt in the song "Kate Kearney of Killarney," her determined gathering of her skirts and peremptory "Now, Mr. Bell," when her mother balks at the missing four shillings imply the likelihood of future opposition. Only at the end is she again thoroughly under her mother's renewed direction, but only after her mother and father had argued with her. Mrs Kearney finally wraps the girl's cloak, not exactly a green flag, around her daughter. The last we hear is that "Kathleen followed her mother meekly." This is Kathleen Kearney, perhaps not Kathleen Ni Houlahan, but visibly a daughter of old Ireland.

Mrs Kearney is of course the mother of the story—although every female contributes something to an odious Ireland's unfortunate feminine gender if not her motherhood. The name Devlin itself, as Edward MacLysaght traces it, was best known in the person of "Anne Devlin (1778–1851), the faithful servant of Robert Emmet, who though imprisoned and tortured would not give information against him."[12] Her persistence, though not her selflessness, inheres in Mrs Kearney. Yet, as a mother, she must also somehow resemble Ireland herself.

And Ireland, as we know, is graced with at least fourteen ancient names, according to Keating, among them Eire, Banba, Fodla, and Hibernia.[13] But she is usually thought of as a triple goddess, Eire-Banba-Fodla. As Eire she represents sovereignty, as Banba fertility, and as Fodla learning and science. But as a triple goddess she has three phases: mother, lover, and hag of death.[14] Despite her ivory manners and chill accomplishments, despite her being mistress of the silver biscuit-barrel and decanter, like the tempestuous Queen Maeve before her, Mrs Kearney has also a touch of the vulgar. Her mocking retort to Holohan, "I'm a great fellow fol-the-diddle-I-do," is hardly ladylike in its hint not only of swindling but also of the slang for copulation.

In her rage—haggard, colored in face, and glaring—she stands for an instant "like an angry stone image." In doing so, she combines many of the female traits said to be common to Ireland and Dublin. Her imperiousness approaches the heights of the statue Hibernia centered on the Bank of Ireland and on the Post Office (to which Joyce likens her husband), and many another public building in Dublin. Her Dublin counterpart may even extend to the head of famed Anna Liffey, one of the fourteen riverine sculptures on the Custom House.[15] One might even mention another name for Ireland, Inis Fail, deriving from the Lia Fail, or Stone of Destiny. In any event, as sovereign mother of two daughters to whom she has passed on her knowledge (French and music) and the bounties of her fertility, her reign is past. Her role as lover perhaps ended when she gave up Turkish Delight and married for spite. Our view of her is plain: the hag of death, for sovereignty remains her abiding and most deadly trait. The figure of the stone image expressing anger fixes her outburst as a victorious paralysis of Eire-Hibernia confronting detractors among her own.

IV

If, as Yeats claimed, life should be a role played before a great audience, both sides of this internecine drama play wretched roles before each other and, if it were known, before a rather sleazy grand concert audience. Yet the question remains: which side prevails? No doubt, perhaps, the Eire Abu Society does, yet our sympathy—what little the story musters—probably ought to go to the Kearneys, even though Holohan and O'Madden Burke have the last word. Mrs Kearney's persistent romantic ideas, once reduced to her eating secretly

Turkish Delight, and then her marrying out of spite, were balanced by the gossip aimed at her likely spinsterhood. The increased anger that leads to her vulgar remark and subsequent undoing is balanced by all sides turning against her. Her organizing the concerts, buying extra tickets, and making purchases at Brown Thomas are counterbalanced by her mean insistence on her contract. Thus, she comes off as a nicely mixed character whom we might not want to know yet might also sympathize with abstractly. I am recalled to Yeats's poem "Red Hanrahan's Song about Ireland," which had appeared in *The Secret Rose* (1897) as "Kathleen the Daughter of Hoolihan and Hanrahan the Red." Each stanza points to the emotional breakdown of Irish idealism through one internal division or another, each in terms of storm and stress. Yet each stanza also ends with a reaffirmation of the ideal, despite constant defeat. I detect something like this contradiction, though in a much more comic vein, with the ideal itself seriously held in question, when we remember Kathleen's resemblance to her mother and distance from Holohan.

I would hark back, then, to the establishment of Sinn Fein just as Joyce was writing the story, though before the convention of November 1905. The picture exposed in the story is indeed "ourselves alone" in history by way of contemporary parody. To pursue the three divisions of the story—from Mrs Kearney's background and acquaintance with Holohan to the first two nights of the concert series to the fearsome and divided last evening—is to trace Yeats's hopes, doubts, and affirmations over the violent fallings-out in the poem. Of course Joyce was to show more hope in Griffith, his analogy with Hungary, and the creation of the Irish Free State in *Ulysses*. Nevertheless, before that, from a galaxy of little national clubs, like the Celtic Literary Society or the Daughters of Ireland, given to debates, classes, and tableaux vivants in the Ancient Concert Rooms,[16] came the Cumann na nGaedheal, the National Council, the Dungannon Clubs, and finally in November 1905 the annual convention of that Council wherein the name Sinn Fein was given to its policy. The Sinn Fein League was an outgrowth declared in 1907, with the organization simply called Sinn Fein in September 1908.[17] Although he wrote of it with some approval in his 1907 essay "Fenianism," Joyce has taken a hard and unsympathetic look at the roots of that organization which, for all its future heroism, was to make the artist's life so difficult in Ireland. Joyce has also maintained a mixed look at that likely independence that brought Ireland to civil war and its two powerfully contending parties ever since.

V

Curiously enough, Joyce may also have another subtle contrast in mind for his confused Dublin audience, the story of yet another familial falling-out, a mysterious and beautiful queen, and her death as a mother, for Miss Healy's mention of Mrs Patrick Campbell not only dates the story but also makes quiet reference to the Dublin production of *Pélléas and Mélisande*. Despite the first tenor's praise—and his seems to be the only sensible mind in the story—the play was not altogether well received in Dublin. After all, Pélléas was played by Sarah Bernhardt, aged around 61, and Mélisande by Mrs Patrick Campbell, then 41. A Dublin critic surmised that the two actresses were "both old enough to know better."[18] To a degree, the vague locale of the play, the mysterious Mélisande, the innocent love affair, and the dreamy symbolism seem to have titillated Dublin. The reviewer in the *Freeman's Journal* praised the symbolism of the play but had to admit that the audience laughed during the scene in the tower "when Pélléas apostrophised the flowing locks of Mélisande."[19] The ordinary Dubliner, a member of the Eire Abu Society, probably shared with that Dublin reporter Stephen Dedalus' ironic assurance that of course Maeterlinck would be difficult, "next to impossible," to put on the stage.[20] True to form, in "The Day of the Rabblement," written earlier in 1901, Joyce berated that audience which would "titter coyly when Mélisande lets down her hair."[21]

Earlier he had driven home this distinction between the moral and patriotic audience and the real drama played before them:

However subdued the tone of passions may be, however ordered the action or commonplace the diction, if a play, or a work of music, or a picture concerns itself with the everlasting hopes, desires and hates of humanity, or deals with a symbolic presentment of our widely related nature, albeit a phase of that nature, then it is drama. Maeterlinck's characters may be, when subjected to the searchlight of that estimable torch, commonsense, unaccountable, drifting, fate-impelled creatures—in fact, as our civilization dubs them, uncanny. But in whatever dwarfed and marionette-like manner, their passions are human and so the exposition of them is drama.[22]

The indirect reference to Pélléas and Mélisande, then, would not only force the contrast between the national stage and true drama but it might also point the moral of Joyce's story. The end of the play finds Mélisande dying, but not before giving birth to a girl like herself, tiny, wan, and symbolic. The two brothers have fought over this mother, the older having killed Pélléas. But the result is a symbolic and tragic drama. Joyce's story, on the other hand, is a bitter, nearly farcical comedy, with little to be commemorated on either side. Moreover, if the Yeats play and the Mangan poem "Kathaleen Ny-Houlahan" begin with a hag and end with a queen, Joyce's story begins with a rather frozen queen and ends with a hag enraged. If we remember Mangan's poem that reiterates Ireland's awaiting rescue by a Stuart prince, "the king's son," then Mrs Kearney's husband lends further embarrassment to an already farcical ending that discovers something like a "king's son," O'Madden Burke, approving her unchivalric treatment. Another king's son, Pélléas, son of Arkël, had died for the expiring mother, Mélisande; in fact he was killed by Arkël's older son, Golaud. Different from Yeats's poem and play, Mangan's poem not only finds Kathleen awaiting a king's son; she is also honored with a daughter:

Think her not a ghastly hag too hideous to be seen,
Call her not unseemly names, our matchless Kathaleen!
Young she is, and fair she is, and would be crowned a queen,
Were the king's son at home here with Kathaleen Ny-Houlahan! . . .

Woollen plaids would grace herself, and robes of silk her child,
If the king's son were living here with Kathaleen Ny-Houlahan!

No amount of charmeuse from Brown Thomas can answer that
noble lack.

NOTES: CHAPTER 13

1   After Stanislaus Joyce, *My Brother's Keeper* (London: Faber, 1958),
    p. 79, and *Joseph Holloway's Abbey Theatre*, ed. Robert Hogan and
    Michael J. O'Neill (Carbondale/Edwardsville, Ill.: Southern Illinois
    University Press, 1967), pp. 42–3, see Richard Ellmann, *James Joyce*
    (New York: Oxford University Press, 1959), pp. 173–4, 375; Mary
    Power, "The naming of Kathleen Kearney," *Journal of Modern
    Literature*, vol. 5, no. 3 (September 1976), pp. 532–4; Ben L.
    Collins, "Joyce's use of Yeats and of Irish history: a reading of 'A
    Mother,'" *Eire-Ireland*, vol. 5, no. 1 (September 1970), pp. 45–66;
    Don Gifford, *Notes for Joyce* (New York: Dutton, 1967), p. 65; John
    Scarry, "The 'first tenor' in James Joyce's 'A Mother,'" *Eire-Ireland*,
    vol. 7, no. 4 (Winter 1972), pp. 67–9; Eugene Sheehy, *May It Please
    the Court* (Dublin: C. J. Fallon, n.d.), p. 27; *Freeman's Journal*, 22
    August, p. 6, 24 August, p. 7, 25 August, p. 6, 27 August, p. 6,
    and 29 August 1904, p. 6; and Michael J. O'Neill, "Joyce's use of
    memory in 'A Mother,'" *Modern Language Notes*, vol. 74, no. 3
    (March 1959), pp. 226–30.
2   David Hayman, "'A Mother,'" *James Joyce's Dubliners: Critical
    Essays*, ed. Clive Hart (New York: Viking Press, 1969), pp. 132–3.
3   Patrick Woulfe, *Irish Names and Surnames* (Dublin: M. H. Gill,
    1923), p. 437.
4   Edward MacLysaght, *Irish Families* (New York: Crown Publishers,
    1972), p. 145.
5   Woulfe, op. cit., p. 574.
6   ibid., p. 593.
7   ibid., p. 251. See also John O'Donovan, *The Annals of Hy Maine*
    (Dublin: Irish Archaeological Society, 1843), pp. 129–59, and
    Roderic O'Flaherty, *A Chorographical Description of West or H-Iar
    Connaught*, ed. James Hardiman (Dublin: H. M. Gill, 1846),
    pp. 34 n., 146, 321–3. Also relevant is H. T. Knox, "The De Burgo
    clans of Galway," *Journal of the Galway Archaeological and Historical
    Society*, vol. 1 (1900–1), pp. 124–31.
8   T. M. Madden, *Genealogical, Historical, and Family Records of the
    O'Maddens of Hy-Many and Their Descendants* (Dublin: W. Powell,

1894), pp. 12–13.

9   ibid., pp. 12–20.

10 *Stephen Hero*, ed. John J. Slocum and Herbert Cahoon (New York: New Directions, 1955), pp. 258, 227.

11 W. B. Yeats, *Irish Fairy and Folk Tales*, Modern Library Edition (New York: Random House, n.d.), p. 85.

12 MacLysaght, op. cit., p. 116.

13 Geoffrey Keating, *The History of Ireland*, ed. David Comyn (London: David Nutt/Irish Texts Society, 1902), Vol. 1, pp. 97–105.

14 See letter from Caitlin Ni Mhadadain to the editor of the *Irish Times*, 6 December 1975, p. 16.

15 Harold G. Leask, "Dublin Custom House: the riverine sculptures," *Journal of the Royal Society of Antiquaries of Ireland*, vol. 75 (1945), pp. 186–94; Viola Barrow, "Dublin Custom House: the river heads," *Dublin Historical Record*, vol. 29, no. 1 (December 1975), pp. 26–7; A. M. Fraser, "Statues on public buildings in Dublin," *Dublin Historical Record*, vol. 2, no. 1 (September 1939), pp. 30–7.

16 Maire Nic Shiubhlaigh, *The Splendid Years*, foreword by Padraic Colum (Dublin: James Duffy, 1955), pp. 2–3.

17 F. S. L. Lyons, *Ireland since the Famine* (London: Weidenfeld & Nicolson, 1971), p. 252.

18 Mrs Patrick Campbell, *My Life and Some Letters* (London: Hutchinson, n.d.), p. 139. See also Alan Dent, *Mrs Patrick Campbell* (London: Museum Press, 1961), p. 156.

19 "Bernhardt in Dublin. 'Pélléas and Mélisande,'" *Freeman's Journal*, 18 July 1905, p. 5.

20 *Stephen Hero*, ed. John J. Slocum and Herbert Cahoon (New York: New Directions, 1955), pp. 39–40.

21 "The day of the rabblement," in *The Critical Writings of James Joyce*, ed. Ellsworth Mason and Richard Ellmann (New York: Viking Press, 1959), p. 71.

22 "Royal Hibernian Academy 'Ecce Homo,'" in ibid., p. 32.

14

"Grace":
Drink, Religion,
and Business as Usual

To write on "Grace" is more than a challenge. So many assertive essays have been written on the story that yet another must truly seem excessive if not downright impertinent. As any reader who has studied the story must know, Stanislaus pointed out the relevance of Dante's *Divine Comedy* to "Grace" a long time ago. Critics have not been slow to take the hint and have pushed on in pursuit of all and any religious implications for a story with such a title and classic parallel. Joseph E. Baker, for instance, has argued for the relevance of man's fall from grace and the subsequent efforts of the Trinity to restore him. F. X. Newman has pointed to the likely parody of the Book of Job. Most ingeniously, Carl Niemeyer has speculated that the flatterers in Dante's eighth circle of Hell might well provide the real key to the moral dereliction of Tom Kernan and his friends, including Father Purdon the apologist for businessmen. To round off such commentary, Robert Boyle has expanded on the above and has distinguished Dante's four levels of meaning as providing an even more detailed allegory and extended parody in the story.[1]

I shall thus devote myself to lesser tasks, specifically what most critics have hinted along the way—the unholy binding of drink, bad business, and perfunctory though no less devout religious observance. Bound together as I think they are, these topics have nevertheless been slighted as a whole. Though the second or Purgatory section of the story is the longest, I shall probably give it the shortest treatment since the meandering intellectual flummery of the section has been thoroughly explored by critics like Kain, Adams, and Beck, to name but three. So I shall try to reconstruct the Dantean scheme anew for the entire story and in passing relate the concept of grace to those enduring perhaps endearing, Dublin traits—drunkenness, anomalous business practice, and religious duty, which all come to a head in the final scene at the Jesuit chapel in Gardiner Street.

But before launching my argument from the Hell of the first part I ought to say something briefly about the concept of grace referred to in the story's title. At best this theological term demands that distinctions be made.

One such distinction lies between actual grace and sanctifying grace. Generally speaking, both are not only supernatural but also come as a gratuitous gift awarded without regard for natural merit or fitness. Actual grace is temporary, an assist from God—because of the virtue of Christ—allowing fallen man to pursue his salvation by performing a good act or avoiding a sinful one. This help from God is momentary, passing, and intermittent. Yet the final end is permanent salvation. On the other hand, sanctifying grace is more than the necessary and gratuitous force that moves us to acts of faith, hope, charity, inspiration, right thoughts and so forth. Fear, contrition, and often the renewal of baptismal vows attend the soul when sanctifying grace becomes a habit and provides a beatific vision of God in His heaven. This rebirth in God is of course the aim of actual grace, so that the usual meaning of grace has come to signify sanctifying grace.

In any event, this second kind of grace is essentially an internal thing, in contrast to the external actual grace, and resembles that grace bestowed on children baptized. As a habit or disposition, sanctifying grace is sometimes called a "permanent, supernatural quality of the soul." This habit is a disposition, supernatural and virtuous, superinfused from above, allowing us to take part in the divine nature. Such a soul is marked by sanctity, beauty, and the friendship and soulship of God. In addition to faith, hope, and charity, the four cardinal virtues—prudence, justice, fortitude, and temperance—are also infused. Yet sanctifying grace (or just plain grace) contains qualities that leave it fragile, mysterious and finally tentative. These qualities include uncertainty of salvation—who but God can be the final judge? Moreover, grace is unequal, even among those sanctified. Yet a third quality is amissibility, a possible fall from grace or a losing of charity that can result from habitual mortal sin.[2]

I shall argue that these distinctions apply in a secular way, both directly and ironically, in each section of the story. But before I join Kernan in the jakes of a Dublin pub off Grafton Street a reader might do well to remember what almost no commentator on the story has forgotten, namely that the word "grace" itself takes on not only secular but even trivial meanings. The fortunes of Kernan's hat alone give something of this ironic progression in the story. Charm, luck, respectability, and gratitude are among the more delectable synonyms that crowd the mind as secondary meanings of the word. In *Ulysses*, Kernan has remained his incorrigible self, hat and all, and even recalls the Sham Squire—and he is something of the same, comically—for his violet gloves. But in Ireland the word "grace" may also proclaim an altogether sharper contrast to that of the theological doctrine. The goddess and therefore the name Grainne, for instance, is usually translated as the name "Grace" in English but means "ugliness" in Gaelic. No less, the English word "grease" often finds itself pronounced "grace" in English-speaking Ireland. So, in addition to the distinctly nontheological uses of the word, Joyce appears from time to time to hint that the grace he points to is downright ugly or just plain greasy. While, then, I shall touch on each of the Dantean levels of the story, I shall also avoid the highroad of biblical allegory and theological equivalents urged by writers like Baker, Newman, Niemeyer, and Boyle. Instead, I shall hold to the obvious staples of the story, the intertwined skeins, as I have mentioned: drunkenness, bad business, and something like *pro forma* religion that bind so many of the meanings of grace.

I

In stressing the comic nature of "Grace"—yet at the same time not forgetting that it once concluded *Dubliners*—I cannot find the Dublin denizens of Hell to be so atrociously wrong as to deserve the punishment of the fraudulent. To discover Kernan curled up at the front of the stairs in the filth of the toilet may indeed herald the fall of angels or men yet might also betoken the aftermath of a pratfall. For this consequence of demon rum, Kernan's last drink, I don't hesitate to place Kernan among the gluttons of the third circle in canto VI, especially after we catch him on his way to recovery upstairs within a ring of his fellow-topers. But at the start we learn that he had lain face down in the lavatory, covered in wet filth, grunting in the stench of the place, bleeding from the mouth. In a moment, two of the men already in the toilet and one of the bartenders bundle Kernan upstairs where he is ringed by his fellow-drinkers. The picture has a rough correspondence to the following lines at the opening of canto VI:

> I am now in the Third Circle: that of rain—
>   One ceaseless, heavy, cold, accursed quench,
>   Whose law and nature vary never a grain:
>
> Huge hailstones, sleet and snow, and turbid drench
>   Of water sluice down through the darkened air,
>   And the soaked ground gives off a putrid stench.
>
> Cerberus, the cruel, misshapen monster, there
>   Bays in his triple gullet and doglike growls
>   Over the wallowing shades; his eyeballs glare
>
> A bloodshot crimson, and his bearded jowls
>   Are greasy and black; pot-bellied, talon-heeled,
>   He clutches and flays and rips and rends the souls.
>
> They howl in the rain like hounds; they try to shield
>   One flank with the other; with many a twist and squirm,
>   The impious wretches writhe in the filthy field.[3]

Cerberus may well reside in the three heads giving Kernan a lift upstairs but more than likely we are asked to see the parallel with the large surly policeman. Though most readers have observed the graceful talisman, Kernan's hat, as it, too, is redeemed in the story, the immediate scene in this first section is thoroughly slimy and wet, and then, with Kernan on the outsider headed for Glasnevin, freezing cold—all the ingredients of Dante's composite picture of rain, cold, stench, and greasy, black, gorbellied monster. As a final bit of evidence for false grace, Kernan attempts to ingratiate himself with his rescuer in true Dublin fashion by offering to buy yet another drink.

Actual grace, however, arrives in the person of the "young man in the cycling suit." His appearance is fortuitous—by the grace of God, as the phrase goes. Only later does Mr Power step forward. Though he claims that his presence is accidental, we may well doubt it. Since he works in the Royal Irish Constabulary office in Dublin Castle, his help is that of a friend also fortunately close to the police. Perhaps he may be thought of as Virgil's sop to Cerberus later in the same canto. Moreover, Kernan's bitten tongue may be punishment enough for gluttony. That mutilated member also leaves him almost without communication with his fellow-gluttons, or so Dante characterizes the solitary indulgence and self-absorption of these creatures. A bitten tongue is also a hazard for a tea salesman whose chores include tea-tasting; so begins the unhappy theme of business failure. Then Mr Power also remarks of the hurt tongue, "That's ugly." If "ugly" can also suggest grace by way of an Irish antonym, then ugliness also extends to business.

On that subject, even though Kernan is full of the pompous dignity of a so-called knight of the road, Joyce's narrative informs us that at best "modern business methods had spared him." In other words he is a near-failure as a businessman, redeemed only by the continued esteem of certain of his old friends. And one of them, Mr Power, however successful, has large, unexplained debts. But Kernan's decline has even touched his children. Though living on the Glasnevin Road—in an area associated with the gracious Mrs Delaney, Delville, and Addison's Walk—Kernan's own house contains three brash young children, most ungracious in both accents and manners.

Accordingly, drink, actual grace, bad business, and outright inelegance band together at the story's beginning. The comic conclusion to this section is rightly put into Mrs Kernan's mouth. She had been waiting for Kernan's return with the week's money. She would also like to offer Mr Power a drink: "I'm so sorry . . . that I've nothing in the house to offer you.

But if you wait a minute I'll send round to Fogarty's at the corner." Any drink she might buy will doubtless be on tick, as we shall learn.

II

If that medal of blood at the beginning of the story recalls those medals given after first communion, we may still have hopes for Mr Kernan's baptismal renewal of grace. Perhaps a retreat will make a new man of him. But, preliminary to that, we must witness the beginning process in the purgatorial episode of Mr Kernan's sickroom where in tried Dublin fashion an escape from true righteousness may yet be possible. That scene's parallels in Dante's *Purgatory* are no less than outrageous, for the blend of business failures, religious superstitions, misinformation, and popular idolization with a sizable amount of drink continues to move the story in its ludicrous course. The grace that should follow upon purgatorial suffering in Dante's work will be singularly unlikely to follow upon Joyce's second scene in Glasnevin.

Nevertheless, Dante's very organization in *Purgatory* is schematized in a loose sense in Mr Kernan's bedroom. With the arrival of Fogarty we have the counterparts to the five sinners assembled in Dante's Upper Purgatory. In her translation of the *Divine Comedy*, Dorothy L. Sayers offers a schematic chart of Purgatory's organization where the Gluttons are to be found in Upper Purgatory, victims of a "Disordered Love of Good," specifically an "excessive Love of Secondary Goods." They are gathered in the Sixth Cornice where they must do penance, that is, starve amidst plenty, meditate on temperance, pray under the guidance of the Angel of Temperance from whom they will finally receive Benediction: "*Beati qui sitiunt*." Joyce's sinners' love of the good or Catholic doctrine is disordered enough; instead of penance, they go on drinking. The nearest they come to starvation or abstinence may echo in Cunningham's utterance, "So we're all going to wash the pot," and this declaration comes after the comic confession that "we may as well all admit we're a nice collection of scoundrels." The prayer in Dante, *Labia mea*

Domine, is a shortened version, as Dorothy L. Sayers explains, of "O Lord, open Thou my lips and my mouth shall show forth Thy praise." And this praise in "Grace," as many commentators have shown, is a high and continuing level of misinformation on the Roman Catholic church. The Angel of Temperance may seem to be Martin Cunningham here, a man blessed with a hopelessly alcoholic wife. Later, of course, it will be Father Purdon, like the Angel of Temperance also red of face and ready to lead the former Gluttons down the Path of Pardon. But here, as in Dante's Purgatory, the day is Tuesday, and the cantos of the Gluttons, XXII–XXIV, present the travelers with the Tree of Temperance and the clear, crystal flood of water. In Joyce's story, stout is produced in a second-floor bedroom and, after Fogarty's arrival, we hear "the light music of whisky falling into glasses." So grace follows purgation in the Sixth Cornice of Dublin. And before confronting Father Purdon the five have agreed to meet in McAuley's, doubtless a public house, on Thursday at 7:30.

But this new grace also has its admixture of business failure or questionableness, along with doubtful religious observation. Each of the five men, for instance exhibits something of a failure or questionable practice in his business or professional life. Then, too, all hold up for pious praise or adulation figures in the Catholic church that earn Joyce's contempt. All five also condemn the Grays, who in public and private life had lent grace to the Dublin world despite being of the Protestant persuasion.

Dante's gluttons in *Purgatory*, for instance, found themselves purged by being reduced to dearth and drought in the midst of plenty. Joyce's are filled with drink in the presence of dwindling fortunes. Kernan, as we have seen, has barely been spared "by modern business methods" and is socially in decline. Only his silk hat and gaiters seem to lend him any grace. His friend Power, for all of his air of the "debonair young man" about town, nevertheless has a position with the hated Royal Irish Constabulary office and suffers under "inexplicable debts [that] were a byword in his circle." Martin Cunningham, perhaps the most sympathetic and intelligent of the five, nevertheless had married an alcoholic lady described as "unpresentable" who had pawned their furniture six times.

He also has had "long association with cases in the police courts" and, despite his resemblance to Shakespeare, is also employed in the Royal Irish Constabulary office. McCoy, who has lived by his wits more than once and has meandered from job to job, often resorts to the old Dublin ruse (as Bloom well knows) of borrowing luggage, supposedly for his wife's musical engagements, but in fact to pawn for his own profit and the lender's loss. Even Mr Power had been one of his victims. Finally Fogarty, the latecomer, fits the description of "a modest grocer," one "who bore himself with a certain grace." Yet he, too, has failed, the last time as the proprietor of a licensed house in Dublin. Kernan also owes him money.

Dubious business or professional practice and a fondness for drink join hands with religion in this section with the mention of Father Tom Burke, Archbishop John McHale (Joyce spells the name MacHale), and Pope Leo XIII. To round off these exemplars of Dublin's religious accommodations—in a house where Mrs Kernan believes in the banshee *and* the Holy Ghost—stand the reviled Grays, father and son, one who brought pure water to Dublin, and the other a noted editor, patriot, and public conscience.

Father Tom, as the Reverend Thomas Burke was called, Cunningham regards as not altogether orthodox in his sermons—and so, as we shall see, they appeared in print. Joyce heightens this hint by having Kernan remember that the Orangeman Crofton accompanied him one time at one of Burke's sermons. Mr Power then affirms their enthusiasm by remarking, "There used always be crowds of Protestants in the chapel when Father Tom was preaching." Kernan has also kept in mind the voice and style of Father Burke when preaching on the late Pope Pius IX. The sermon was probably close to the lecture given in Yonkers, New York, on 16 December 1872. There, amid his exaggerated praise of the so-called beleaguered Pope, Father Burke lamented his fate as "a sad prisoner in the abandoned halls of the Vatican."[4] The phrase is echoed in Kernan's admiration for Father Burke: "'Upon my word it was magnificent, the style of the oratory. And his voice! God! hadn't he a voice! 'The Prisoner of the Vatican,' he called him.'" In fact, Kernan for a moment thinks he and Crofton were in the pit of a theatre. Ironically, Burke's biographer reminds us that one critic said his voice resembled that of "great tragedians," and the biographer himself proudly says of Burke that "histrionic tastes were with him no passing fancy. Though as a priest the theatre was forbidden to him, he showed to the end dramatic passion and power."[5]

Fittingly, Father Burke was quick to celebrate Pius IX's espousal of Immaculate Conception and Papal Infallibility, two of the great and comic topics among the five topers. Burke's inspired Irish nationalism, like that of the Archbishop of Tuam, John McHale, roundly approved and found support in Pius IX's appointment of Archbishop Paul Cullen to the cardinalship.[6] In keeping with Joyce's themes—drinking, business and unabashed patriotism, and religious twaddle—other highly representative sermons and oratorical triumphs ought to be named: "Drunkenness the Worst Degradation—Temperance the Greatest Blessing of Man," "No Salvation outside the Catholic Church," and "The Genius and Character of the Irish People."[7] These together with his phenomenal funding successes are summed up in a passage from the *Dictionary of National Biography*:

> In 1872 he visited the United States, having been appointed visitor to the houses of the Dominican community on the American continent. He delivered sermons and lectures in all parts of the Union, and acquired extraordinary popularity as an orator. The sum collected for American charities by his sermons reached £100,000. His lectures in answer to Mr. J. A. Froude, the historian, on the relations between England and Ireland, caused much excitement and produced an animated controversy.

The son of a Galway baker, Father Burke may indeed have had an inner life as one biographer claimed;[8] but, as Joyce hints, his crude wit, awkward jokes, florid oratory, vulgar attacks on Darwin and women's rights are what most attach to his memory.[9] He was just the priest to appeal to a failed businessman, a penitent drunkard, and a confused Catholic convert. Even as a boy, Father Burke was wild and mischievous. At his best, as a grown man he was esteemed as a "*raconteur*, the lion of social life and the centre of attraction wherever he went."[10] The anonymous fellow-Dominican who wrote these words is resolute in explaining the supposed two sides of the jolly father on virtually every page of his book.

Nevertheless, the blunders in Father Burke's printed sermons were notorious; careless editing and printing once had him claiming that "our Lord is one *in person* with the Father;" in Dublin, Protestant ladies and American visitors often made of his public appearances dangerously crowded spectacles; rigidity, severity, and churlishness marked his early career; he once danced a jig with his sister to shock a pompous and mystified stranger priest. While all the accounts of him that I have located are defensive, the real theatricality of the man makes Joyce's innuendo look mild.[11]

A like character, John MacHale, as Joyce spells the name, was the Archbishop of Tuam and was fondly called the Lion of Tuam. The son of an innkeeper, he was also a fervent supporter of the Irish language, a hater of the English (he opposed Newman on that ground), a physically energetic man, and a failure as a prose stylist. As the *Dictionary of National Biography* puts it, "most of his English writings are turgid and violent, without being forcible." Such a loud, noisy creature lends even more irony to this purgatorial section by thus combining in his person these doubtful companion traits of childlike bumbler, patriotic priest, and ineffectual opponent of drink. A passage like the following, where the Archbishop defends Pius IX, is but one long and ungracious rant from a speech given at Castlebar otherwise laced with condemnations of Italians, English, Turks, and Jews:

> Much as the English may boast of their excellence in the works of fiction, they outrage in this instance the laws of fiction itself. Story tellers of more dramatic skill would have selected times and countries far more remote for the exhibition of their horrors. The passionate descriptions of the Pope's tyranny might have done very well in those distant days, when the intercourse with far countries was so rare and difficult, and when a traveller returning from the remote Indies would tell a gaping crowd the wonders which he witnessed—and how he saw the sun coming up out of the very bosom of the ocean, and heard the hissing and the roar of the steam, as he ascended from its agitated

waters (cheers and loud laughter). But now to expect to impose upon public credulity, when a journey to China, or Australia, or California, costs less of anxiety and preparation than it would have cost our fathers to cross the Shannon; when the Alps can be reached in three days, from the summit of which you may behold the beautiful plains of Italy; when mountains of granite are perforated for the facility of communication, and oceans are traversed with the velocity of a hurricane, without its danger; when narrow seas are bridged by a level tube, through which hundreds of passengers are wafted in a moment of time; when the most distant lands are linked together by sliding chains of iron, over which trains of larger bulk, and heavier weight, and huger length than the sluggish caravans of Bagdad are whirled, sweeping along with a rapidity of speed, which leaves far behind the bounding sledge of the deer over the frozen snows of Lapland; when, in fine, all the marvels of the ancient mythology are more than realized, and the lightning from the clouds of Heaven—swifter than the fabled descent of Iris or of Mercury, conveying the thoughts of the mind along a metal thread, becomes an ordinary messenger of mankind;—it is too much even for the insolence of an English press, except through the stupid and bigoted and brutalized portion of its own population, to strive to persuade the world of an Italian oppression which has not been felt, and of the weight of a Papal tyranny that has no existence (enthusiastic cheering).[12]

On the other hand, Leo XIII's public irritation with the Irish peasantry's violent physical reaction against their landlords, like Captain Boycott;[13] and then Leo's presumption to the role of poet, along with his flowery sermons, one of which Joyce parodied,[14] stand most ironically behind the fulsome praise accorded that Pope by Kernan and his friends. The Grays, however, are a different matter.

Doctor, political editor of the *Freeman's Journal*, and later its proprietor, Sir John Gray consistently backed O'Connell, his great Catholic contemporary, in his efforts to repeal the Union. For his stand he was indicted with O'Connell and sentenced to prison, though the decision was finally reversed. Sir John had also pushed the scheme for bringing fresh water from the basin of the River Vartry in Wicklow and was knighted for his success. As the *Dictionary of National Biography* adds, he also "advocated the abolition of the Irish protestant church establishment, reform of the land laws, and free denominational education." He was three times elected MP for Kilkenny city and once turned down the office of Lord Mayor of Dublin. Perhaps most ironical for the theme of drink in "Grace," he was best remembered for those strenuous efforts, against strong opposition, to bring fresh water to Dublin. For that deed, a statue, the Gray Memorial by Thomas Farrell, was erected for him on Lower Sackville Street; none other than Archbishop McHale, an old friend of Gray's, unveiled the statue and spoke with great fervor in his praise. Contrary to Kernan's memory of the event, Edmund Dwyer Gray did not speak at the unveiling but was host and main speaker at a banquet in the Antient Concert Rooms that evening in honor of his Grace, the Archbishop, who could not attend because of his failing health. This young Gray also managed the *Freeman's Journal*. Far from being indecisive, as two critics of the story remark,[15] Edmund Dwyer Gray at the age of 20 rescued five persons from a wreck in Dublin Bay. He also, as chairman of the Department of Public Health, reformed Dublin's municipal health system, was MP for Tipperary from 1877 to 1880, and became the elected Lord Mayor of Dublin in 1880. Indefatigable in organizing famine relief, he also strove to his utmost to alleviate the distressed peasantry in the West. Like his father, he, too, was sentenced to prison for political statements in the *Freeman's Journal* and, indeed, served a six-week term. He was also a determined backer of Parnell. But I need not dilate on any more of his and his father's identification with oppressed Catholic Ireland to underline the hollowness of Mr Power's cry, "None of the Grays was any good."[16]

III

In concluding this chapter with a direct glance at the characters in the Jesuit Church of Francis Xavier in Gardiner Street, I shall settle on some old, some new problems. Most critics, however, have been quick to catch Father Purdon's misinterpretation of the parable of the unjust steward. Some have questioned the legitimate use of Father Bernard Vaughan as the model for Father Purdon.[17] Most realize that Kernan's progress to that chapel allows Joyce to promote him ironically to Paradise in Dante's scheme. Niemeyer and others have offered sensible guesses as to which scene in *Paradise* Joyce had in mind. I shall suggest one myself, then take another look at the assembled worshipers named in the story, and finally compare Father Purdon and his interpretation of the verses in St Luke, chapter 16, with Father Vaughan's own sermons and utterances. Needless to say, I shall discover the triple theme of drink, shabby professional or business life, and routine religious observance most highly bound together here, despite that conclusion from the passage in St Luke, "Ye cannot serve God and mammon."

St Luke, chapter 16, begins, however, with the sentence "And he said also unto his disciples, There was a certain rich man, which had a steward. . . ." This solemn beginning is directly parodied by Joyce in making Father Purdon the guide through the eighth and ninth verses of St Luke, chapter 16, for twelve other disciples specifically named among the other worshipers before the altar. They include the five we have already studied. Added to them are seven more, equally Pharisaic, disciples: a notorious moneylender, Mr Harford; the notorious receiver of bribes, Mr Fanning, registration agent and mayor-maker; then Michael Grimes, owner of three pawnshops. Following him, we hear of Dan Hogan's nephew hoping for the "job in the Town Clerk's office"; then Mr Hendrick of the *Freeman's Journal* whom we recall from "A Mother," doubtless on to a good thing; at last, a nondescript labeled "poor O'Carroll," an old chum of Kernan's and now a commercial failure. The twelfth man is hinted to have curried Fanning's favor and sits beside him: "one of the newly elected councillors of the ward." Their Christ and pastor is a large man, red of face, one of the usual signs of drink in Joyce's work, Father Purdon.

If, indeed, Christ addressing his disciples is parodied in this assembly, then so, too, may be Dante's Circle of Twelve Lights in his *Paradise*. Another possibility, if we remember the figure of the quincunx in the story, and then the red light signaling the presence of the host, is that Joyce may be parodying Dante's canto XIV, the ascent to Mars with its ruby splendors and vision of the Cross. Nor are Joyce's twelve men in any way Mars-like warriors for Christ; at least, that is a convincing part of Carl Niemeyer's educated guess.[18] The red light, of course, also ties in with the notorious Purdon Street. On the other hand, the ascent to the sun in canto X presents us twelve spirits—or children—of light, who could also pass muster for Joyce's twelve Dublin souls and Purdon's allusion to the children of light. For what it's worth, then, this is my choice from Dante's *Paradise*, especially because there begins Dante's progress beyond the sensual world, a world that Joyce's twelve never leave. An added irony is that the first of Dante's wise spirits is St Thomas Aquinas, and Thomas Kernan is the first though reluctant ascender in "Grace."

Before turning, however, to what has often been called the most difficult parable in the Bible we ought to look first at Father Purdon's original, Father Bernard Vaughan, because he has often been defended, even once against Joyce's picture of him in the Gardiner Street chapel. That defender, William T. Noon, SJ, has drawn attention to the good father's zeal, his kindness, popularity, and spirituality. Father Noon concludes by countering Stanislaus Joyce's revelation of his brother's source, Father Vaughan, as "a vulgarian priest in search of publicity," with this rejoinder: "It would seem that only such Irish initiates as Stanislaus could have sensed this, and that few of them would have accepted such a portraiture as a human likeness faithful or just."[19] Yet I shall maintain that Father Noon has fastened on one side of Father Vaughan that, if it existed, remained buried under the more egregious side that Joyce, his brother, and most thoughtful Irishmen held in contempt.

The *Dictionary of National Biography* acknowledges that Vaughan had been a mediocre but enthusiastic student, remained unconventional as a preacher, popular yet given to vulgar epigrammatic language, sensational and crude, a real hound for publicity—he was selling Christianity, as he once put it—yet withal privately unassuming, simple, and obedient.

Even one of his well-wishers, however, C. C. Martindale, another Jesuit, cannot hide the unspeakable crudity of the man, nor can he forget Vaughan's frequent doctrinal errors as a preacher, though his printed sermons and speeches usually were meticulously edited. To go on and list all of Martindale's admissions would be tedious but, to be fair to Joyce, here are some of the most outlandish instances of the Vaughan notoriety that his biographer reveals: Vaughan delighted in the limelight; he was a boastful fund-collector; and, despite his sojourns and following in Ireland, he was unpopular there for his praise of the spirituality of the poor, defense of the Duke of Norfolk, and condemnation of Lord Mayor McSwiney's hunger strike. In San Francisco he had the temerity to advertise a retreat as the "'Golden Gate' Limited Express" headed for the "Paradise of the Soul." He once played up to a miners' audience by announcing that they, like good Christians, would strike gold, the "symbol of charity": "It, too, was the current coin in the Kingdom of Christ." Vaughan in fact acknowledged himself to be God's advertising man, the drummer of the church. One critic likened him to Parson Trulliber.[20] Those readers who would like to mine more of this gold ought to read some of Vaughan's sermons, speeches, and tracts boldly pushing businessmen's commonsense, capitalism, and the Jesuit order itself as composed of just "plain blunt men."[21] Joyce's portrait catches the man exactly in Father Purdon's appearance, resonant and confident delivery and absurd interpretation of the parable.

His source is the Rheims version of the New Testament.[22] Although I might not agree with Robert Sumner Jackson that Kernan is to be identified with the unjust steward himself, that critic's summary of what Joyce is up to in rendering Purdon's misinterpretation impresses me as just right: "The condemnation of the church is made by presenting a Jesuit priest who turns the parable into a defence of pharisaism, making out of it the point exactly the reverse of its plain literal sense."[23] But let me add that Joyce does this reversal, if possible, even one better, for Joyce changes a key word in the Rheims version when he puts the ninth verse of St Luke, chapter 6, in Father Purdon's mouth. That version reads: "And I say to you, Make unto you friends of the mammon of iniquity; that when you shall *fail* [my italics], they may receive you into everlasting dwellings." For "fail" Joyce has Father Purdon utter "die." In doing so, he has the good father reconstruct the text to make it even less offensive to his audience of "business men and professional men" and so widen even more the gap between a religious accounting system and the mysterious operation of grace that accords nothing to any man's efforts to set right his spiritual ledger. Christ's final admonition, "Ye cannot serve God and mammon," is everywhere violated in Father Purdon's peroration.

In so doing, Joyce's "Grace" concludes a story of drink, business and professional sloth, and humdrum religious practice loudly and clearly with a reassurance of the worst sort. Such a story also stood as the conclusion of the original twelve stories that began with three treating one by one Dublin's faith, hope, and charity, all centered in a boy who failed to discover any of these quintessential virtues in his young life as a Dubliner. These are the virtues that lead Dante's soul to God in canto XXIV of the *Paradise* and cannot be gained by human determinations but only by God's grace operating through the agency of divine revelation. Finally, the repeated allusion to providence in the earliest version of "The Sisters" got its ironic undercutting from a priest whose life seemed to deny its most powerful workings. From the beginning Father Flynn knew that he was not long for this world, though other Dubliners did not. Perhaps Joyce wisely enough omitted mention of providence in the published versions of the story and left the absence of grace to the more likely drift of fate for which Father Bernard Vaughan must have seemed to be a perfect model. Moreover, faith, hope, and charity are fated in Dublin to be expressed in their opposites: a religion of habitual accounts; the visionary hopes in another drink; and the charity that lies in usury, sharp business practice and professional collusion with an avaricious oppressor.

NOTES: CHAPTER 14

1 Stanislaus Joyce, "The background to *Dubliners*," *Listener*, 25 March 1954, p. 526; Joseph E. Baker, "The Trinity in Joyce's

'Grace,'" *James Joyce Quarterly*, vol. 2, no. 4 (Summer 1965), pp. 299–303; Carl Niemeyer, "'Grace' and Joyce's method of parody," *College English*, vol. 27, no. 3 (December 1965), pp. 196–201; F. X. Newman, "The Land of Ooze: Joyce's 'Grace' and the Book of Job," *Studies in Short Fiction*, vol. 4, no. 1 (Fall 1966), pp. 70–9; and Robert Boyle, "Swiftian allegory and Dantean parody in Joyce's 'Grace,'" *James Joyce Quarterly*, vol. 7, no. 1 (Fall 1969), pp.11–21. Perhaps the ablest general treatment of "Grace" is still Marvin Magalaner's in *Time of Apprenticeship: The Fiction of Young James Joyce* (London/New York/Toronto: Abelard-Schuman, 1959), pp. 129–43. Nevertheless, Richard M. Kain's "'Grace,'" in *James Joyce's Dubliners: Critical Essays*, ed. Clive Hart (New York: Viking Press, 1969), pp. 134–52, strikes me as both the shrewdest and most commonsensical of all commentaries so far.

2 I have been summarizing, perhaps too briefly and loosely, the article on Grace in the *Catholic Encyclopedia* (New York: Encyclopedia Press, 1913), Vol. 6, pp. 689–714.

3 Dante, *The Divine Comedy: Hell*, trans. Dorothy L. Sayers (Harmondsworth: Penguin Books, n.d.), pp. 202–3.

4 Thomas N. Burke, "Pontificate of Pius IX," *Lectures and Sermons*, 2nd ser. (New York: Excelsior Catholic Publishing House, 1873), p. 156.

5 William J. Fitz-Patrick, *The Life of the Very Reverend Thomas N. Burke* (London: Kegan, Paul, Trench, 1885), Vol. 1, p. 53.

6 ibid., p. 158.

7 ibid., pp. 446–65, 506–23 and 533–42.

8 Anon., *The Inner Life of Father Thomas Burke* (London: Burns & Oates, n.d.), pp. 2–3.

9 Thomas N. Burke, "The Catholic church and the age we live in," *Lectures and Sermons*, ed. J. A. Rochford, 2nd edn (New York: P. F. Collier, 1878), pp. 273, 282.

10 *Inner Life of Father Thomas Burke*, p. 101.

11 Fitz-Patrick, op. cit., Vol. 2, pp. 97–103, 276–9.

12 *The Great Catholic Demonstration . . . Held at Castlebar, Mayo, January 7, 1860* (Dublin: A. M. Sullivan, 1860), p. 4.

13 See, for instance, Justin McCarthy, *The Life of Leo XIII* (London: Bliss, 1896), pp. 104–12, 142–6.

14 *Letters of James Joyce*, ed. Richard Ellmann (New York: Viking, 1966), Vol. 2, p. 210.

15 *Dubliners*, ed. Robert Scholes and A. Walton Litz, Viking Critical Library (New York: Viking, 1969), p. 499.

16 For a detailed summary of the Grays' careers, see the *Dictionary of National Biography* entries for each. On the elder's efforts on behalf of Dublin's sewerage and water systems, see his *Observations on*

House and General Sewerage . . . (Dublin: Hodges & Smith, 1855), passim, and *Speech of John Gray* . . . *in Vindication of the Municipal Council of Dublin* (Dublin: John Falconer, 1864), passim. For a full account of the unveiling of his statue and subsequent celebrations, see "The Gray testimonial," *Freeman's Journal*, 15 August 1861, p. 5. The statue's importance was noted in articles in the *Irish Builder*: "The Gray testimonial," 15 August 1861, p. 605, and "The Gray memorial," 1 July 1879, p. 201 respectively. Typical in reflecting his son Edmund Dwyer Gray's sympathies are *The Plantation at Coolgreany* . . . (Dublin: The Freeman's Journal Ltd Printers, [1890]), pp. 15–27, and *The Treatment of Political Prisoners in Ireland* (Dublin: The Freeman's Journal Ltd Printers, 1889), pp. vi–viii, 1–41.

17 William T. Noon, "James Joyce: unfacts, fiction, and facts," *PMLA*, vol. 76, no. 3 (June 1961), pp. 272–3.

18 Niemeyer, op. cit., p. 199.

19 Noon, op. cit., p. 272.

20 C. C. Martindale, SJ, *Bernard Vaughan, SJ* (London: Longman's Green, 1923), pp. 103–4, 148–9, 171, 173, 230 and 233.

21 See Bernard Vaughan, "The Jesuit in fact and fiction," *Irish Times*, 25 March 1903, p. 4; "'Our Lord before the people,'" *Freeman's Journal*, 6 April 1903, p. 2; *Socialism—Is It Liberty or Tyranny?* (London: George Allen, 1910), pp. 14–21; *Socialism from the Christian Standpoint* (New York: Macmillan, 1912), pp. 242–3, 246–53, 263–6 and 276–7; and such Catholic Truth Society pamphlets as *Faith and Reason* (London, 1889), and *Father Bernard Vaughan's Free Trade Hall Lectures* (London, n.d.) that reply to the Bishop of Manchester on *Roman Claims*.

22 Robert Sumner Jackson, "A parabolic reading of James Joyce's 'Grace,'" *Modern Language Notes*, vol. 76, no. 8 (December 1961), p. 720.

23 ibid., p. 723.

15

"The Dead":
I Follow St Patrick

In a memorable article, "The background to *Dubliners*," Stanislaus Joyce reflected on his brother's inspiration for "The Dead":

The idea for "The Dead" was suggested . . . by a letter of mine to my brother when he was already in Trieste. It came about in this way. The principal singer in a Moore Centenary Concert in Dublin—such was the name I remember, though 1805 was no special date in Moore's life—was a very well-known Irish baritone who lived in London, Plunket Green. As my father had sung with him in concerts when he was a young man and often used to speak of him, I went to hear him. The quality of his voice was somewhat harsh, I thought, but he could do what he liked with it. One of Moore's Irish melodies was "The Dead" [Stanislaus probably means "Oh, Ye Dead"]. When in the second verse of the song the dead speak, Plunket Green, instead of singing in sepulchral tones, used a plaintive pianissimo. The effect was electrifying. It reminded me of the lines of a cradle-song of Yeats':

> The angels are stooping
> Above your white bed;
> They are weary of trooping
> With the whimpering dead.

It sounded as if the dead were whimpering and jealous of the happiness of the living. My brother liked the idea and asked me to send him the song. I did so, but when he wrote the story some six or seven years later—so long did it take to mature!—he preferred to use a west of Ireland ballad for the song which is the turning point of the story.[1]

Now, while Stanislaus, slight confusions aside, has further remarks to make about the story—for them, later—we might well listen to both verses of the song. In summarizing Stanislaus' reminder, Richard Ellmann has quoted the second in his famous essay, "The background of 'The Dead,'" and has made the point that the dead and the living alike are jealous of each other. Nevertheless, both verses strike me as germane to the story; here is the first:

Oh, ye Dead! oh, ye Dead! whom we know by the light you give
From your cold gleaming eyes, though you move like men who live,
    Why leave you thus your graves,
    In far off fields and waves,
Where the worm and the sea-bird only know your bed;
    To haunt this spot, where all
    Those eyes that wept your fall,
And the hearts that bewail'd you, like your own, lie dead?

Then, in the second stanza, the Dead answer:

It is true—it is true—we are shadows cold and wan;
It is true—it is true—all the friends we loved are gone;
    But, oh! thus e'en in death,
    So sweet is still the breath
Of the fields and the flow'rs in our youth we wander'd o'er,
    That ere, condemn'd, we go
    To freeze 'mid Hecla's snow,
We would taste it awhile, and dream we live once more![2]

In other words, even with the later substitution of "The Lass of Aughrim" for "Oh, Ye Dead," the interaction, contention, dependence, and connection of the living and the dead— obvious to all critics in the final concentration on Michael Furey—seem to have been Joyce's subject from the very first.

Be that as it may, perhaps John V. Kelleher more than any other reader of the story has shown the many levels where this interaction takes place.[3] He has determined the date to be 6 January, the Feast of the Epiphany, 6 January called also in Ireland Old or Small Christmas. As Stanislaus also reminds us, on this night ghost stories are told. And, since a reference to "the

Dead" in Ireland usually points to the illustrious dead, Kelleher also parades before us some of the ghosts of an earlier Catholic Dublin that Gabriel may be said to have neglected. Kelleher also argues convincingly that the marital surprise to befall Gabriel may also parallel the fate of King Conaire in the old saga "The Destruction of Da Derga's Hostel." Yet "The Dead" strikes me as going even beyond the retelling of one more Irish destruction and the mere inclusion of Joyce's own auto-biography. I have in mind Joyce's concentration on Irish hospitality, yet at the same time a hospitality that is something more than a nearly outlandish Morkan display of food and drink at the end of the Christmas season.

Perhaps I should then add here some of Stanislaus' further observations on the story to prepare the reader for my own argument:

> There is a mastery of story telling in the skill with which a crescendo of noise and jollity is gradually worked up and then suddenly silenced by the ghost of a memory that returns to blight the happiness of the living. Yet "The Dead" is not merely a Christmas ghost story and not merely technically clever. In "The Dead" the two polar attitudes of men towards women, that of the lover and that of the husband, are presented compassionately. It is not the eternal triangle of falsity and deception. The two men at different times in the woman's life have loved her with equal sincerity each in his way, and there is no guile in the woman. But one love is the enemy of the other, and the dead lover's romantic passion, outliving his mortal flesh, is still dominant in the woman's heart.[4]

Contention, even enmity, bind the living and the dead, yet something else enters the story at the end, and Gabriel truly becomes a changed man. He is roused from something more than his complacency.[5]

Since the story takes place on Wednesday, 6 January 1904—*Mignon* started the next day, the Conference on the University Question had already met that Wednesday in Galway City, and the Negro chieftain had just been introduced to Dublin[6]—the change in Gabriel was probably not yet apparent to those who recalled the earlier Conroy couple in

Ulysses. To be sure, death-in-life lurks just beneath the party's noisy surface. To punctuate almost every scene at the party with something like a full stop, Joyce uses Mr Browne as might Holbein in his series of woodcuts, *The Dance of Death*. Browne smiles, he grins, waxes ironic with Gabriel's speech, claims Julia as his discovery and, as we shall see, "laughs as if his heart would break" before gathering Freddy and his mother, certainly two more of Death's likely victims, into something like the Irish death-coach. My point, then, in this already overlong introduction, is that the story's ending accents something quite opposite to this death-in-life, something best called life-in-death. Like the descent of grace that hovers over the final pages, Gabriel's proposed trip westward is prepared for from the very start. The answer to the paralysis in the story and the book lies in the West of Ireland, survives a destruction, finds its example at Mount Melleray, not in the anglicized Ireland of the eastern seaboard but in the Joyce country itself. That change that I shall claim for Gabriel is possibly summed up in the claim that Joyce once made for St Patrick: he did not convert the Irish but was converted by them.[7]

I

Most comments on "The Dead" since the seminal essays by Ellmann and Kelleher take their direction either by totally surveying the story or by elucidating a puzzling detail. I shall do something in between. Accordingly I would first draw attention to Joyce's tripartite structure made by two lines of periods: first the entrance of Gabriel, Gretta, and Freddy; then the singing, dancing, feasting and after-dinner speech; and at last the party's break-up, the trip to the Gresham, and then the final scene, itself broken into two parts by the extra space preceding the paragraph "She was fast asleep."

But in that first section our initial encounter is with the servant girl Lily, truly an enigmatic, minor, yet important character. I need not elaborate on the various theories affixed to her. While I agree that her name signals from the beginning the connection between this Christmas story and Easter,[8] I would first see her plain. She is the caretaker's daughter. He is mentioned but three times in the story. The next thing we learn about Lily is that she "was literally run off her feet." Evidently she does the housework for the Morkans three. Now she must announce those who arrive. For instance, she greets Gabriel, directs his wife upstairs, later endures a scene with him. At table, she brings three potatoes to Gabriel that she has kept back after serving the rest of the guests. We also learn that Gabriel's aunts have found a recent change in her. The last we see of Lily is her removing the guests' plates after Gabriel has begun eating. All this I offer by way of summary. But Lily's singular appearance is of course her oft-remarked exchange with Gabriel.

As John Kelleher has noted, her pronouncing Gabriel's surname in three syllables suggests a reference to King Conaire. I would add that such a pronunciation also hints that she, too, like Gretta, comes from the Gaeltacht. We may come to see that Gabriel's treatment of a Connacht servant resembles in part his treatment of his Connacht wife. This likelihood may also be emphasized by the distant fact that Lily's name, like that of Gretta's servant Bessie, derives from the same Elizabeth, and in Ireland a Connacht wife would be likely to hire a Connacht servant—Bessie. Lily is also somewhat soured, as the Dublin idiom would have it. Moreover, her mistresses are fussy, though Lily usually gets on with them. But, again, Aunt Kate has seen a change in her, presumably her back answers, something like the one that surprised Gabriel. She has also asked Gabriel pointedly if it is snowing again. My speculations here are capped in Joyce's description of her as "a slim, growing girl, pale in complexion, and with hay-coloured hair. The gas in the pantry made her look still paler. Gabriel had known her when she was a child and used to sit on the lowest steps nursing a rag doll."

Here, then, is my point. The references to snow, to Lily's being literally run off her feet, to her disappointment in men, to her likely West of Ireland origin, her paleness in the gaslight, Gabriel's memory of her nursing a doll, her status as servant and daughter to a servant, perhaps even to her serving potatoes (an association with a Western tenantry), all point to "The Lass of Aughrim." Gabriel was quite right to tip her in the true fashion of an eighteenth-century gentleman; and she

227

was right in trying to refuse the tip, for, in doing so, Gabriel placed himself and his fussy aunts perilously close to the original Lord Gregory and his superior mother.[9] Already, then, if my reading has any force, a distant ghost lodges in Lily's bitter complaint to Gabriel. He may learn to understand her, her origins, and one of her counterparts better before the night is over.

Perhaps, then, we might also turn in this first glimpse of Gabriel to the Morkan family that Joyce sketches in, following the first paragraph of the story. Many a critic has caught the parallel between the boy of "The Sisters" and this Gabriel of the two aunts. I concur, even though Gabriel was not an orphan. But I shall go further in seeing that boy as a Gabriel grown to something like a wise man or magus. He may even hold the university post that Joyce himself rejected, though more than likely he teaches in what we Americans call a preparatory school. He is certainly not the artist, however, that Yeats in his essay might have wished. Gabriel is not the imaginative heir to Yeats's Father Rosencrux. Instead, Gabriel serves as a commentator, an instructor, a teacher who writes reviews and keeps up his languages on the Continent. His physical being, plumpness aside, certainly resembles Joyce's, although Richard Ellmann has shown that others may also enter the portrait. Nevertheless, Gabriel's class-consciousness, his solicitude for his family, peculiar servitude to this annual Morkan Christmas affair, and residence in south County Dublin only add to what I have argued to be the boy's fate in "The Sisters." Yet I shall stick to my prediction that Gabriel will return to one kind of Irishtown, as Father Flynn did not.

But Gabriel's parents and family must engage us further. Later in the evening he will declare his aunts and their niece the Three Graces. He will also liken his difficulty in praising them to that of Paris before the three goddesses. I would rather, however, point to the real sisterhood—the Three Fates again from my first chapter—the sisters Morkan who have determined Gabriel's fate, till the end of the party, however hazy he may be of the fact. We may even liken them, and I look back to my chapter on "A Mother," to the three Irish goddesses—daughters of Cain as tradition holds them—Banba, Fodla and Eire, with Banba, the eldest, like Gabriel's mother, usually identified with Death. They were called by the Irish historian Keating the first settlers of Ireland. In any case, these three women demand a second look, for Gabriel's mother, and then her sisters, at least for this evening, have powerfully shaped him for his self-discovery. As John Kelleher has pointed out in the essay I have mentioned, the curse on King Connaire, and so on Gabriel, has descended through the female line. The blame rests on Gabriel's mother. She had been the brains of the family; she had also lacked musical talent. She led the way in thrusting herself into the Protestant enclave of Monkstown, just as her sisters had removed to Usher's Island. All this and more Kelleher cites as part of the social climbing, the religious and racial denial in Gabriel's family. I shall argue that the process had started even earlier, probably with grandfather Morkan himself.

He seems to have been, in Gabriel's words, "a very pompous old gentlemen." His dressing up to go to a military review in the Phoenix Park might well qualify in part his patriotic association with the Back Lane Parliament that met in Tailor's Hall. In fact, though his starch mill was in that neighborhood, his home was in Stonybatter. Some thirty years before, around 1874, I take it, with the death of his son, also named Patrick, the pomposity that the elder Morkan had passed along to his three daughters took them to their more highfalutin abodes. Even the solicitous Mary Jane has something of old Patrick's pomposity. In his youth, Stonybatter had been known for its corn- and frieze-market. It was also an Irish-speaking locale known for its May Day festival.[10] None of these can be associated with the present family. Meaning "paved or stony road," Stonybatter is Ireland's most ancient road, one of the five great roads leading from Tara, and was constructed in the second century. The road's ultimate importance for "The Dead" may be implied in the words of D. A. Chart: "Aughrim Street . . . later became Manor Street and Stonybatter . . . Part of the old route from Meath to the ancient crossing over the Liffey at Bridge Street [just below Usher's Island], and from thence along the sea coast to Wicklow. The footsteps of S. Patrick followed this path,"[11] on which later. But Gabriel's mother stopped at the more fashionable Monkstown. Her example may not have been wasted on Mary Jane, daughter and granddaughter of a Patrick, who teaches children from families along the Kingstown and Dalkey line. She has also attached herself to the recently completed and beautified St Mary's Church in Haddington Road where, under the leadership of Canon Dillon, a new organ constructed by Telford & Company had recently been installed. In 1901 the parish included 4,506 Catholics and 3,252 of other denominations, another suggestion of the upper-class tone that still blesses Haddington Road.[12] The church also had the added distinction of being a bishop's church; in this case the pastor was the Bishop of Nara, an African diocese still unconverted. More superiority.

So far, then, in reviewing the first section of the story, I have concentrated on the embittered Lily and on Gabriel and the female line in his family where the name of Patrick has disappeared. But Gabriel's later tale of grandfather Patrick Morkan and his horse Johnny may well underline more comically this continuity of pretension. Although the name Morkan is a diminutive of *Murcad*, "sea warrior" in Irish, old Patrick had nevertheless set out to see a British military review in the Phoenix Park. His horse Johnny, certainly no Gray of Macha, had even emulated his master on the way by slowly circling the equestrian statue of William III in College Green. His movements apparently duplicate the same circling identified with Orange celebrations in November and July when loyal Williamites and their historical progeny would troop the statue in solemn commemoration of the battle of the Boyne and the muster of the Volunteers.[13] Gabriel will later wince at the same arrogance evident in the social careers of his aunts, his mother, and Mary Jane. But what about himself? Small wonder that Mr Browne vies with him, the master of ceremonies who feels himself above his fellow-merrymakers, at the end of this section. For the dead have already laid their hands on Gabriel through the family of his mother. Mr Browne lingers especially with the ladies to whom he feels himself most dear—just as Death was to endear himself to Eve. "Death is here, death is there, death is busy everywhere," as the old Dublin saying has it. The sound of the dance upstairs, then, in reality is no trilling counterpoint to such thoughts, yet on the darkened ground floor, listening to the clacking and shuffling that sound in his ears, Gabriel ponders his social difference and the inappropriateness of his prepared speech. The section ends with Freddy's arrival, Gabriel put in charge of him, and then Browne heard amidst his jokes, libations, and attentions, at last paying court to Freddy, whom he indifferently calls Teddy. Browne's solicitude and the memory of Ellen Morkan are unheedingly joined in Gabriel's mind.

II

The second section begins with Mary Jane's impossibly mechanical playing and ends with Freddy Malins leading the company in an equally mechanical song. Now, Freddy could very well be playing the role of Fer Caille, the churl of cropped hair, one hand, and one eye in the Da Derga tale. Twice we hear that he rubs his left hand in his left eye. Indeed, the hag wife of the tale might easily be seen in Freddy's mother. Both are friendly to Conaire/Gabriel and both encumber him. Mary's playing is a nice introduction to such boring interference, and I shall return to her flying hands that occasionally pause "like those of a priestess in momentary imprecation" later. But Freddy, already introduced in the first section, has been paired with Gabriel from the beginning.

In fact, he seems to be a grosser edition of Gabriel, a less sober counterpart, still in some ways an equally sensitive man. He has broken his pledge after but five days, and Gabriel is now in charge of him almost as if Freddy were a strayed lamb or black sheep, yet the name Malins is probably meant to recall the Celtic *maelan*, that is, monk or disciple. The proper name Malins derives from *Meallan* and is described by Father Woulfe as "the name of an ecclesiastical family in Ulster—a branch of the Cinel Eoghain—who were hereditary keepers of the Bell of St Patrick, known as the Bell of the Testament."[14] I shall not linger over Freddy's compliment to Aunt Julia, his lauding the Negro chieftain—G. H. Elliott, who had just made his first appearance in Dublin as the dark servant in the Gaiety Christmas pantomime version of *The Babes in the Wood*.[15] I shall even put aside for a moment Freddy's explanation of Mount Melleray where he is going to dry out. No, it's Freddy the

231

seller of the Christmas cards in a Henry Street stall, the man of monkish but jovial nature, the victim of Mr Browne's patronizing, the drunk sometimes hard to manage and also saddled with an impossible mother, that I would push to the fore in this section, for all his churlishness. Besotted or not, he represents the negative of all that Gabriel stands for and serves as an unannounced bellwether to a world of song, drink, holiness, and death that Gabriel refuses and Gretta knows.

The dinner itself must wait upon at least three ludicrous if not ugly scenes that Gabriel endures from the enthusiasms of Mrs Malins, Freddy, and Miss Ivors, the last especially irritating. She, too, is friendly, at least ostensibly so, to Gabriel—some have said more than friendly. But, just as Freddy's later remarks on music, monks, and Negro chieftains may delicately contrast with Gabriel's strenuous carving and fulsome oratory, so Miss Ivors's enthusiasm for Gaelic, as all have noted, contrasts with his pose as the good European. Two things about her, however, may deserve added stress. First, she wears an Irish device, more than likely the famed Tara Brooch that contains "two minute human faces of cast violet glass" (as the National Museum pamphlet on the Brooch tells us), a device particularly favored by members of the Gaelic League. She is Gabriel's partner in Lancers; they cross together, and then go visiting, as the dancing terms go. I might also add that her good evening to him, *Beannacht libh*, is in reality a blessing in Irish. Despite her repeating the slur "West Briton" to him, the question remains: will they *both* go visiting to the West after all? Are they in any way connected? In any case, with Miss Ivors's plaint that he knows neither his own people nor his own country, we are again prepared here for the heavy revelation to come.

A fourth movement in this section prior to Gabriel's fatuous speech is his gazing on the Phoenix Park, clearly visible from the second floor of 15 Usher's Island. And just before Aunt Julia's song, and then the dinner, Gabriel imagines the scene again. He muses that he would rather be walking through the snow along the Liffey and then take his way through the Park. He visualizes the trees full of snow and the Wellington Monument itself gaining a cap of snow. Trees, monument, and snow enter this vision again just before Gabriel gives his speech, this time with the Fifteen Acres added. The purity of the air and snow, the beauty of the moment, and the bracing vision westward take a powerful hold on him. Yet this specific locale may further align Gabriel with his grandfather, for the Monument, a gigantic obelisk 205 feet in height, is adorned with the names of the Iron Duke's victories.[16] Designed by an Englishmen, Sir Richard Smirke, and popularly known as "the overgrown milestone," the monument is an obvious symbol of English and Protestant might. Moreover, the Fifteen Acres—actually more like fifty Irish acres and once a duelling-ground—had been the site for many a British military review and sham battle. As recent to the story as 23 July 1903, the visiting king and queen had reviewed 10,000 troops and 2,000 bluejackets there. Thinking to endear himself to his Irish Catholic subjects, Edward VII had offered, among other remarks, these condescending words on the death of the late Pope, Leo XIII:

> The death of his Holiness the Pope, though expected for some time, has, I know, brought sadness to the hearts of multitudes among my subjects—a sadness in which I share, remembering, as I do, the kindness with which his Holiness so recently received me at Rome, and the interest he took in the welfare of my people.[17]

The snow in Phoenix Park, like that lodged on Gabriel's toes and overcoat, has touched on the living and the dead who also harbored distinctly un-Irish sympathies. So far in this second section, the unnoticed contest between living and dead, English and Irish, while fierce, has been very nearly invisible to Gabriel.

To turn now to Gabriel's speech is in part to move to the story's praise of Irish hospitality and otherwise to a gentle parody of typical Irish postprandial rhetoric, in this case rhetoric that contains no little irony when viewed against the final revelations of the evening ahead. Yet, except for Gabriel's phrase "thought-tormented music," taken from his review, as far as I can see the quotation from Browning was probably dropped. Still, the likely volume that Gabriel reviewed had some telling poems in it that cast a rather harsh light on his enthusiasms.

In his call for a life of striving and bustle, about which he
may have private reservations, Gabriel in his speech is very
close to the Browning of the eighties. Nevertheless, Gabriel
may well have reviewed one of the selections of Browning's
poetry that appeared in 1903.[18] The reference in the story is
simply to "Browning's poems." More than likely, however, the
poems were those in the seventeenth volume, the last in the
collected edition of *The Poetical Works of Robert Browning* (New
York and London: Macmillan, 1903), the first volume of which
had been published in 1894. But this seventeenth volume
contained an index to the entire collection, an index to the first
lines of shorter poems, biographical and historical notes to the
poems, and Browning's last book of verse, *Asolando*, published
on the day of his death.

As my friend Mr John Feeley has reminded me, *Asolando* was
dedicated to Mrs Arthur Bronson, the American hostess, and
celebrates her hospitality and that of her town, Asolo, in
northern Italy about nineteen miles from Treviso. The dedication itself includes the words "yet another experience of the
gracious hospitality now bestowed on me since so many a
year," words strongly reminiscent of the introduction and
conclusion to Gabriel's own speech. The subtitle of the volume,
"Facts and Fancies," stresses the constant theme of the
illusions of youth that contrast sharply with what Browning
assumes to be the realistic vision of the aged man, something
like the difference that Gabriel insinuates about Miss Ivors's
view of life and his own. The poem "Epilogue," coming at the
end of the evening, like Gabriel's speech, is a likely source for
his Browning quotation since the poem so closely resembles
that speech. Gabriel touches on our memories of the dead and
gone, on our melancholy recall of youth, change, and those
absent faces. Just as quickly, however, Gabriel directs his
audience to the claims of the present: "We have all of us living
duties and living affections which claim, and rightly claim, our
strenuous endeavours." The "Epilogue" is symptomatic and all
too reminiscent of Browning the diner-out of those last years.
Browning's sentiments seem, then, to be Gabriel's, perhaps
even more fulsomely proclaimed in the "Epilogue":

"The Dead"

At the midnight in the silence of the sleep-time,
  When you set your fancies free,
Will they pass to where—by death, fools think, imprisoned—
Low he lies who once so loved you, whom you loved so
      —Pity me?

Oh to love so, be so loved, yet so mistaken!
  What had I on earth to do
With the slothful, with the mawkish, the unmanly?
Like the aimless, helpless, hopeless, did I drivel
      —Being—who?

One who never turned his back but marched breast forward,
  Never doubted clouds would break,
Never dreamed, though right were worsted, wrong would triumph,
Held we fall to rise, are baffled to fight better,
      Sleep to wake.

No, at noonday in the bustle of man's work-time
  Greet the unseen with a cheer!
Bid him forward, breast and back as either should be,
"Strive and thrive!" cry "Speed,—fight on, fare ever
      There as here!"

Fatuous enough in orating to vulgarians, as he later admits, Gabriel will finally distinguish another kind of hospitality. Nevertheless, here Gabriel continues in his orotund way, much like the Browning he has reviewed: "Therefore I will not linger on the past. I will not let any gloomy moralising intrude upon us here to-night. Here we are gathered together for a brief moment from the bustle and rush of our everyday routine." And so forth.

While any number of poems in Browning's last volume can match the theme and tone of "Epilogue," a good number of others come near to apotheosizing a girl's love. One in particular, "A Pearl, a Girl," seems powerfully relevant to Gretta's hidden thoughts about Michael Furey. The poem also allows the connection between her name Margaret and Margarite or Pearl. At the beginning of the story, when Gabriel remarked lightheartedly that Gretta would just as soon walk home in the snow—and I leave "The Lass of Aughrim" aside—he may have spoken once more a great deal more than he knew. Here is the poem:

235

A simple ring with a single stone
  To the vulgar eye no stone of price:
Whisper the right word, that alone—
  Forth starts a sprite, like fire from ice,
And lo, you are lord (says an Eastern scroll)
Of heaven and earth, lord whole and sole
  Through the power in a pearl.

A woman ('tis I this time that say)
  With little the world counts worthy praise
Utter the true word—out and away
  Escapes her soul: I am wrapt in blaze,
Creation's lord, of heaven and earth
Lord whole and sole—by a minute's birth—
Through the love in a girl!

While pointing to his discovery and reversed expectations of the final third of the story, this poem also catches at Gabriel's fancied role as Paris in his speech; he will more closely resemble Agamemnon. Even the name of the volume, *Asolando*, may stem from *asolare*, as Browning states in his dedicatory note, which means "to disport in the open air, amuse one's self at random," the very antithesis of the evening thus far.[19]

This second part of the story, consequently, has paired Gabriel with Freddy Malins, whose names identify him on one hand, Malins, with a monk and with the guardians of St Patrick's bell and, on the other, Freddy, with all those symptoms of the national failing that draw Mr Browne so close to him. Gabriel has also been blessed and tenderly mocked by an Irish enthusiast probably wearing a Tara brooch. She has called him a "West Briton," with the usual rebuff allowed that phrase, yet also a description that might be taken seriously. The Phoenix Park has twice drawn Gabriel's attention, and both times he has looked westward only to view those memorials that best align him with his grandfather Patrick Morkan. Finally, though putting aside his quotation from Browning, he has more than likely drawn heavily on the poem concluding a volume celebrating hospitality that would round out his heavy-handed tribute to the Morkan evening. Yet the pompous and rather clumsy Browning of the last ten years seems to have overtaken Gabriel unawares as he urges the strenuous life, the bustle, and daily routine to stiffen his officious flattery—with little real regard for his own Margarite and her love.

III

The last section, then, must find Death in its most hilarious mood. Mr Browne had offered "No, no" and "Here, here," Joyce's drops of irony, at important junctures of Gabriel's speech. At last Browne is all but beside himself. For this final section of "The Dead," although beginning with a great burst of late party hilarity, heralds the start of a journey eastward toward death. Aunt Kate requests that the door be closed to keep out the cold air, or "Mrs Malins will get her death of cold." Yet in the same instant Mary Jane reminds her that "Mr Browne is out there." We then get Aunt Kate's retort that overtly links Browne with the figure of Death that I derive from Holbein. Mary Jane, without catching the gravity of her own words, remarks on Browne's attentiveness. Aunt Kate promptly pushes the implication. Browne's heavy presence on "the Christmas," meaning during the party, has been like that of the gas. The word begins to take on its original meaning of spirit, in this case a malevolent one, especially since Browne has also been sporting in that cold, early-morning air. "Airy" has the connotation of "ghostly, fearsome," as P. W. Joyce explains—"a survival of the old Irish pagan belief that air-demons were the most malignant of all supernatural beings."[20] For Death does enter. That is, Browne comes in "laughing as if his heart would break," Holbein's laughing, mimicking nemesis at his grimmest. Mary Jane, indeed like a Druid priestess in this scene, adds that she wouldn't want Gabriel's and Browne's—note the new pairing—journey home in this cold. Browne then further identifies himself with that skeletal specter, often pictured armed with a dart or spear, when he allows that "a *rattling* fine walk in the country or a fast drive with a good spanker between the *shafts*" would please him most (my italics). A moment later, after Gabriel's story of grandfather Morkan and his horse, Aunt Kate gives the Irish salutation to the dead, "The Lord have mercy on his soul."

Then another burst of laughter explodes from Freddy as he adjusts his mother in a cab and gives directions to the driver. Mr Browne of course assumes direction of the cab, which for a moment becomes something like the traditional Irish death-coach what with heads in and out of it, that will make like a bird, perhaps the angel of death, for the gates of Trinity College. Supposedly, Death may not enter the Holy Trinity. But with the Protestant Browne directing the coach Joyce may well be reversing that imperative. Thus, we are prepared for Gabriel's beholding Gretta in the shadows of the stairway, for the ancient tonality singing of "The Lass of Aughrim," for the memory of a boy who worked in the gasworks, and for Bartell D'Arcy's celebrated cold.

But before marking Gabriel's wonderment before the figure of Gretta among those shades, we might hark back to another instance of music, the discussion of opera just before Gabriel's speech in the previous section. As we have seen, Mary Jane has been given a pass to *Mignon* by one of her pupils. That opera opened for the holiday season the next day, Thursday the 7th, at the Theatre Royal, and would be repeated three times the next week by the Moody Manners Opera Company.[21] Already Bartell D'Arcy has "praised very highly the leading contralto of the company," despite Miss Furlong's suggesting her vulgarity. The singer was more than likely Miss Tiefy Davies in the role of the Gypsy Queen, a contralto part in *The Bohemian Girl*, performed on 30 December.[22] She was praised in the *Irish Times* for her singing in *Faust*—she took the role of Siebel—on 30 December. Mr Browne then comes forth with his favorite operas, *Lucrezia Borgia* and *Dinora*, to which he adds Don Caesare's song from *Maritana*, "Let Me like a Soldier Fall." What these operas have in common, simply put and not surprisingly enough, are youthful lovers and the threat of an older wealthy man, statesman, or wizard. Faust vies with Marguerite and Siebel; the king and his gold oppose the love between Maritana and Don Caesare; a suspicious husband causes a wife to kill herself and her son in *Lucrezia Borgia*; her father nearly kills Mignon, in love with Wilhelm Meister; Dinora believes her lover Hoel has betrayed her for the money hidden by the wizard Tonick.

All these instances point to the plight of the Lass of Aughrim and just as poignantly to Gretta's continued love for Michael Furey—whether the bane be a disdainful mother, a rich lord, or an heir to Patrick Morkan's pomposity. Moreover, D'Arcy's cold, the delicate lungs of Michael Furey, even his job in the Galway gasworks—as a Catholic he doubtless clerked standing up or shoveled coal—have barely made the song's rendition possible. And the snow this evening is the heaviest in thirty years, the length of time the Morkans have been at 15 Usher's Island. Apparently, the night is memorable for more than one memory of failed or hampered or stricken health.

Yet throughout Gabriel's uncomprehending observation of Gretta her bronze hair is stressed, so is the blue of her hat, the "grace and mystery of her attitude," her flushed cheeks and shining eyes: all make up a picture of something indeed, a remembrance of distant music certainly, perhaps something more. A long-dead poet-singer had perished for Gretta. Even if D'Arcy couldn't get the song right and Gretta had forgotten the title, in "The Lass of Aughrim" something of an air spirit, something or someone, dead but alive, vies with the malignant Mr Browne. Another breath, another ghost has come, still very much alive, however delicate.

But immediately the farewells are given after yet one more imprecation from Mary Jane. In his happiness Gabriel longs to protect Gretta but he has forgotten his phrase "thought-tormented music." He nevertheless recalls intimate moments that strike him as fiery stars—not a Furey star, which as a magus from the East he is really following. He even remembers her watching a roaring furnace yet he cannot know how she might identify it with a coke furnace in the Galway gasworks. The same might be said for his pressing a ticket in her hand or even his fond memory of a letter on the table, for pebbles at a window and her departure for Dublin are also distant parallels. Gabriel is a deluded man in the presence of the living dead.[23]

In fact the night is cold along the Liffey, and death or hostile forces surround D'Arcy the hoarse singer, Gretta the listener, and Gabriel the observer. For instance the lamps along the quay "still burn redly in the air," much like the Celtic omen of disaster—bloody red clouds or the washer at the bloody ford (and we are close to the original ford of the hurdles) that presaged death. The menace of the Four Courts John V.

Kelleher has already noted. The "rattling cab" itself and Winetavern Street, once associated with funeral homes, maintain that dread. Then to remark a white horse at O'Connell Bridge is to see the symbol of William III's victory at the Boyne. A white horse usually adorned the fanlight of a Protestant house. Perhaps we are also meant to fix on the white horse in Moore's poem "O'Donoghue's Mistress" that brings the dead hero back every spring. The poem follows "Oh, Ye Dead" in the *Melodies*. Moreover, to pass O'Connell's statue is to pass the major statue of Hibernia in Dublin. Here she is displayed trampling her fetters. By contrast, Gretta bows her head and seems laden with a burden as she ascends the Gresham stairs. These hostile forces and omens strike me as in open view at last when Gretta walks into the "ghastly light" from the street. While gazing at that light, she admits to being tired—the beginning of a series of her powerful West of Ireland understatements. Soon her mention of the song "The Lass of Aughrim" and then her memory of Michael Furey follow. We then behold a beautiful weeping woman, the final Irish harbinger of death's approach. The famous exchange between Gabriel and Gretta follows.

IV

Its force has seldom if ever been recognized. Gretta slips into the local but formal and general language and gestures of the Galway girl that she was, language and gestures that understate the powerful emotions roused in her and now sweeping through her. To begin with, she is said to dry "her eyes with the back of her hand like a child," but one sign of her powerful retreat into her buried self. Then she speaks of Michael Furey as a "person," employing the usual West of Ireland generality, a furtive and protective device. Then he immediately becomes a "young boy"—"boy" in Ireland also meaning an unmarried man. Gretta's calling him "delicate" can further point to his sensibility but, more directly of course, to his tubercular lungs—10,000 a year died of this affliction—the white plague in Ireland.[24] When asked if she loved Michael, she answers with all the power of Galway reticence in such matters: "I used to go out walking with him," the West of Ireland phrase for courtship. To underline the threat to his delicacy, Joyce has Gretta reveal that Michael worked in the gasworks. As I have suggested, a 17-year-old Catholic probably shoveled coal to be heated for coal-gas or clerked standing up. The tie between such a deadly job and Browne's being laid on like the gas is perhaps too powerful. Mention, too, of his great dark eyes and their expression forcefully comments on Gabriel's "glimmering gilt-rimmed eyeglasses" and the restless though sensitive eyes behind them. Asked again if she were in love with Michael Furey, Gretta innocently offers another ax-blow of understatement: "I was great with him at that time." Her reticence and force combine to deepen the implications of her next admission: "I *think* he died for me" (my italics), something very close to the demand that the traditional Kathleen Ni Houlihan made on the youth of Ireland but with what a difference. Aware that some ghostly presence is speaking through Gretta, Gabriel nevertheless gets the full, gentle, mantled narrative of a countrywoman's overmastering early love. Michael Furey "was in decline;" he "wouldn't be let out." Then she waits a moment and sighs—as Irish women do to control such an account. But she continues. He was a "poor fellow," "fond" of her, a "gentle boy." Note the enforced generalities that nevertheless make her truthtelling so acutely personal and penetrating. They went out walking, she and Michael Furey, "like the way they do in the country." He was "to study singing only for his health"—how much is packed into that qualification. Then came her leavetaking and his worsening, yet she "wouldn't be let see him." Note again the radical switch in her syntax and usage from the Gretta of the first few pages of the story. Gretta now stops to control herself. So Joyce signals the depth of truth and confession from a still guileless West of Ireland woman. Then her last sight of Michael, for distant music is with her still. She can still "see his eyes as well as well." The rain, the tree, the wall, the pebbles at the window follow and summon up the scene of "The Lass of Aughrim." The action, however, is the opposite.

Since Gretta left for the convent at the beginning of winter, and Michael Furey died but a week later, the suggestion is that she left close to the winter solstice and that he died near the end of the year. The day Gretta heard that he was dead—"O the day I heard that, that he was dead!"—might very well have been near 6 January, the end of the holiday season in Ireland, the season that ends with the day of the Morkan party.[25] I speculate, then, that Michael Furey has been in her heart, perhaps even during her "three mortal hours of preparation," all evening. The fully accelerated movement toward death at the beginning of this section has none the less brought a dead man into near-visibility on a beam of light through the seemingly offhand, casual, understated, generalized soft speech of his own Ireland. Wildness is not quite the substantive for him, although the surname Furey is most often found in Galway.[26]

V

Before we contemplate Gabriel after Gretta has fallen asleep, we probably ought to consider first where the story has taken us beyond the Gresham Hotel. Perhaps Monkstown, Gabriel's home, is the best place to start. The name itself derives from Monkstown Castle "erected in the 12th or 13th century by the monks of the Abbey of the Blessed Virgin Mary near Dublin. St Mary's Abbey," as F. Elrington Ball continues the account, "had been affiliated early in the 12th century to the Cistercian Order" and—with the coming of the Anglo-Normans—"fresh tenants were supplied by the great Cistercian House of Buildwas in Shropshire, under whose cure and disposition it was placed." As a defence against Irish invaders from the Wicklow mountains, the monks built Monkstown Castle. Until its suppression by Henry VIII in 1539, the castle served, as will Mount Melleray for Freddy, as hospitable lodgings for travelers landing at Dalkey and making their way by an innless path to Dublin.[27]

Yet Usher's Island and Phoenix Park—perhaps not unexpectedly—have also brave religious antecedents favoring hospitality, care, and protection. I refer of course to the Knights Templars and later the knights Hospitalers or Knights of St John of Jerusalem, military and religious orders that held the lands now Phoenix Park and Usher's Island.[28] Further, I might add, the humanity and kindness of Lord Moira of Usher's Island for the Catholic and Irish cause were especially celebrated in the presence of Lord Edward Fitzgerald at Moira House in 1798. Although it became the Mendicity Institution in 1826 and was virtually dismantled as a house, in its service to paupers (121,820 meals were served during one year at the turn of our century)[29] it echoes the charitable note I associate with so many places in the story. While such meals may not have been as sumptuous as that of the Misses Morkan, the Association for the Prevention of Mendicity working through the former Moira House had as its chief task "the providing of daily meals (over 100,000 per annum are given), the transmission of strangers to their homes, and the supplying of cheap baths."[30] Something perhaps of the same solicitude attaches to the history of the Franciscan chapel, where Aunt Julia toiled for so many years in the choir, the noted Adam and Eve's Church, a clandestine Catholic chapel during Penal times named from a neighborhood tavern.

Of course what I'm preparing for is the importance of Mount Melleray and the embarrassing table discussion of the monks there. While the monks did not indeed sleep in their coffins, yet Freddy may avail himself of part of their hospitality—Mount Melleray was then a noted dry-out center. Dedicated to silence, the monks also give themselves to contemplation and the redeeming penitential practice of their order. As Reformed Cistercians of the Strict Observance, these Trappists also devoted themselves to manual labor, virtual unceasing prayer, and severe self-denial. A day at Mount Melleray at the foot of the Knockmealdown Mountains, near Cappoquin, County Waterford, has been thus described:

The day's work began at 2 a.m., when every monk was called from his cell to begin the Matins of Our Lady's office.

At 3 o'clock began the Matins of the Divine Office, and at 4 o'clock, Masses. The Office of Compline concluded the day's work. Six hours of every day were devoted to the works of God alone by the choir monks of the Order.

The monks did not eat meat, fish or many other things on any day of the year. To all this was added the penances and severe fasts prescribed by the Rule. The whole life of the Cistercian was a life of self-immolation and the mortification involved in the Holy Rule was the greatest sacrifice of all.[31]

And, in another account, these similar words mark the divisions of the day for the Cistercian Choir Religious:

Four hours of the day for Divine Office and the Little Office of the Blessed Virgin.

Two hours for Masses, though only one is of obligation by rule.

Two hours for study and spiritual reading.

Four hours for manual labor.

Four hours for reading, minor duties of the monastery and private devotions.

One hour for meals.

Seven hours for sleep.[32]

The strange, not to say jarring note that Mr Browne's incomprehension brings out may contrast—especially when the austerity and selflessness of the monks are pointed out by Freddy—with the self-discovery of the famed reformer of the order, Armand-Jean de Rancé. For all at table lapse into a silence, lugubrious, even anticlimactic, when Mrs Mallins adds: "They are very good men, the monks, very pious men." Fruits, sweets, chocolates, port, and sherry follow, doubtless more understandable at that season for Mr Browne, yet contrasting markedly with the custom of ancient Irish Christmas—after all, a holy time.[33] But Mary Jane had interjected on the subject of the monks sleeping in their coffins—"The coffin is to remind them of their last end." And herein lies the relevance of Rancé, most particularly for Gabriel's last end, so to speak.

Throughout the conversation, Gabriel has remained silent. Yet his discovery at the end of the night will be a revelation of the power and nearness of death in life yet at the same time the life-giving force of an early, selfless, passionate death. His attitude will become wholeheartedly charitable as generous tears fill his eyes. To a degree he repeats the surprising alteration once seen in the brilliant cleric Rancé, the supposed lover of the Duchess of Montbazan, and ultimately the great

seventeenth-century reformer of the Cistercian order. She died
suddenly on 28 April 1657, after a three-day illness. One
account has him discovering her dead in her coffin. In any
case, her death very nearly prostrated him. Tormented by her
lingering image, he also found that the sumptuous life of Paris
and country house had palled upon him. Out of this travail,
however, came what can be called another conversion,
attended by contrition for his past and the beginning of a new
humility. Eventually, Rancé disposed of his wealth, and, being
an abbot in name, retained his smallest possession, the Abbey
of La Trappe, where he retired in 1662 to become a Cistercian
monk, now the abbot in fact, and reinvigorated the Strict
Observance.[34] Whatever the force of this parallel—Rancé and
Gabriel—the Mount Melleray episode lies at the center of the
growing theme of abnegation, selflessness, and devotion in the
story. We ought also to remember that the discussion of Mount
Melleray follows upon the mention of opera and singing in
Dublin. Music and a devotion superior to death will also come
together when Gretta hears D'Arcy sing "The Lass of
Aughrim" and then makes her admission to Gabriel about
Michael. In turn, Gabriel's triumph will be his self-denial and
humility before the hosts of the dead.

We should also pause over the place of that last meeting
between Gretta and Michael, Nun's Island. Named for the
Community of Poor Clares, the island is formed by the Galway
river stemming from Lough Corrib which divides, indeed
arches to the right, after passing the salmon weir bridge and
forms a mill race on either side of the subsequent island.
Removed to that island in 1649—then called Ilaun Altanagh—
the convent was destroyed by Cromwellian forces in 1653 and
was again burned and the community dispersed after the
Williamite victory in 1691. However, the Clares returned in
1825 and are known as the Angel Guardians of Galway.[35]
Inspired by St Clare of Assisi, the order's purpose is to pray
and do penance for the sinners of the world. Strictly cloistered,
the life of a Poor Clare is one of austerity and mortification.
Somewhat like the Trappists, the Clares rise at midnight to
pray, especially for the conversion of sinners. Needless to say,

Their rule is one of the most rigorous in the Church. The

nuns live entirely on alms and cannot accept any endowment, or own any property, even in the name of the Community. Their food is for the most part brought to them day by day as an offering of charity, the very poor being often the foremost in this good work. Of what is received only a limited supply may be stored up. The nuns never eat meat, and fast on all days except Sundays. They rise at midnight for Office and Meditation. Besides the Divine Office, the Offices of the Blessed Virgin and of the Dead are said. Except during Advent and Lent there is "recreation" twice a week, silence being observed at all other times. The "enclosure" is extremely strict. Only one reception room, with one heavily veiled grille, is allowed in these convents, so that visitors can never be numerous. The admission of outsiders within the convent itself is, even in cases of absolute necessity, subject to the most stringent regulations. The habit is of rough brown serge; and instead of the usual stiff coif, a large "kerchief" of unstarched linen frames the face, beneath the black veil, one point falling to the waist. Except in the garden, where sandals are worn, the nuns go barefoot.[36]

Thus fasting, night vigils, austerities, silence, and contemplation mark this holy death-in-life, a "dying to oneself, to the world, to its attractions,"[37] the height of self-denial, a quelling of self-will, perhaps the extreme of hospitality. This accent in the story may quietly include the Joyce association with the order as part of the Galway connection so important to Joyce both within and without the story itself. For the early chalice still preserved by the community is inscribed with the date 1701 and the words "Pray for the soule of John Joyes and his wife Agnes Joyes who made this challis for the use of the convent of St. Clare in Galway, 1701."[38] A successful Galway goldsmith, Joyce ultimately bought the estate of Rahoon from a Colonel Whaly, a former officer in Cromwell's forces—and Rahoon is one of a number of possible sites for Sonny Bodkin's grave.

But in the story itself the graveyard for Michael Furey is Kilcummin cemetery at Oughterard. Usually termed the gateway or base for visiting the Joyce country, Oughterard, a small town seventeen miles northwest of Galway City, is known not only for its associations with the Joyce country, but also, fittingly for Michael Furey, with St Michael himself. As a seventeenth-century historian of Iar-Connacht wrote of the River Fuogh that flows through Oughterard, "On the north side of the river, not far from the bridge, westward, was discovered by revelation, about the year 1654, a well in honour of St. Michael, archangel."[39] Of more mortal if no less sacred memory is the famed Lugnaedon Stone, identified with Oughterard, on the Lough Corrib Isle of Inchnagoill, which also has the ancient church of Templepatrick. And the name Inchnagoill means "the isle of the devout foreigner," since Lugnaedon was the nephew and pilot for no less than St Patrick himself.[40]

VI

Gabriel's charitable journey westward, then, would take him toward that Joyce country and possibly to that graveyard where Michael Furey lies buried. In so journeying, Gabriel would also have paralleled, if not exactly duplicated, St Patrick's journey to the West of Ireland in response to something of the same vision—"the form of a young man standing under a dripping tree." For the evening at the Misses Morkan's has demonstrated, as I hope to show, how very close to St Patrick's path Gabriel's has been. Just as important places in the story have been linked to the hospitality, charity, and selflessness found among the Trappists and Poor Clares, not to forget the solicitude of St Michael of Oughterard, so Gabriel at the end of "The Dead" may well undergo St Patrick's conversion as Joyce interpreted it—he had not converted the Irish but, instead, had been converted by them.[41] While Adaline Glasheen and Hugh Staples, among others, have shown the importance of St Patrick in *Finnegans Wake*, here I would like to speculate on Gabriel's parallel experience not only in being converted by the Irish—and in this case the ur-Irish—but also in his enlightened role as man of letters, something like Joyce's later Yawn Patrick in *Finnegans Wake*.[42]

The St Patrick associations in the story far outnumber, if they do not outshine, those charitable ones at the end, yet they are also something the same. And I bear in mind the fixed and general nature of the saint's influence throughout Ireland. First of all, Patrick is thought to have been from the west of Roman Britain, and from a family of some minor distinction. To Miss Ivors, Gabriel not only denies that Irish is his language, but she in turn calls him a West Briton. Irish sea-pirates supposedly captured Patrick and enslaved him. His task was that of a shepherd of swine and maybe sheep. Morkan in Irish derives from the term "sea-warrior" or "pirate."[43] Every year, apparently, Gabriel has been captured, after a fashion, by his aunts; this year he must also tend Freddy. By the end of the story, Gabriel recognizes himself as his aunts' pennyboy or slavey. Freddy, the black sheep, has recently sold Christmas cards—featuring many a lamb, no doubt—and has returned what is seldom returned in Ireland, the loan of a pound. His name Malins was long associated, as we have seen, with the hereditary keepers of St Patrick's bell in the North. But, again, the Morkans are from Stonybatter. Their path from there thirty years before to Usher's Island was also St Patrick's in his visitation to Wicklow, along the way passing Monkstown. Then also the Irish device worn by Miss Ivors, more than likely a Tara brooch, may also recall Patrick's contention with the Druids at Tara before King Laoghaire's court. Indeed, Mary Jane aware of Mr Browne's attentiveness, and then Mary Jane laboring at the piano—her "hands like those of a priestess in momentary deprecation"—may also give back that scene. In any case, Gabriel feels more than one eye upon him when Miss Ivors upbraids him for neglecting Ireland. Yet St Patrick had won his case against the Druids. And Miss Ivors does cast blessings in Irish on Gabriel for all the shower of metaphorical fire and blood she had poured upon him as was the actual custom of ancient Druidesses.[44] An added irony may be Gabriel's worshipping in Monkstown's only Catholic church, St Patrick's, opened and dedicated by Cardinal Cullen in 1866.[45]

Yet the parallel between Gabriel's imaginative vision of "the form of a young man standing under a dripping tree" and the vision that brought Patrick back to Ireland after his escape most powerfully arrests at least one reader. Gabriel, after all, preferred to spend his holidays cycling in France, Belgium, or Germany, that is, on the Continent, where indeed Patrick had sojourned after escaping Ireland. Yet as article 23 of his *Confession* states:

> After a few years I was in the country of the Britons again with my parents, who accepted me as a son, and in good faith begged me that at any rate now, after such suffering as I had borne, I should not leave them to go away anywhere.
>
> And of course it was there that, in a night vision, I saw a man called Victoricus who seemed to come from Ireland with innumerable letters, and he gave me one of them and I read the beginning of it, containing the Voice of the Irish. And when I read the beginning of the letter aloud I seemed in that moment to hear the voice of those who were beside the Wood of Foclut, which is near the Western Sea, and they shouted out as if with one voice: We beg you, holy boy, to come and walk among us once again and it completely broke my heart and I could read no more, and woke up. Thank God, after many years the Lord did for those people as they had called on him to do.[46]

In section 24, St Patrick hears the spirit again and understands only the end of his speech: "The one who gave his life for you is speaking in you." I tend to link these words to the spears, thorns, and crosses at the very end. St Patrick concludes this portion with the fact that he "woke up in delight."[47]

In most accounts of the saint, we learn that he returned to Ireland and made his several journeys westward. These I take to be reflected in Gabriel's statement, "The time had come for him to set out on his journey westward." Thus, if we further examine the topography listed here between Dublin and Oughterard—all touched by the same general snowfall—we may again find the path of St Patrick some fifteen centuries earlier on his route to do penance in Connacht; that is, his progress to what became Croagh Patrick parallels when it doesn't coincide with Gabriel's imaginative sweep of terrain. Gabriel names these locales to himself: "the dark central plain," "the treeless hills," "the Bog of Allen," "the dark mutinous Shannon waves" and "the lonely churchyard on the hill where

Michael Furey lay buried." St Patrick had hurled the devils of the world into the sea at the end of his pilgrimage. Although not quite in consecutive order, these locales are apt checkpoints for Gabriel's own return to the wider Ireland and his rejection of the devils of a Dublin world of paralysis, serpentine enough.

That dark central plain is usually identified with County Westmeath—Meath in Gaelic means "middle"—with its Tyrrell's Pass, site of one of many wells made famous by the saint. These treeless hills may also include what Joyce once declared Ireland's Jerusalem or Mecca,[48] the Hill of Tara in Meath, where on Slane Hill, before he was to meet King Laoghaire on Easter Sunday, Patrick lit the Paschal Fire and broke the power of the Druids. The Bog of Allen in Kildare recalls the stronghold of Finn McCool, of whom in a moment, for Patrick's colloquy with his followers may yet be glanced at. The mutinous Shannon waves may hint of Patrick's crossing at Drumboylan but more than likely apply to the Shannon estuary below Limerick, where the sluggish river occasionally appears to flow backwards when embraced by the Atlantic waves at Loop Head. On the estuary at the village of Foynes stands Knockpatrick, the Hill of Patrick, from the summit of which Patrick is said to have blessed the land and people surrounding the estuary.[49]

As Richard Ellmann has pointed out, our final view in the story is of the Crucifixion. Yet I would add that the view may also include a qualifying irony. For Gabriel to contemplate sympathetically the figure of Michael under the tree, then to put himself in touch with other shades from Michael's world, idly to follow the snow as it touches on St Patrick's path to that very hill in Oughterard, and then to acknowledge the final judgment, the last end that awaits us all, these details can also play out one last major theme in the Patrick legend, the famous Colloquy of the Old Men. For Michael—archangel and singer—and Gabriel—archangel and reviewer/teacher—bring together poet and critic. Michael Furey may also include that side of Oisin—warrior, poet and lover—lured ultimately to his death by Niamh (or Gretta), the Oisin who previous to that death disputed with St Patrick the values of the pagan and Christian world-views. Some accounts are comic, some tragic, some merely politely contentious. But in showing Gabriel converted by the Irish, so to speak, Joyce may have gone one step further by giving the poet-lover, here Oisin, the person of the singer-lover-ghost Michael Furey, now recognized, understood, and appreciated by the critical, cleric-appearing, middle-class Gabriel.

As I have argued earlier in Chapter 1, the opening story, "The Sisters," pictures a boy's fate, his likely future defeat as a priest of the imagination, something like the fate of Father Flynn, a genuine and no less scrupulous priest. Misunderstood by his sisters and the boy's aunt, condemned by the uncle and Mr Cotter, the priest in his relationship to the boy serves as an ironic parallel to the figure of Father Christian Rosencrux, W. B. Yeats's symbol for the imagination dormant for some two hundred years. In both his essay "The Body of the Father Christian Rosencrux" and in the later poem "The Mountain Tomb" Yeats elaborates on this symbol and his hopes for a new literature. Yeats frequently went on to speculate that this imaginative rekindling in literature would soon break out in Ireland, the hoped-for effulgence of the Irish Literary Revival. I hold Joyce's first story, then, to be a strong demurrer against such a possibility in the Dublin of 1895 and after. Part of Joyce's method throughout *Dubliners* would be his setting his face against such extravagant hopes, hopes voiced with such fervor in Yeats's essay in the *Bookman*, September 1895, "Irish National Literature, III"; rather than turning back to Chapter 1, let me repeat some of Yeats's message from this magazine version of his essay "The Body of the Father Christian Rosencrux":

The followers of the Father Christian Rosencrux, says the old tradition, wrapped his imperishable body in noble raiment and laid it under the house of their order, in a tomb containing the symbols of all things in heaven and earth, and in the waters under the earth, and set about him inextinguishable magical lamps, which burnt on generation after generation, until other students of the order came upon the tomb by chance. It seems to me that the imagination has had no very different history during the last two hundred years, but has been laid in a great tomb of criticism, and had set over it inextinguishable magical lamps of wisdom and romance, and has been altogether so nobly housed and apparelled that we have forgotten that its wizard lips are closed, or but opened for the complaining of some melancholy and ghostly voice. . . .

It seems to a perhaps fanciful watcher of the skies like myself that this age of criticism is about to pass, and an age of imagination, of emotion, of moods, of revelation, about to come in its place; for certainly belief in a supersensual world is at hand again; and when the notion that we are "phantoms of the earth and water" has gone down the wind, we will trust our own being and all it desires to invent; and when the external world is no more the standard of reality, we will learn again that the great Passions are angels of God, and that to embody them "uncurbed in their eternal glory," even in their labour for the ending of man's peace and prosperity, is more than to comment, ever so wisely, upon the tendencies of our time, or to express the socialistic, or humanitarian, or other forces of our time, or even "to sum up" our time as the phrase is; for Art is a revelation, and not a criticism. . . .

   This revolution may be the opportunity of the Irish Celt, for he has an unexhausted and inexhaustible mythology to give him symbols and personages, and his nature has been profoundly emotional from the beginning.[50]

According to Yeats's description of the literature of the past two hundred years, Gabriel, the boy from "The Sisters" grown up, seems to have been equally fated to represent it as a mere reviewer, teacher, speaker, and commentator given to summing up.

   Returning to "The Dead," then, we may now see Gabriel released from the fate of the boy in "The Sisters," the original fate of the priest spelled out by three old women. Despite the urgings and success of Gabriel's father and mother (substitute the aunt and uncle of the first story) and the domination of all three Morkan sisters (substitute aunt and sisters Flynn), the dead uncle and grandfather, both named Patrick, may have still prevailed, as Father Flynn may not have with the boy. For the fate of the boy had seemed to cling to Gabriel, subservient as he has been to the wishes of his mother and the yearly expectations of his aunts. Yet, if Gabriel has not helped usher in the imaginative revival that Yeats had urged on Ireland, and Joyce doubted, Gabriel has nevertheless come to some ancient patrician accommodation and sympathy that blend the pagan joy and Christian circumspection that usually sit so ill together in Ireland. The dead, then, may have some reason to rejoice, renewed as Michael Furey is in the understanding though uncreative swooning soul of the living Gabriel. The grace of snow that binds both together has indeed about it something of the harbinger of the Easter Lily. Moreover, a wise man from the East of Ireland has experienced an epiphany, just as the feast, service, and ending of the book demand. And, though snow was not general over Ireland on 6 January 1904, Joyce makes sure that it is on this conclusive night, for snow at Christmas—as Seán Ó Suilleabháin tells us—traditionally leads to a mild, early, and hopeful spring in Ireland.[51] St Patrick's Day is usually thought to be for practical purposes the beginning of that spring. All may be well, then, for, after all, a corn factor owns the house where the Morkan Christmas party is once more celebrated at Usher's Island. "The Dead" in the long run is a story of growth and life and spring.

NOTES: CHAPTER 15

1 Stanislaus Joyce, "The background to *Dubliners*," *Listener*, vol. 51, no. 1308 (25 March 1954), pp. 526–7.
2 Moore added the note: "Paul Leland mentions that there is a mountain in some part of Ireland, where the ghosts of persons who have died in foreign lands walk about and converse with those they meet, like living people. If asked why they do not return to their homes, they say they are obliged to go to Mount Hecla, and disappear immediately."
3 John V. Kelleher, "Irish history and mythology in James Joyce's 'The Dead,'" *Review of Politics*, vol. 27, no. 3 (July 1965), pp. 414–33.
4 Stanislaus Joyce, op. cit., p. 527.
5 cf. John MacNicholas, "Comic design in James Joyce's 'The Dead,'" *Modern British Literature*, vol. 1, no. 1 (Fall 1976), pp. 56–65, and John D. and Ruth A. Boyd, "The love triangle in

Joyce's 'The Dead,'" *University of Toronto Quarterly*, vol. 42, no. 3 (Spring 1973), pp. 202–17.

6 Mary Jane has a pass for *Mignon*, which opened the next day, Thursday, 7 January. The *Freeman's Journal* for that day announced the opening on page 4. The same issue reports on the Galway meeting, called by Captain John Shawe-Taylor, that was supposed to settle the University Question. See the leader on page 4 and the accompanying article, "The Irish University Question," also the long account of the meeting, "The Irish University Question," on page 5. The Negro chieftain, G. H. Elliott, was also appearing for the first time in Dublin at the Gaiety performance of *Babes in the Wood*. See "Platform and stage," *Irish Times*, 19 December 1903, p. 9. See also John Scarry, "The 'Negro chieftain' and disharmony in Joyce's 'The Dead,'" *Revue des langues vivantes*, vol. 39, no. 2 (Summer 1973), pp. 182–3.

7 *Letters of James Joyce*, ed. Richard Ellmann (New York: Viking, 1966), Vol. 3, p. 79.

8 The Easter–Christmas connection is fairly widely accepted. For an elementary discussion of this and other juxtapositions in the story, see Robert Bierman, "Structural elements in 'The Dead,'" *James Joyce Quarterly*, vol. 4, no. 1 (Fall 1966), pp. 42–5.

9 George L. Geckle, "The dead lass of Aughrim," *Eire-Ireland*, vol. 9, no. 3 (Autumn 1974), p. 94, feels that the song reflects on all of Gabriel's problems with women, Lily included.

10 James Collins, *Life in Old Dublin* (Dublin: James Duffy, 1913), p. 72.

11 D. A. Chart, *The Story of Dublin* (London: Dent, 1907), p. 320. See also E. MacDowel Cosgrave, *Dublin and Co. Dublin in the Twentieth Century* (Brighton/London: W. T. Pike, 1908), p. 8. Also M. H. Daly, "A ramble from St Mary's Abbey to Oxmantown," *Dublin Historical Record*, vol. 21, no. 3 (June 1967), pp. 107–8.

12 Rev. N. Donnelly, *A Short History of Some Dublin Parishes* (Dublin: Catholic Truth Society of Ireland, 1905), Pt 2, pp. 72–5. For a picture of the design for the new St Mary's, see *Irish Builder*, 15 February 1894, p. 47.

13 John T. Gilbert, *A History of the City of Dublin*, Vol. 3 (Dublin: McGlashan & Gill, 1859), pp. 40–56.

14 Patrick Woulfe, *Irish Names and Surnames* (Dublin: M. H. Gill, 1923), p. 615. The current National Museum of Ireland pamphlet offers a picture and brief description of this beautiful bell.

15 He was extremely well received, as the article "Platform at the Gaiety Theatre," *Irish Times*, 28 December 1903, p. 6, reports.

16 E. MacDowell Cosgrave and Leonard R. Strangways, *Visitors' Guide to Dublin and Neighbourhood together with Supplemental Guide*

to the *Irish International Exhibition of 1907 Giving a Complete Dictionary of Dublin* (Dublin: Sealy, Bryers & Walker/London: Simkin, Marshall, Hamilton, Kent, n.d.), p. 224.

17   "Annals of the year," *Irish Times*, 1 January 1904, p. 7.

18   Blackie & Son (London) brought out such a selection in 1903 as did Cassell & Co. See Leslie Nathan Broughton et al., *Robert Browning: A Bibliography, 1830–1950* (Ithaca, NY: Cornell University Press, 1953), items A384, A389.

19   cf. William T. Going, "Joyce's Gabriel Conroy and Robert Browning: the cult of 'broad-cloth,'" *Papers in Language and Literature*, vol. 13, no. 2 (Spring 1977), pp. 203–7.

20   P. W. Joyce, *English as We Speak It in Ireland* (London: Longmans, Green, 1910), p. 210.

21   See the *Irish Times* review for 8 January 1904, p. 6.

22   "Moody Manners Opera Company," *Irish Times*, 31 December 1903, p. 6. Miss Tony Lester had been slightly criticized for her performance of the same role by the same newspaper, "English opera company at the Theatre Royal," *Irish Times*, 29 December 1903, p. 6. Miss Davies, the contralto, was praised again for her role as Siebel in *Faust* by the *Irish Times* the day before the party: "Moody Manners Opera Company," 5 January 1904, p. 6. For a general background on these and earlier operas in Dublin, see Carmel McAsey, "Dublin and opera," *Dublin Historical Record*, vol. 23, nos 2–3 (December 1969), pp. 45–55.

23   After writing these words, I came across a similar thought in John P. McKenna, "An ill-starred magus," *James Joyce Quarterly*, vol. 9, no. 1 (Fall 1971), p. 127.

24   "Consumption," *Irish Times*, 18 October 1900, p. 5.

25   I am indebted to John Kelleher for this suggestion.

26   Woulfe, op. cit., p. 527.

27   F. Elrington Ball, *A History of the County of Dublin*, Part First (Dublin: A. Thom, 1902), p. 2.

28   Relevant here are C. Litton Falkiner, "The Hospital of St John of Jerusalem in Ireland," *Royal Irish Academy Proceedings*, vol. 26, section C (1907), pp. 275–317, and Herbert Wood, "The Templars in Ireland," in ibid., pp. 327–77.

29   Gilbert, op. cit., Vol. 1, pp. 393–400. Also "Dublin charities," *Irish Times*, 26 December 1900, p. 6.

30   Cosgrave and Strangways, op. cit., p. 149. For fuller information today, see Joan Tighe, "The Mendicity Institution," *Dublin Historical Record*, vol. 20, nos. 3–4 (June–September 1965), pp. 100–15.

31   Ailbe J. Luddy, *The Story of Mount Melleray* (Dublin: M. H. Gill, 1946), p. 308.

32 H. J. McDermott, *The Trappist Monk* (Peosta, Iowa: New Melleray Abbey, 1924), p. 66. For the daily life of a Cistercian monk in our time, see Thomas Merton, *The Waters of Siloe* (New York: Harcourt Brace, 1949), pp. x–xi.
33 A. M. P. Smithson, "Christmas in old Dublin," *Dublin Historical Record*, vol. 6, no. 1 (September–November, 1943), pp. 1–7.
34 Ailbe J. Luddy, *The Real Rancé* (London/New York/Toronto: Longmans, Green, 1931), pp. 50–69; McDermott, op. cit., pp. 27–41.
35 Hely Dutton, *Survey of the County of Galway* (Dublin: Dublin University Press, 1824), p. 504. Also Hubert Quinn, "Trials and triumphs," in *Poor Clare Ter-Centenary Record 1629–1929*, ed. Sylvester O'Brien (Galway: Published by the Editor, 1929), pp. 15–16.
36 Helena [Mrs Thomas] Concannon, *The Poor Clares in Ireland* (Dublin: M. H. Gill, 1929), p. 170 n. 1.
37 Sylvester O'Brien, "The secret of the grille," in *Poor Clare Ter-Centenary Record 1629–1929*, ed. Sylvester O'Brien (Galway: Published by the Editor, 1929), p. 31.
38 Helena Concannon, "Trophies of our faith," in ibid., pp. 18–19.
39 Roderic O'Flaherty, *A Chorographical Description of West or H-Iar Connaught*, ed. James Hardiman (Dublin: M. H. Gill/Irish Archaeological Society, 1846), p. 53.
40 James Henthorn Todd, *St Patrick, Apostle of Ireland* (Dublin: Hodges, Smith, 1864), p. 365; *Ireland*, ed. L. Russell Muirhead (London: Ernest Benn, 1949), p. 175; and Oliver St John Gogarty, *I Follow Saint Patrick* (London: Constable, 1950), pp. 238–9. Gogarty's account, hardly scholarly, is firsthand, repeats the many legends attributed to the saint, and is thoroughly local in its knowledge. See also Sir William R. Wilde, *Lough Corrib*, 2nd edn (Dublin: McGlashan & Gill, 1872), pp. 133–49.
41 *Letters of James Joyce*, ed. Richard Ellmann (New York: Viking, 1966), Vol. 3, p. 79.
42 In outlining these general parallels, I have relied on the general accounts of St Patrick's life in Todd, op. cit.; Whitely Stokes (ed.), *The Tripartite Life of Patrick, with Other Documents Relating to That Saint*, 2 pts (London: Rolls Series, 1887); and J. B. Bury, *The Life of St Patrick* (London/New York: Macmillan, 1905). According to James S. Atherton, *The Books at the Wake* (London: Faber, 1959), p. 145: "St Patrick's *Confessio* [to be found in all three books] is a book which Joyce is certain to have read. There are several half-quotations from it and Joyce had also read most, perhaps all, of the biographies, including the *Tripartite Life*, but whether he took his information from this or from one of the modern lives that

includes material from it cannot be determined from internal evidence."

43 Woulfe, op. cit., p. 623.
44 For Joyce on St Patrick at Tara, see *Letters*, Vol. 3, pp. 344–6.
45 Carmel McAsey, "Monkstown, Co. Dublin," *Dublin Historical Record*, vol. 24, no. 4 (September 1976), p. 147.
46 Instead of Bury's literal translation of 1905, I have used the more modern one from Arnold Marsh (trans.), *Saint Patrick's Writings* (Dundalk: Dundalgan Press, 1961), p. 11.
47 ibid.
48 *Letters*, Vol. 3, p. 345.
49 Richard Hayward, *Where the River Shannon Flows* (London: Arthur Barker, 1950), pp. 304–5. See also "Estuary of the Shannon," *Irish Times*, 4 September 1900, p. 6.
50 *Uncollected Prose by W. B. Yeats*, ed. John P. Frayne, Vol. 1 (London: Macmillan, 1970), pp. 376–7.
51 "Traditional Christmas in Ireland," *Ireland Today* (Bulletin of the Department of Foreign Affairs), no. 941, 15 December 1978, p. 3.

Conclusion:
Joyce, Dublin, Dubliners, and After

The subject of Joyce, Dublin, and *Dubliners* remains as impossible here at the end of this book as it is inevitable. For an American to write briefly on the topic seems equally impossible—yet, I suppose, also inevitable. Frankly, then, as an American and cisatlantic Irishman, I am especially daunted since almost every major critic has sworn to the absolute importance of Dublin for Joyce's life and work. Thus I am many, many times indebted to the frequently eloquent testimony on Joyce and his city by such as Ellmann, Kain, Hutchins, Hart and Knuth, Atherton, Staples, and very many others. But perhaps my best aids have been the short—hence pleasingly terse—essays by F. S. L. Lyons, J. C. C. Mays, Terence Brown, and Thomas Kinsella.[1] Lyons, for instance, insists upon the historian's right to distinguish the real turn-of-the-century Dublin from the imagined but limited city that Joyce serves up. Joyce, as Lyons maintains, was alienated from both Dublin worlds, the fading Ascendancy culture and that of the growing Catholic nationalist movement. Mays, in a similar vein, scrutinizes *Ulysses* and pronounces it utterly different from the Dublin of the standard guidebooks and the equally happy Dublin usually touted by its two distinct societies. The same differences exist in *Dubliners*. Joyce, as Mays's account goes, chose to fix on that third of Dublin north of the Liffey, largely northeast toward the Royal Canal. Joyce's triumph, then, lay in persuading a reader that this world of the inept and the lower-middle class, with the exception of the Monto district, was all Dublin. Clearly the slums of O'Casey and

O'Flaherty were very near. Terence Brown, on the other hand, applauds Joyce's originality in turning such squalor into a universal metaphor. Kinsella does him one better by claiming for Joyce a continuity with native Irish literature by limiting his subject to Yeats's despised "filthy modern tide": Dublin. All these astute observations have helped me, yet I still may take a different course.

In addition, then, to questioning this so-called difference between the actual Dublin and Joyce's imaginative but limited city, I shall also face in this afterword that perennial assertion of his warring hatred and love of Ireland. Virtually every critic repeats it—in this year alone such seasoned and important Joyceans as Richard Ellmann and David Norris.[2] They may well be right. The amalgam of hatred and love, however, I see as but another form of the argument for a bifurcated Dublin, the real thing and the product of Joyce's imaginative persuasion. Far closer to his actual attitude might be the comic view of Dublin from Eccles Street or any other street; at least, that's Frank Budgen's claim:

> It is not easy to define the mood of *Ulysses*, but it seems to me that Joyce neither hates nor loves, neither curses nor praises the world, but that he affirms it with a "Yes" as positive as that with which Marion Bloom affirms her prerogative on the last page. It is not to him a brave new world. . . . Rather it is a brave old world, forever flowing like a river, ever seeming to change yet changing never. The prevailing attitude of *Ulysses* is a very humane scepticism—not of tried human values, necessary at all times for social cohesion, but of all tendencies and systems whatsoever. There are moods of pity and grief in it, but the prevailing mood is humour.[3]

All this strikes me as well said by way of cutting beneath the surface of *Ulysses*. But can Budgen's words also pertain to *Dubliners*? I think so. An even deeper response to all of Joyce's work, however early or late, might take off from a statement by his brother Stanislaus:

> The two dominant passions of my brother's life were to be love of father and of fatherland. The latter was not the

love of a patriot, which is an emotion of the market-place, part hatred of some other country, part falsehood. It was the comprehending love of an artist for his subject. Both passions stemmed, I believe, from his ancient love of God, and were already at that time spreading tough roots underground in a most unpropitious climate: love of his country, *or rather of his city* [my italics] that was to reject him and his work; love of his father, who was like a millstone around his neck. The roots of feeling in some men sink all the deeper for the difficulties that surround and frustrate them; and I wonder that people do not see how much higher than the divine love, which is the preacher's theme, is that human passion which can love an unworthy object utterly without return and forgive without waiting to be supplicated.[4]

Acutely aware of Joyce's oft-uttered fury, rage, disgust, lament, scorn, contempt, and fear for Dublin, I nevertheless agree with Stanislaus on Joyce the artist and his love of his subject and city. To establish my agreement, then, I shall first look briefly at Dublin at the turn of the century and then explore Joyce's reaction to it as a man. Only then shall I turn briefly to the Dublin of *Dubliners* and his other major works. Thereby I also hope to arrive at several tentative conclusions about those supposed contraries, fact and imagination, hatred and love.

I

Dublin at the beginning of this century certainly was a city where motley was worn. Tourist guides, memoirs, histories, statistical surveys, and even the curious in our time who direct their gaze at Dublin, all obtrude a different-colored Dublin on us. The guidebooks, for instance, are fairly standard, especially those by Cosgrave and Strangways, Wakeman, Whammond, Sullivan, Peter, Dignam, and no end of anonymous compilers. But my favorite is a guide to the luminaries of Dublin by E. McDowel Cosgrave where Mahaffy, Traill, Dowden, McGuckin, and Count Markiewicz are among the few fabulous survivors in the arts and humanities amid a galaxy of doctors, lawyers, corporation members, merchants, and the like.[5]

Perhaps the most unbeatable of these guides for sheer patronizing banality is Frances Gerard's *Picturesque Dublin*— dedicated appropriately enough to the Countess of Cadogan, the Lord-Lieutenant's wife—full of lavish praise for Castle and military life in Dublin. After parrying former untoward accounts by the likes of Carlyle, Thackeray, and George Moore, the author can, at one point, admonish the reader with this typical observation: "Few tourists have ever penetrated into that curious, old-world quarter the Liberties, where once the nobility of Ireland had fine houses, where is situated the old Dutch and Huguenot quarter, and where in the Coombe five hundred weavers plied their shuttles manufacturing those lovely brocades which were sent to all parts of the world, and which fetched high prices."[6]

The romance of Castle and military life has rarely been put more fetchingly than in this passage:

> The dark-eyed daughters of Eblana are said to dote upon the military uniform—not in the vulgar manner, let it be understood; as a matter of fact, Irish girls are far less forward than the more demure belle of English society, and Saxon warriors recognize this fact by choosing them for partners, not only for a dance, but for life.[7]

Of course, the expected, doubtless true, admission follows: "I love every corner and nook of the quaint old town where the happy days of my youth were spent."[8] Such guides, bland as they are at best, *do* indeed offer factual information about districts, institutions, monuments, streets, and public buildings and areas, like the important Phoenix Park, in Joyce's fiction. But Joyce's affection is of an altogether different kind.

I do not intend to dwell overlong on the value of all these witnesses to Joyce's relatively small, communal, divided, eighteenth-century, drink-ridden city of personalities and historical memories. Moreover, the brutal statistics for Dublin's slum life—soaring infant mortality, miserable living conditions, TB, prostitution, and alcoholism[9]—have been dramatized to the world in O'Casey's famous Dublin trilogy and auto-biographies. Hints of these statistics are usually just around the corner in *Dubliners*. On the other hand, George Moore, W. B. Yeats, the Colums, and P. L. Dickinson can look back at the period as signaling the beginnings of high culture and artistic hopes. Dublin might be dirty but she was also friendly, even joyous. Thus Dickinson in a book with two chapters on the new Arts Club.[10] Yeats lamented the end of romance in Ireland with John O'Leary's funeral in 1907. Padraic Colum bemoaned the passing of that Dublin of opera, orators, recitations, and at-homes,[11] also lamented by George Moore. Trinity College, too, had its own brilliant life as the Stanford and McDowell biography of Mahaffy shows.[12]

As far as historians go, Samuel FitzPatrick waxes ecstatic over the amenities of the modern Dublin of 1901. Dublin is no longer dirty; the streets are wide, well lighted, and well kept; her electric trams are the best in Europe; the population has risen to 289,108 from 170,094 in 1805 (though the figures for the immediate pre-Famine days appear to be missing); 32,004 houses stand on their own two legs within the municipal boundaries; the viceregal court is still resplendent; public buildings dazzle the fortunate onlooker; most citizens are now in easy reach of Kingstown, Howth, Lucan, Killiney, and the Phoenix Park.[13] The author then concludes the praise of his fair city with these words: "In the trading competition of the times we live in Dublin has, as a manufacturing or even as a distributing centre, fallen into the background; but she still possesses her social traditions, her literary and artistic culture, and her unique advantages of natural situation."[14]

No less emphatic (we might say blind) is D. A. Chart. In 1907 his great claim was that peace reigns in Ireland: "The turbulence of 1882 is not likely to be repeated. The fenian of 1866 could not arouse the people as the United Irishmen did in 1798. . . . King Edward has twice visited Dublin since his accession. His unequalled tact and diplomacy has made a whole half-hostile nation his warm admirers."[15] In those years Dublin struck one English visitor as more free than even Britain herself.[16] As shortsighted as some of these statements appear, coming before the violence of 1916 and after, they do bear a truth for the time that Joyce portrayed. But the stories on public life alone—"Ivy Day in the Committee Room," "A Mother," and "Grace"—cast another light on such facts.

Perhaps the whole matter has been put best by Conor Cruise O'Brien in his essay "1891–1916" that leads off his *The Shaping of Modern Ireland*:

It was a time in which nothing happened; nothing except (as we find when we look into it) a revolution in land ownership, the beginning of a national quest for a lost language and culture, and the preparation of the two successful rebellions which were, among other things, to tear Ireland in two. Yet despite these momentous events it is not only to us with our memories of school history that the period seems empty; it seemed so to many contemporaries. For James Joyce, as we know, the seething Dublin of 1904 was "the centre of paralysis," a place in which the maudlin mumbled helplessly about "poor oul' Parnell."[17]

But I shall claim that Joyce was aware of both the nothingness and the ferment, though he also laughed at much of the latter. Nevertheless, both peek out in his best work, most aptly perhaps in the Citizen in the "Cyclops" episode, or so I shall claim, but no less endearingly in the studied particulars of not only "Ivy Day in the Committee Room" but also the stories of childhood, youth, and maturity. Perhaps no story combines "seething Dublin" and period emptiness so deftly as "The Dead."

II

Young and old, Joyce the man reacted to Dublin in extremes— extreme disdain and extreme affection, sometimes both at once. We are all familiar with the furious outbursts, sometimes the ravings, in his letters. Who, for instance, can forget his avowed hatred of home and church in the famous 1904 letter to Nora?[18] His contempt for the writers in AE's anthology, *New Songs*, specifically George Roberts, led Joyce to break out with "O blind, snivelling, nose-dropping, calumniated Christ wherefore were these young men begotten?"[19] In the next year he castigated contemporary Irish literature as "ill-written, morally obtuse formless caricature."[20] And then another plea to Nora: "How sick, sick, sick I am of Dublin! It is the city of failure, of rancor and unhappiness. I long to be out of it."[21] At this point, Joyce could exclaim: "I loathe Ireland and the Irish."[22] Even in the thirties he feared returning to Dublin, thinking he might be shot.[23]

Though Joyce might condemn Dubliners as charlatans, windbags, whiners after Home Rule, lechers, and drunks who concluded most besotted evenings by "arsing along" home, he could also be quick to add that Ireland still furnished most of the brains of the United Kingdom and had fixed the imprimatur of her genius on its language.[24] Alessandro Francini Bruni remembered Joyce in his cups weeping over Ireland's wrongs yet scorning her at the same time—trying to drown *her* tears in "a river of eloquence."[25] Thus "the sorrow of the laughing Pagliacci," at least according to Bruni's bravura Italianate memory.[26] This double reaction that I have turned to—part, as I repeat, of Joyce's deep affection—may also be echoed in his impassioned words addressed to Nora in 1909: "One moment I see you like a virgin or madonna, the next moment I see you shameless, insolent, half-naked and obscene."[27]

Yet this also was the man who treasured Dublin newspapers, books, maps, and gossip from his friends. We know that he had read or owned such well-known accounts of Dublin city and county as those by D. A. Chart, F. Elrington Ball, John D'Alton, Charles Haliday, Walter Harris, W. J. FitzPatrick, probably West St John Joyce, and certainly *Thom's Directory* and its Dublin annals for 1904 and 1905. These materials may help underline John Eglinton's observation, borrowed from Stephen Dedalus, that "Dublin was of importance because it belonged to him [Joyce]."[28] As Richard Ellmann and others have reminded us, Joyce in Paris adorned the walls of his flat with pictures and sketches of old Dublin. His large rug presented a design based on the Liffey in all its twisted course. He once declared of Dublin: "For me it will always be the first city of the world."[29] Had he his choice, Joyce once admitted, he would rather be the burgermaster of a free city state like Dublin than be a king. He would be in genuine control with everything at his fingertips, precisely the role he assumed in re-creating the Dublin of his youth. Thus, on Shaw's receiving the Nobel Prize, Joyce congratulated him with the appellation "distinguished fellow townsman."[30] He felt that the Dublin of his youth, lacking much responsibility, possessed more real freedom than it did under the Free State.[31] Moreover, for him Dublin was a medieval city still where evil was not only recognized but was also acknowledged as the complement of good, as Joyce made clear in his medieval-modern *Ulysses* where among other combinations he juxtaposes Molly Bloom with the Virgin Mary.

Seventh city of Christendom, second city of the Empire, the very heart of Ireland, Dublin became the site for the two main problems that beset Joyce: "that of human behaviour and that of human environment."[32] Now, most of Joyce's delectable admissions apropos of his own city came later in life, came from exile, that breeder of the deepest communal affections, but also came, I submit, as revelations of a constant love from *Dubliners* on rather than of some gradual surface change. In Paris a reproduction of Vermeer's painting of Delft hung over Joyce's mantlepiece, characteristically, because it, too, celebrated a city.[33] As Joyce once answered Mrs Sheehy Skeffington, who was astonished at his near-maniacal pre-occupation with Dublin during his exile: "There was an English Queen who said that when she died the word 'Calais' would be written on her heart, 'Dublin' will be found on mine."[34] Something of the same attachment comes through in a remark Joyce made to Arthur Power: "For myself, I always write about Dublin, because if I can get to the heart of Dublin I can get to the heart of all the cities of the world."[35]

III

But now I must turn to Joyce's work, especially *Dubliners*, and to his brother's claim that it signals Joyce's real love for his city, the comprehending love of an artist for his subject—father and fatherland. Harry Levin has labeled Simon Dedalus "the embodiment of Dublin."[36] Joyce himself remarks that *Ulysses* was his father's and his father's friends' book. Given the originals of so many of the characters in *Dubliners*, Joyce might have said the same about that book. To Adolph Hoffmeister, however, he did confess:

Each of my books is a book about Dublin. Dublin is a city of scarcely three hundred thousand population, but it has become the universal city of my work. *Dubliners* was my last look at that city. Then I looked at the people around me. *Portrait* was the picture of my spiritual self. *Ulysses* transformed individual impressions and emotions to give them general significance. "Work in Progress" has a significance completely above reality; transcending humans, things, senses, and entering the realm of complete abstraction.[37]

But, as I shall claim, that first look at Dublin persisted, and in all of the seediness of its backstreets. As Joyce once admitted of himself, he had the mind of a grocer's assistant; in other words he knew where everything was and how to arrange it. In what may be an apocryphal story, Mahaffy is said to have read *Ulysses* only to conclude that such was the result of educating corner boys who spit in the Liffey. Joyce might have taken that for a high compliment.

To be sure, rancor enough displays its fearsome head in Joyce's early satirical poems, "The Holy Office" and "Gas from a Burner," just as indignation bursts out in nearly every sentence of the essay "The Day of the Rabblement." Essay and poems are clearly attacks on the Dublin literary establishment, in the end an attack on one of its more egregious practitioners, George Roberts.

A Portrait of the Artist is a related book and is consequently beyond the pale of my argument since the Dublin depicted is largely that of souls—so very many—hostile to the one soul, Stephen's. That dreaded page of Stephen's condemnation of family, nation, religion, and language—in the face of that sempiternal Irish innocent, Davin—the English-speaking world knows well enough. But even here it generally forgets Stephen's generous praise of the Jesuits who educated him, and then Stephen's passionate embrace of the Irish soil after the flesh-and-blood vision of his Irish muse, and this in the wake of his troubled journey to Cork that included the benefactions of his father's shaky cup and the glories of the College's medical hall. Even in one of the final diary entries that mirror Stephen's ultimate isolation at the end of the

Portrait, we are confronted with the humorous caricature of the Dubliner Mulrennan and even more so with the fact that Stephen refuses to fear Mulrennan's ancient detractor or even harm him. Let me turn, then, to *Dubliners*.

IV

First, despite Joyce's concentration on north-side Dublin, the stories frequently spill over with hints of the variegated life of the entire city and its environs. One example is "The Dead." The social presence of Monkstown, Kingstown, and Dalkey occasionally confounds the Morkan party in the stiff formality and sometimes the downright snobbery of Mary Jane, both in her music and in her arch remarks. No less, Gabriel's mental reservations about his fellow-partygoers, the heavy shuffling dancers, and not the least about his own aunts—two ignorant old women—probably stem from his haughty mother in Monkstown. In "After the Race" the elder Doyle, now a merchant prince, made his start in Kingstown; Farley's yacht is anchored there in the harbor; and of course Jimmy returns to be fleeced on that yacht. In one story or another, we discover ourselves in the relatively suburban Drumcondra, Ballsbridge, Sidney Parade, and as far out as the western suburb Chapelizod. All provide significant locales for, respectively, "Clay," "Araby," and "A Painful Case." Further mention of Skerries, Glasnevin, and the Phoenix Park provide keenly ironic qualifications for the pomposity of Mrs Kearney, Tom Kernan, and Grandfather Morkan. Much more might be said on the subject of Joyce's insinuation of a total Dublin, city and county, in these fifteen stories, but clearly the charge of his misrepresenting the real Dublin is thin.

More important for me is to establish that matter of his affection for his city as attested to by his brother. Victims of one kind of paralysis or another, shortsighted and disappointed as so many of the main characters in *Dubliners* are, Joyce nevertheless handles them with a sureness of grasp, even with a gingerly touch and command, that makes the famous phrase "scrupulous meanness" seem at certain moments virtually a term of endearment. For instance, the sisters Flynn, malapropisms, grammar, and all, are none the less victims of hopes that had brought them from Irishtown to Great Britain Street. What matter that they but dimly comprehend their sensitive brother's plight? At the end of "An Encounter," Joyce confronts the boy with a confused, aged pederast who still has a good accent, a remote literary sensibility, and a behavior that betokens a constraint, repression, or puritanism that has somehow turned him crazed in romantic Ireland. On the other hand, the truly charitable dead priest in "Araby" seems for some reason to have failed in his calling. Yet his books and the boy's for a moment are the same, perhaps a possible suggestion that both came to the same harsh realization that they were somehow double agents.

Eveline herself in the next story recognizes that recent kindness in her otherwise brutal father may possibly redeem him. If, then, she is seemingly reduced to something like a helpless, passive animal as she refuses her real savior, Frank, at the north Wall, her cry of anguish has what might be called a double might. I could continue to cite either wasted potential or smothered worth in characters like Little Chandler, Farrington, Maria, Joe Donnelly, Mr Duffy, Martin Cunningham, Joe Hynes, Freddy Malins and Julia Morkan, to name but a handful of victims, which Joyce resolutely presents in a steady light of pathos without a scintilla of malice. Even the more questionable creatures like Polly Mooney, Lenihan, and Mrs Kearney are not without our passing sympathy when we discover them suddenly alone and bewildered yet fraught with hope.

Finally, Joyce's detailed scrutiny of Dublin's topography and setting, no less his studied revelation of a Dubliner's gestures and responses both insinuate a genuine fascination with his city and a fond understanding of its derelictions, its native erring ways. Here I recall "An Encounter" with the ferry boat crossing the Liffey transporting the boys, some laborers, and a little Jew. That incongruity Joyce catches in the narrator's observation, "Once during the short voyage our eyes met and we laughed." In the same story, a tall man with green eyes sings out cheerfully to an amused crowd on the quays, "All right! All right!" as planks are discharged from a ship. Just as arresting are the lady who moves her full arm frequently yet gracefully for Farrington's benefit in "Counterparts"; the screwed up countenance meant to inspire trust offered by the hopeless Miss Beirne in "A Mother"; the curt salute to Jimmy Doyle from the railway porter in Kingstown; Lily's sharp retort to Gabriel in "The Dead"; the sight of the Protestant parishioners before St George's Church in the oppressively Catholic atmosphere of "The Boarding House"; and even the absurd religious conversation in "Grace"—all are proof of a vital life, however paltry and diminished, observed, recorded, and artistically rendered in exquisitely selected detail. Joyce's very idea of the epiphany—to be found in practically every story—testifies to his solicitude for the apparently trivial phrase that turns out to be so powerfully stocked with an arresting moment and penetrating light.

V

In *Ulysses* the city of Dublin, far from being the lonesome borough of American comment, became, as Joyce once said, something else: "I tried to give the colour and tone of Dublin with my words; the drab, yet glistening atmosphere of Dublin, its hallucinatory vapours, its tattered confusion, the atmosphere of its bars, its social immobility. . . ."[38] In other words, the degradations and exultations of a city.

Thus, that City of Dis, whom his fellow-exile Dante formulated, is not Joyce's Dublin. Rather, as Stephen acknowledged, while leading its pressmen to drink in the "Aeolus" episode, he had much to learn from them and the city, especially language and gesture. At that moment, Joyce ensured that Stephen's own parable of the plums be clever yet remain somewhat pointless, much like his earlier riddle for the schoolboys. Already in the "Proteus" episode Stephen had begun to come to terms with his city, himself, and his talent. Even something like healthy Dublin skepticism forces him to laugh at himself. And not for the last time in the novel. Nor the first, for Joyce, perhaps against his will, has Mulligan do it earlier and in a most malicious, witty Dublin fashion. Neither can we miss Joyce's delight in the carping glory of the Citizen of the "Cyclops" episode with its shameless narrator, a

Thersites with the voice of Joyce's father, or, for that matter, the reference to one of the minor gods of the book, Pisser Burke, of the cocked ear, an authority on the British Empire, Queen Victoria herself, and of course Mrs Riordan. If Dublin City appears to some no more than a mechanized body politic, Joyce has nevertheless also offered us the dear Father Conmee to lead us to the center of the "Wandering Rocks" episode from the start, though he, to be sure, intentionally overlooks that center—love—laughably. Perhaps no other episode testifies to the fond laughter of *Ulysses* as much as this one of the "Wandering Rocks" where Dubliners talk at odds with each other but leave us, in eye and memory, the whimsical impression of one of the last cities to combine comically Christ and Caesar in English. This certainly supersedes Henry James's Rome. Finally, if *Finnegans Wake* is never any one city in particular, it certainly includes a place to grow up absurd between Howth and Chapelizod. And the builder of that city in the twenties and thirties seems to have remained serenely unperturbed by 1916, the Anglo-Irish war, the Treaty, the emerging Free State, and the De Valera years, although they all get mentioned, usually comically and ploddingly. Love, not hate, subsumes such an exiled memory, for love makes even hatred comic between brother and brother, father and son, mother and daughter, and God knows whatever else goes on between any other couples in *Finnegans Wake*.

VI

But my conclusion must be tentative. My final impression of Joyce's work is that he saw himself as a citizen of a city of which he himself was a builder. So indeed, early in *Ulysses*, Stephen sees himself as at once part yet not part of fourteenth-century Dublin:

> Galleys of the Lochlanns ran here to beach, in quest of prey, their bloodbeaked prows riding low on a molten pewter surf. Dane Vikings, torcs of tomahawks aglitter on their breasts when Malachi wore the collar of gold. A school of turle hide whales stranded in hot noon,

spouting, hobbling in the shallows. Then from the starving cagework city a horde of jerkined dwarfs, my people, with flayers' knives, running, scaling, hacking in green blubbery whalemeat. Famine, plague and slaughter. Their blood is in me, their lusts my waves. I moved among them on the frozen Liffey, that I, among the spluttering resin fires. I spoke to no-one: none to me.

Precisely. But Joyce went Stephen one better, for he believed that one might reconstruct the Dublin of his day a thousand years later on the basis of *Ulysses*. That claim has been denied. But the spirit of it is right. Yearly most inveterate readers of Joyce attempt to reconstruct it—out of an undeniable if odd kind of joy that reading him brings. As Stanislaus once wrote in his *Diary*, "Dublin is an old, small, seaport Capital with a tradition. Yes, Dean Swift is the tradition."[39] I would substitute Joyce for Swift. An American critic has written of *Ulysses*: "The loneliness of its citizens is paralleled by an unperceived disintegration in all the aspects of Dublin life."[40] His example is the "Wandering Rocks" episode. Yet no episode is more highly integrated in the whole book and Dublin day. Like so much in Joyce, supposed disunity can reveal the highest unity, the greatest hatred the deepest love. Joyce's love and Joyce's scorn, then, are a blend, not mere contraries, and love more and more predominates. The resulting picture of Dublin emerges as personal, partial, distanced, objective, ancient and, as far as I can see, soon to be recognized as timeless. In the long run, one asks, has not Joyce done for Dublin what Yeats and the Revival have done for Ireland? If he has, the discovery has simply taken us a little longer to make.

NOTES: CONCLUSION

1 F. S. L. Lyons, "James Joyce's Dublin," *Twentieth Century Studies*, no. 4 (November 1970), pp. 6–25; J. C. C. Mays, "Some comments on the Dublin of *Ulysses*," in *Ulysses cinquante ans après*, ed. Louis Bennerot (Paris: Marcel Didier, 1974), pp. 83–98. Terence Brown, "Dublin in twentieth-century writing: metaphor and subject," *Irish University Review*, vol. 8, no. 1 (Spring 1978), pp. 7–21; and Thomas Kinsella, "The Irish writer," *Davis, Mangan, Ferguson?*,

ed. Roger McHugh (Dublin: Dolmen Press 1970), pp. 57–70.

2 Richard Ellmann, "An Irish European art," *Ireland of the Welcomes*, vol. 31, no. 3 (May–June 1982), p. 5; David Norris, "'Teems of times and happy returns': a celebration of James Joyce at 100," *Ireland Today* (Bulletin of The Department of Foreign Affairs), no. 985 (February 1982), p. 6.

3 Frank Budgen, *James Joyce and the Making of "Ulysses"* (Bloomington, Ind.: Indiana University Press, 1960), p. 71.

4 Stanislaus Joyce, *My Brother's Keeper* (London: Faber, 1958), p. 234.

5 E. MacDowell Cosgrave, *Dublin and Co. Dublin in the Twentieth Century* (Brighton/London: W. T. Pike, 1908), n.p.

6 Frances Gerard, *Picturesque Dublin Old and New* (London: Hutchinson, 1898), p. xi.

7 ibid., pp. 159–60.

8 ibid., p. xii.

9 Lyons, op. cit., p. 11. And see especially Joseph V. O'Brien, *"Dear, Dirty Dublin"* (Berkeley, Calif.: University of California Press, 1982), passim.

10 P. L. Dickinson, *The Dublin of Yesterday* (London: Methuen, 1929), p. 168.

11 Mary and Padraic Colum, *Our Friend James Joyce* (New York: Doubleday, 1958), p. 57.

12 W. B. Stanford and R. B. McDowell, *Mahaffy* (London: Routledge & Kegan Paul, 1971), passim.

13 Samuel A. Ossory FitzPatrick, *Dublin* (London: Methuen, 1907), p. 328.

14 ibid., p. 340.

15 D. A. Chart, *The Story of Dublin* (London: Dent, 1907), pp. 126–7.

16 John Harvey, *Dublin* (London: Batsford, 1949), p. 74.

17 Conor Cruise O'Brien (ed.), *The Shaping of Modern Ireland* (London: Routledge & Kegan Paul, 1960), p. 13.

18 *Letters of James Joyce*, ed. Richard Ellmann (New York: Viking Press, 1966), Vol. 2, pp. 48–50.

19 ibid., p. 51.

20 ibid., p. 70.

21 ibid., p. 163.

22 ibid., p. 174.

23 Arthur Power, *Conversations with James Joyce* (New York: Harper & Row, 1974), p. 43.

24 Alessandro Francini Bruni, "Joyce stripped naked in the Piazza," in *Portraits of the Artist in Exile*, ed. Willard Potts (Seattle, Wash./London: University of Washington Press, 1979), p. 28.

25 ibid., p. 33.

Conclusion

26 Alessandro Francini Bruni, "Recollections of Joyce," in *Portraits of the Artist in Exile*, ed. Willard Potts (Seattle, Wash./London: University of Washington Press, 1979), p. 41.
27 *Selected Letters*, pp. 166–7.
28 Robert Scholes and Richard M. Kain (eds), *The Workshop of Daedalus* (Evanston, Ill.: Northwestern University Press, 1965), p. 203.
29 Jacques Mercanton, "The hours of James Joyce," in *Portraits of the Artist in Exile*, ed. Willard Potts (Seattle, Wash./London: University of Washington Press, 1979), p. 220.
30 *Selected Letters*, p. 318.
31 Power, op. cit., p. 65.
32 ibid., p. 50.
33 ibid., p. 103.
34 Scholes and Kain, op. cit., p. 180.
35 Richard Ellmann, *James Joyce*, rev. edn (New York/Oxford/Toronto: Oxford University Press, 1982), p. 505.
36 Harry Levin, *James Joyce* (London: Faber, 1944), p. 43.
37 Adolf Hoffmeister, "Portrait of Joyce," *Portraits of the Artist in Exile*, ed. Willard Potts (Seattle, Wash./London: University of Washington Press, 1979), p. 132.
38 Power, op. cit., p. 98.
39 *The Complete Dublin Diary of Stanislaus Joyce*, ed. George H. Healey (Ithaca, NY/London: Cornell University Press 1971), p. 73.
40 Douglas Knight, "The reading of *Ulysses*," *Journal of English Literary History*, vol. 19, no. 1 (March 1952), p. 76.

Index

Abbot, The (Scott) 6, 54
Abiff, Hiram 27
Adam and Eve's Church 112–13, 115
Adversaria Hibernica 127
AE 131–2, 137–8; *A Celtic Christmas* 131, 136; *New Songs* 3, 133–8, 263
"After the Race" 8, 10, 77–90, 161, 267, 269; betrayal/self-betrayal 83–5; Doyle senior 10–11, 77, 80, 85, 87, 267; Jimmy Doyle 8, 10–11, 77, 79–88, 267
alchemy 25–6
Alton, John D' 16; *History of the County Dublin* 39, 264
Angel Guardians of Galway 245
Annesley, Lord (Viscount Glerawley) 40
Annesley House 115
Annunciation in "The Boarding House" 10, 114, 116–17, 122
Aoife 9, 69
"Araby" 31, 52–67, 267–8; the boy 5–6, 13–14, 31, 52–3, 55–6, 60–2, 200; dead priest's books 4–6, 52–6, 268; double agents 6, 31, 52–6, 62, 268
As I Was Going Down Sackville Street 129
Ascendancy, Protestant 4, 91–4, 98, 100–1, 103, 105–6, 115, 153, 156, 258
Asolando (Browning) 3, 234, 236
Association for the Prevention of Mendicity 243

"Background of 'The Dead', The" (Ellmann) 224, 226, 228, 250
"Background to *Dubliners*, The" (S. Joyce) 223–5
Bagenal, Mabel 160

Baggot Street 97–8, 102, 104–5
Baker, Joseph E. 205, 207
Baker, Rev Pacificus (Father Bernard Baker) 6; *the Devout Communicant* 6, 54
Balfe, Michael William; "I Dreamt" 150, 156, 158, 161
Ball, F. Elrington 16; *A History of the County of Dublin* 98, 242, 264
"Ballad of Joking Jesus, The" (Joyce-Gogarty) 113
Ballinamuck 81–2, 84
Ballsbridge 151, 153, 267
Barataria 99
Barrington, Sir Jonah 102
Beaux's Walk 98
Beck, Warren 151, 188, 206
Beggar's Bush Barracks 5, 146–7
Behan, Brendan 153–4
"Believe Me if All Those Endearing Young Charms" (Moore) 118
"Bells of Shandon, The" (Mahony) 119
Benstock, Bernard 19
Beresford, John 40
Bernhardt, Sarah 189, 201
betrayal 4; "After the Race" 83–5; "An Encounter" 37; "Ivy Day in the Committee Room" 13; "A Mother" 188; "Two Gallants" 91–3, 96, 100–1, 103
Black Eagle pub 179–81, 186
Black Pig, the 161–2
Blake, Anne 95
Blotner, Joseph 10, 176
"Boarding House, The" 6, 12, 109–24, 269; Annunciation 10, 114, 116–17, 122; Crucifixion 10, 109–13, 117, 122, 142; Bob Doran 10, 13–14, 109–16, 120–2; Mrs

274

Mooney 6, 10, 14, 109–13, 115–16, 120–2; Polly Mooney 6, 10, 14, 109–22, 268

"Body of the Father Christian Rosencrux, The" (Yeats) 2, 23–4, 27, 30, 32, 228, 251–2

Bohemian Girl, The 73, 159–60, 238

Boromean Tribute 11, 87–8

Boru, Brian 7, 40

Bowen, Elizabeth 101

Bowen, Professor Zack 77, 80, 121

boy, the: "Araby" 5–6, 13–14, 31, 52–3, 55–6, 60–2, 220; "The Dead" 3, 13, 31, 228, 252; "An Encounter" 7, 13, 36–7, 44–5, 47–9, 220; "The Sisters" 2, 6, 13, 19, 22–3, 25–31, 220, 228, 251–2

Boyle, Rev Father Robert 91–2, 134, 205, 207

Boyne, Battle of the 6, 92, 96, 230, 240

Brabazon family 97

Bronson, Mrs Arthur 234

Brown, Terence 258–9

Browning, Robert 233–6; *Asolando* 3, 234, 236; "Epilogue" 3, 234–5; "A Pearl, a Girl" 235–6; *The Poetical Works of RB* 234

Bruni, Alessandro Francini 264

Budgen, Frank 17, 259

Burgo family, De 193–5

Burke, Father Tom 212–14

Burke family 193–4

Butler family 38, 45, 194

Byrne, Captain 81, 84

Byron, George Gordon Lord 125, 130–1, 138–9; "On the Death of a Young Lady" 125, 130, 138–9; *The Prisoner of Chillon* 3, 125–6, 130, 139

"Call, The" (Roberts) 135

Campbell, Mrs Patrick 189, 192, 201

Caoilte 184, 192

Capel, Arthur (Earl of Essex) 103, 127

Capel Street 103–4, 128

Case of Wagner, The (Nietzche) 173

Cathleen Ni Houlihan (Yeats) 188, 202

Catholic Emancipation (1829) 6, 21, 37, 92, 99, 115, 121

Catholic Encyclopedia 117

Cauldron of Dagda 61

Cavandish, Sir Henry 93

Caves du Vatican Les (Gide) 22

Celtic Christmas, A 131, 136

Celtic Twilight 3, 125, 131, 135

Chapelizod 5, 165–7, 173–4, 267

Charitable Infirmary in Cook Street 56

Charlemont, Lord 95, 160

Chart, D. A. 229, 262, 264

Children of Lir 9, 69

Christ: "The Boarding House" 109–14, 116; "Clay" 170; "Counterparts" 142–4, 147; "Eveline" 72–5; "Grace" 217–18; "Ivy Day in the Committee Room" 11, 176; "The Sisters" 19; *see also* crucifixion

Christian Brothers Schools 55, 65, 66n, 177

Cistercians 243–5, 247

City Hall 104, 181

City of Dublin Hospital 173

"Clay" 8, 150–64, 267; Joe Donnelly 151, 156–60, 162, 268; Maria 8, 150–63, 168; neighbour girls 8, 151, 157–8, 162

Clontarf, battle of 7, 39–40

Colloquy of the Old Men 186, 250

Colombière, Father Claude de la 71, 73

Colooney, battle of 82

Colum, Padraic 136, 262; "A Drover" 137

Conaire, King 9, 31, 225, 227, 229, 231

Conference on the University Question 225, 254n

Connolly, Thomas 168; "Joyce's 'Three Sisters': a pennyworth of snuff" 19; "Marriage divination in Joyce's 'Clay'" 157

Conyngham, Rt Hon. William Burton 93

Coote, Sir Charles 41

Corless's 126, 133

Cornwallis, General 81

Cosgrave, Dillon 16, 161

Cosgrave, E. McDowel 260–1

Cosgrave, William 129

"Counterparts" 4, 13, 141–9;
  curcifixion 5, 142–4, 146–8;
  Farrington 4–5, 13–15, 141–7,
  268–9; heaven and hell 4–5,
  141–5, 147; Six Sins against the
  Holy Ghost 145–6
Countess Cathleen, The 188
Craig, Maurice 104
Cromwell, Henry 43
Cromwell, Oliver 7, 36, 43, 45, 47
crucifixion: "The Boarding House" 10,
  109–13, 117, 122, 142;
  "Counterparts" 5, 142–4, 146–8;
  "The Dead" 250; "Ivy Day in the
  Committee Room" 176
"Crucifixion in 'The Boarding House',
  The" (Rosenberg) 109–11
Cuchulain 69, 192

Daly's Club 4, 92–3
Dame Street 97, 104
Dance of Death, The (Holbein) 226, 237
Dante, Alighieri: *The Divine Comedy*
  205–11, 217–18, 220, 269
"Dark Rosaleen" (Mangan) 63
Davies, Miss Tiefy 238
"Day of the Rabblement, The" 201,
  266
"Dead, The" 1, 3, 9, 18, 31, 161,
  223–57, 263, 267, 269; Mr Browne
  226, 230–2, 236–9, 241, 244;
  Gabriel Conroy 3, 14, 31–2,
  225–42, 244–5, 247–53, 267;
  Michael Furey 32, 224, 235,
  239–42, 245–7, 250–1, 253; Gretta
  31, 226–7, 232, 235, 238–42, 245,
  250; "The Lass of Aughrim" 224,
  227, 235, 238–41, 245; Freddy
  Malins 226, 231–2, 236, 238,
  242–3, 248, 268; Morkan family
  228–30, 236–7, 239, 252–3, 267–8;
  West of Ireland 16, 31, 161,
  223–4, 226–7, 232, 240–1, 246–7
Deese, William 101–2
"Destruction of Da Derga's Hostel,
  The" 9, 225, 231
determinism 14–15
Devlin, Anne 198
Devout Communicant, The (Baker) 6, 54

Dickinson, P. L. 262
Dictionary of National Biography 54,
  213–14, 216, 218
Dillon, John 38
Divin Comedy, The (Dante) 205–11,
  217–18, 220, 269
Dodder, River 7, 31, 43, 45–7, 161
Donnybrook 97–8
Dorset Street 97
double agents in "Araby" 6, 31, 52–6,
  62, 268
drink/drinking habits 15;
  "Counterparts" 145; "Grace"
  205–7, 209–10, 212–14, 216–17,
  220; "Ivy Day in the Committee
  Room" 179–80, 182
"Drover, A" (Colum) 137
Drumcondra 151, 153, 160–1, 267
Dublin 260–3; Joyce's feelings
  towards 258–60, 263–71
"Dublin annals" 16
Dublin Bucks 93, 95, 104, 106
Dublin by Lamplight 152, 156, 160
Dublin Opinon 93
Dun Laoghaire 10–11, 84, 86, 88, 161

Earl Street 97
"Earth and the Infinite" (Roberts)
  134–5
Edward VII 38, 97, 105, 180–1, 233,
  262
Egan MP, John 99–100
Eire Abu Society 189, 191, 199, 201
Eire-Banba-Fodla 198–9, 228–9
Elliott, G. H. 225, 231–2, 254n
Ellmann, Richard 94, 118, 125, 188,
  258–9, 264; "The background of
  'The Dead' " 224, 226, 228, 250
Ely Place 98–9, 105
Emmet, Robert 6, 21, 43, 101, 183, 198
"Encounter, An" 7, 15, 30–1, 36–51,
  52, 161, 268; the boy 36–7, 44–5,
  47–9
England/English: "After the Race" 8,
  11, 77–9, 81, 83–8; "Araby" 62–4;
  "Clay" 8, 154–6, 158, 161;
  "Counterparts" 141, 144; "The
  Dead" 233; "An Encounter" 37–8,
  40, 43, 48; "Grace" 214; "Ivy Day

in the Committee Room" 11, 183,
186; "A Little Cloud" 129, 138; "A
Mother" 194–5; "Two Gallants"
4, 92–3, 99–105
English, Buck 93
epiphanies 1, 13, 29, 62, 116, 147, 193,
253, 269
"Epilogue" (Browning) 3, 234–5
Europa qiovane, L' (Ferrero) 94
Eustace, Sir Maurice 147
Eve/Eva 9, 68–9, 121
"Eveleen's Bower" (Moore) 73
"Eveline" 9, 12, 68–76; Eveline 9,
12–13, 68–75, 268; Frank 9, 12–13,
68, 73–5, 268
"Evening Bells, a Petersburg Air"
(Moore) 119

Fane, John (tenth Earl of
Westmoreland) 104
Farman, Henri 78
Fates, the Three 28–30, 228–9
Feast of the Epiphany (day of Old
Christmas) 31, 224
Feast of the Most Precious Blood 6,
21, 25–6
Feeley, John 234
Feis Tigh Chonain (O'Kearney) 197
Fenians 11, 177–8, 182–3, 262
"Fenianism" (Joyce) 183, 201
Ferrero, Guiglielmo: *L'Europa giovane*
94
Fianna 11, 183–6
Fifteen Acres 233
Finn 11, 183–4, 192, 250
Finnegans Wake 17, 153, 247, 270
FitzGerald family 38, 194; Lord
Edward F. 102–3, 243; Silken
Thomas F. 41, 195
Fitzgibbon, John "Black Jack" (Earl of
Clare) 99, 101–2
Fitzmaurice, Hon Thomas 101
Fitz-Patrick, Samuel 262
Fitzroy, Henry (first Duke of Grafton)
103
Fitzwilliam family 99, 102
Fournier, Henri 78
France/French 8, 11, 40, 77–81, 83–8
Freeman's Journal 21, 96, 100, 136–7,

188, 191, 193, 196, 201, 215–17
Freemasonry 22, 26–7, 29, 56, 61–2,
177–8

G or Detective Division 106, 108n
Gabhra, battle of 183
Gabriel, M. 78
Gaelic League 232
Gallaher, Fred 125, 128–30; *Our Irish
Jockeys* 128–9
Gandon, James 126
Garrison, the 91, 93, 106
"Gas from a Burner" 132, 266
George III 96, 105
George IV 84, 102, 105
George's Street 106, 170
Georgian Society Records 102
Gerard, Frances: *Picturesque Dublin*
261
Gibbon, Edward 6, 54
Gide, André: *Les Caves du Vatican* 22
Gilbert, John T. 17; *History of Dublin*
1, 16
Ginkel, General de 43
gnomon 18–19, 27–8
Gogarty, Buck 125, 128–30, 132,
137–8; *As I Was Going Down
Sackville Street* 129; "The Ballad of
Joking Jesus" 113; *Secret Springs of
Dublin Song* 138
Gonne, Maud 88, 90n
Gordon-Bennett Cup Race 8, 77–8
Gore-Booth, Eva 136
"Grace" 10, 205–22, 262, 269; business
failure 205–7, 209–13, 217, 220;
concept of grace 206–11, 220;
drink 205–7, 209–10, 212–14,
216–17, 220; Tom Kernan 205,
207–12, 215, 217–19, 267;
perfunctory religious observance
205–7, 210–13, 217, 220
Grafton Street, 101, 103–4
Gray, Edmund Dwyer 211–12, 216
Gray, Sir John 211–12, 215–16
"Gray Rock, The" (Yeats) 192
Great Britain Street 22, 268
Gregory family 92, 228
Griffiths, Arthur: *The Resurrection of
Hungary* 77, 86, 190, 200

Halfpenny Marvel 37–8
Haliday, Charles: *The Scandinavian
  Kingdom of Dublin* 7, 45–7, 264
Halper, Nathan 118
Hardwicke Street 115, 118, 121, 122n
Harmon, Maurice 125
Hart, Father Charles: *The Student's
  Catholic Doctrine* 145
Hassett, Thomas Henry 43
Hauptmann 166, 168
hell: "Counterparts" 4–5, 141–5, 147;
  "Grace" 206–7
Hell-Fire Club 92, 97
Henrietta Street 126–7, 139n
Herbert, Sidney 170
Hibernian Bank 97
Higgins, Francis (the Sham Squire)
  92, 100, 103, 207
History of Dublin (Gilbert) 1, 16
*History of Ireland in the Eighteenth
  Century, A* (Lecky) 81
History of the County Dublin (D'Alton)
  39, 264
History of the County of Dublin, A (Ball)
  98, 242, 264
History of the Irish Rebellion in 1798
  (Maxwell) 81
HMS Pinafore 73
Hoffmeister, Adolf 1, 265
Holbein: *The Dance of Death* 226, 237
Holloway 188–9
"Holy Office, The" 266
"Home Rule Comes of Age" 176
Humbert, General 8, 81–3
Hume, Gustavus 98–9
Hume Street 4, 98
Hungary 77, 82, 85–7, 200
Hutchinson, General 81
Huxley, Thomas 21

"I Dreamt" (Balfe) 150, 156, 158, 161
Ibsen, Henrick 2; *Ghosts* 20; *Master
  Builder* 27
imagination 2–3, 23–5, 30–2, 251–3
Inchanagoill 247
Ireland/Irish 1–4, 7, 9, 12, 15–16,
  259–60, 264; "After the Race" 8,
  77–81, 83–5, 87–8; "Araby" 6, 60,
  62–5; "The Boarding House" 110,

121; "Clay" 8, 154–5, 158, 161;
  "Counterparts" 141, 147; "The
  Dead" 16, 31–2, 38, 121, 161,
  193–4, 196, 223–4, 226–7, 232,
  240–1, 246–7; "An Encounter" 7,
  36–49; "Eveline" 9, 68–9, 73, 75;
  "Grace" 213–16, 218; "Ivy Day in
  the Committee Room" 11,
  176–87; "A Mother" 189–90,
  198–201; "The Sisters" 6, 20–3;
  "Two Gallants" 4, 91–3, 96, 105
"Ireland, Island of Saints and Sages"
  37
Irish College in Rome 22
Irish Fairy and Folk Tales (Yeats) 197
"Irish history and mythology in
  James Joyce's 'The Dead' "
  (Kelleher) 9, 31, 224–7, 229,
  239–40
Irish Homestead 28, 86
Irish Literary Revival 2–3, 30, 188–92,
  251, 253, 271
Irish Names and Surnames (Woulfe) 16,
  138, 190, 231
"Irish National Literature, III" (Yeats)
  24, 251
Irish Republic Brotherhood 43
Irish Times 57, 78, 238
Irishtown 22, 32, 43, 228, 268
Isolde's font 166–7
Isolde's Fort 166–7, 172, 174
Isolde's Lane 167
Isolde's tower 5, 166–7, 174
"Ivy Day in the Committee Room"
  11–12, 176–87, 262–3; Joe Hynes
  13, 177–81, 183–4, 186, 268;
  Phoenix Flame 11–12, 177–9,
  183–4, 186; Tierney 11, 178–82,
  184, 186

Jackson, Robert Sumner 219
James II 6, 21, 43, 71, 103
Jebb, Frederick 95–6
Jenatzy, Camille 78
Jervis Street Hospital 55–6, 58, 60
Johnston, Francis 118–19
Joseph: "The Boarding House"
  113–16; "A Little Cloud" 134;
  Ulysses 10

Joyce, P. W. 237
Joyce, Stanislaus 16, 20, 43–4, 131,
    166, 188, 218, 259–60, 265, 267,
    271; "The background to
    Dubliners" 223–5
Joyce, Weston St John 16, 264
"Joyce's 'Three Sisters': a pennyworth
    of snuff" (Connolly) 19
"Joyce's use of memory in 'A
    Mother' " (O'Neill) 188–9
Juno and the Paycock 159

Kain, Richard 18, 206, 258
"Kathleen Ny-Houlahan" (Mangan)
    63, 198, 202–3, 241
Kelleher, Professor John V. 22; "Irish
    history and mythology in James
    Joyce's 'The Dead' " 9, 31, 224–7,
    229, 239–40
Kennedy, Olive 188
Kenner, Hugh 18
Keohler, Thomas 136
Kerry House 101
Kerwan, Richard 95
Kickham, Charles 182
Kildare Street 96–7
Kildare Street Club 4, 92–3, 97, 105–6
King James Mint-House 103
King's Inns 126–7, 132–3
Kingsbridge 5
Kingstown 5, 10–11, 83–6, 88, 262, 267
Kinsella, Thomas 258–9
Knights of St John 32, 41, 242
Knights Templars 25, 242
Knyff, Rene the chevalier de 78

Lake, General 81
Lalla Rookh (Moore) 59
Laoghaire, King 10–11, 87–8, 248, 250
Lawless, Buck 93
Lecky, W. E. H.: *A History of Ireland in
    the Eighteenth Century* 81
Leinster House 102
Leo XIII, Pope 38, 212, 215, 233
leprechauns 197
Levin, Harry 265
Liffey, River 5, 7, 31, 39, 41, 45–6,
    119–20, 161; Liffey Ferry Service
    41

"Little Cloud, A" 12, 125–40; Little
    Chandler 3, 13–14, 125–8, 130–6,
    138–9, 268; Ignatius Gallaher
    125–6, 128–30, 134–6, 138–9
" 'Little Cloud, A' Joyce's portrait of
    the would-be artist" (Ruoff) 125,
    136, 138
Lives of the United Irishmen (Madden)
    101–2
Loftus family 99
lords-lieutenant 38, 43, 56, 58, 62, 94,
    96, 99, 103–5, 121, 127
Loyola, Ignatius 125, 130; *Spiritual
    Exercises* 130
Luby, Thomas 182
Lucas's coffee-house 104
Lugnaedon Stone 247
Luttrell, General Henry Lawes 95
Lyons, F. S. L. 176, 258
Lytton, Lord 37, 44

MacLysaght, Edward 132, 190, 198
MacMurrough, Dermot (King of
    Leinster) 69, 91, 160
Madden, Dr: *Lives of the United
    Irishmen* 101–2
Magalaner, Marvin 18, 70, 93, 172
Magazine Fort 166, 172
Magazine Hill 5, 167, 172
Mahony, Francis (Father Prout): "The
    Bells of Shandon" 119
Malone family 138
Mangan, James Clarence: "Dark
    Rosaleen" 63; "Kathleen
    Ny-Houlahan" 63
Manners, Charles (Fourth Duke of
    Rutland) 94–5
Manuo 111, 113
Margaret Mary Alacoque, Blessed
    9–10, 12, 69–74
Maritana 189, 193, 238
Marlborough Street 6, 115–16, 120
marriage, Irish forced 10, 109–11, 116
"Marriage divination in Joyce's
    'Clay' " (Connolly) 157
Martindale, C. C. 219
Mary Magdalene 109, 121
Master Builder (Ibsen) 27
"Maternal Night" (Roberts) 131

Maynooth Catechism 145, 168

Mays, J. C. C. 258

Maxwell, W. H.: *History of the Irish Rebellion in 1798* 81

McCormack, John 188, 192

McHale, Archbishop John (MacHale) 212–14, 216

Meadow of the Swine 160–1

Meath, Earl of 97

Memoirs of Vidocq, The 53

Merrion Square 100, 102–3

Merrion Street 102, 104

Mignon 225, 238

Milligan, Alice 136

Mitchell, Susan 136

Modest Proposal, A (Swift) 155

Moira, Lord 243

Moira House 243

Monkstown 229, 242, 248, 267; M. Castle 242

Montbazan, Duchess of 244–5

Moore, George 261–2

Moore, Tom 37, 44, 92, 223; "Believe Me if All Those Endearing Young Charms" 118; "Evening Bells, a Petersburg Air" 119; *Lalla Rookh* 59; "O'Donoghue's Mistress" 240; "Oh, Ye Dead" 223–4, 240

Mosse, Bartholomew 95

"Mother, A" 3, 14, 188–204, 217, 228, 262, 269; Holohan 3, 14, 189–92, 196, 199–200; Kathleen Kearney 3, 188–9, 191, 196, 198–200; Mrs Kearney 14, 188, 190–3, 198–200, 202, 267–8; O'Madden Burke 13–14, 189–90, 192, 193–6, 199, 202

Motoring Illustrated 79

Mount Melleray 32, 231, 242–5

"Mountain Tomb, The" (Yeats) 3, 251

Mud Island 40, 111

Mulligan, Buck 129, 130

Mystical Marriage, concept of 117

names, personal 9, 16, 48–9, 60, 68–9, 110, 112–13, 130, 132, 134, 138, 141, 146, 149n, 162, 166, 190–1, 193–6, 226–7, 230–1, 235–6, 242, 248

Napper Tandy demonstration 90n

Nassau Street 96

"Nation" tradition 136–7

New Encyclopaedia of Freemasonry, A (Waite) 61

New Songs (ed. AE) 3, 133–8, 263

Newcomen's Bridge 39–40

Newman, F. X. 205, 207

Niall of the Nine Hostages 10–11, 87–8

Niemeyer, Carl 205, 207, 217–18

Nietzche, Friedrich 166, 170–1, 173; *The Case of Wagner* 173

Noon SJ, William T. 218

North, W. S. 59

North Strand Road 7, 39–40, 111

Nun's Island 245

Nuptial Mass 110–12, 114, 116

O'Brien, Conor Cruise 176; *The Shaping of Modern Ireland* 263

O'Casey, Sean 261

O'Connell, Daniel 40, 116, 215

O'Connell Schools 55, 65, 66n

O'Connor, Ulick 129

"O'Donoghue's Mistress" (Moore) 240

O'Leary, John 182–3, 262

O'Madden family 193–5

O'Mahony, John 182

O'Malley, Grace 82

O'Malley, Professor Glenn 52

O'Neill, Hugh (Earl of Tyrone) 160

O'Neill, Michael J.: "Joyce's use of memory in 'A Mother' " 188–9

O'Sullivan, Seumas 136–7; "The Twilight People" 137

"Oh, Ye Dead" (Moore) 223–4, 240

Oisin 183–4, 186, 250–1

"On the Death of a Young Lady" (Byron) 125, 130, 138–9

Order of the Sacred Heart 9, 12, 70–3, 75, 196–7

Ormond Quay 197

Ormond family 38

Oscar 183–4, 186

Oughterard 32, 246–7, 249–50

Oxford Dictionary of English Christian Names 69

"Painful Case, A" 13, 165–75, 257; Mr
  Duffy 5, 13, 165–74, 268; Mrs
  Sinico 5, 15, 165, 167, 169–73
Paracelsus 25
paralysis 1–3, 7, 9, 14, 18–20, 28–30,
  52, 75, 141, 188, 190, 226, 250,
  263, 267
paresis 20
Parnell, Charles Stewart 11, 38, 63,
  103, 176–84, 186, 216, 263
Peacocke, Canon 119–20, 123n–124n
"Pearl, a Girl, A" (Browning) 235–6
Pearse, P. H. 63
Pélléas and Mélisande (Maeterlinck)
  189, 201–2
Petty, Sir William 147
Phoenix Flame 11–12, 177–9, 183–4,
  186
Phoenix Park 166, 169, 172, 229–30,
  232–3, 236, 242, 261–2, 267;
  Phoenix Pillar of 178–9
Phoenix Park Distillery 167, 171
Picturesque Dublin (Gerard) 261
Pidgeon, John 36, 42
Pigeon House 7, 15, 25, 36, 39, 42–3,
  46, 81
Pillar, Nelson's 151, 153, 156, 160
Pim's department store 97
Pius IX, Pope 212–14
Pius XII, Pope 113
Plato's *Republic* 28
Pluck 37
pooka 152, 154, 161
Poor Clares of Nun's Island 32, 245–7
Portrait of the Artist as a Young Man 9,
  27, 30, 46, 100, 121, 266–7
Power, Pat 94
Prisoner of Chillon, The (Byron) 3,
  125–6, 130, 139
"Prisoner of Love, The" (Roberts) 3,
  133
Pro-Cathedral, Marlborough Street 6,
  115–16, 120–1
Protestant Church/Protestants 38, 40,
  141, 154–6, 161, 211–12, 233, 240;
  see also Ascendancy, Protestant
Prout, Father (Francis Mahony): "The
  Bells of Shandon" 119
Providence 18, 28, 220

Puckstown 161
puritanism 7, 45, 47, 268

Races of Castlebar 8, 80–3
Rancé, Armand-Jean de 244–5
Rathmines, battle of 43
"Red Hanrahan's Song about Ireland"
  (Yeats) 3, 200
Reynolds, Thomas 102
Richards, Grant 1, 112
Ringsend 36, 39, 42–3, 45–6
Roberts, George 3, 125, 131–3, 136,
  138, 263, 266; "The Call" 135;
  "Earth and the Infinite" 134–5;
  "Maternal Night" 131; "The
  Prisoner of Love" 3, 133
Roche, Captain Philip 41
Roche, Tiger 94
Roman Catholic Church 6–7, 18, 21,
  27, 36–8, 40, 45, 54, 56, 115–16,
  120, 141, 145–6, 150, 155–6,
  171–2, 210–11
Romanticism in literature 125, 131
Rosa Alchemica (Yeats) 26
Rosenberg, Bruce A.: "The crucifixion
  in 'The Boarding House' " 109–11
Rosicrucians 18–19, 23, 25–9
Rossa, Jeremiah O'Donovan 63–5, 182
Rosycross, Father 25–6, 30–1
Rotunda Hospital 95
Rowan, Hamilton 101
Royal College of Surgeons 101–2
Royal Exchange 104, 181
Royal Irish Constabulary office 209,
  211–12
Ruoff, James: " 'A Little Cloud':
  Joyce's portrait of the would-be
  artist" 125, 136, 138
Rutland Square 4, 94–5, 100–1, 103
Ryan, Thomas 128–9

Sackville, Lionel Cranfield (first Duke
  of Dorset) 96
Sackville, Lord George 96
Sackville Street 96, 103
St Catherine 32
St Catherine's Church, Meath Street
  6, 21
St Francis de Sales 70, 73

St Francis Xavier 37
St George's Church 109, 118–20, 123n–124n
St Michael 247
St Patrick 87, 183, 186, 190–1, 236, 247–50; *Confession* 249
St Stephen's Green 94, 98, 100–1, 104–5
St Thomas Aquinas 218
Samhain 8–9, 151–2, 157, 160–3
Sayers, Dorothy L. 210–11
Scandinavian Kingdom of Dublin, The (Haliday) 7, 45–7, 264
Scholes, Robert 121
Scotland 154–5, 158
Scott, John (Earl of Clonmel) 92, 94, 100
Scott, Sir Walter 37, 44; *The Abbot* 6, 54
Secret Springs of Dublin Song 138
Senchus Mor 11, 87
Senn, Fritz 36, 45
"Shade of Parnell, The" 176
Shan Van Vocht 150–1, 157, 190
Shaping of Modern Ireland, The (O'Brien) 263
Shelbourne Hotel 4, 100–1
Short, Clarice 125
Shovel, Sir Cloudesley 43
Sidney, Sir Philip 170
Sidney Parade 170, 267
Simon Magus 27, 35n
simony 18–19, 27–8, 35n
Sinn Fein 190, 200–1
Sirr, Major 102, 104, 182
"Sisters, The" 2, 14–15, 18–35, 52, 178, 251; the boy 2, 6, 13, 19, 22–3, 25–31, 220, 228, 251–2; death-notice 4, 6, 21–2, 29; Father Flynn 2, 6, 13, 14–15, 18–23, 25–32, 35n, 220, 251–2
Skeat's *Etymological Dictionary* 135
South Circular 97–8
South George's Street 5
Spiritual Exercises (Loyola) 130
Sport 128
Sportsman 128
Spring Gardens 111–12
Stein, Professor W. B. 141

Stephen Hero 86
Stephens, James 182
Stern, Frederick C. 176
Stewart, George 102
Steyne, the 45–7
Stone, Harry 52
Stonybatter 229, 248
Story of the Injured Lady, The (Swift) 151, 154–5, 157
Student's Catholic Doctrine, The (Hart) 145
Sweetman, John 121
Swift, Jonathan 154, 271; *A Modest Proposal* 155; *The Story of the Injured Lady* 151, 154–5, 157
Synge, J. M. 133

Tandy, Napper 90n, 101
Tara Brooch 232, 236, 248
Teeling, Captain Bernard 81–4
Thing 46–7
Thingmote (Thingmount) 7, 46; T. of Dublin 46
Thomas Street 21
Thom's Directory 39, 97, 170, 264
Tindall, William York 18–19, 151
titles, meaning of 6–7, 13, 18, 20, 78, 85, 88, 121–2, 150
Tolstoy, Leo 2
Tone, Matthew 83
Tone, Wolfe 43, 77, 84, 101
Touche, David La 93
"Tower, The" (Yeats) 194
Trinity College 101, 262
Tristan and Isolde legend 5, 165–75
Tuathal, King 11, 87–8
Turgenev: *Sketches* 2
"Twlight People, The" (O'Sullivan) 137
"Two Gallants" 91–108; betrayal 91–3, 96, 100–1, 103; Corley 4, 13–14, 91–100, 102, 104–6; Lenehan 4, 91–3, 95–7, 100–6, 196, 268

Ulysses 4, 6, 9–10, 13, 16–17, 27, 30, 37, 100, 106, 130, 151, 170, 176, 191, 195, 200, 207, 226, 258–9, 265–6, 269–71; "Cyclops" section 111–14, 154, 263, 269–70

Union Jack 37
"United Irishman, The" 136
United Irishmen, 43, 82, 101–2, 262
United States of America 85–6
Upper Sheriff Street 40
Usher's Island 32, 229, 242–3, 248

"Valley of the Black Pig, The" (Yeats)
    161–2
Vaughan, Father Bernard 217–20
Vélo 79
Vidocq, François Eugene 6, 53; *The
    Memoirs of Vidocq* 53
Vikings 7, 36, 39, 41, 45–8
"Villanelle of the Temptress, The" 121
Virgin Mary: "Araby" 6; "The
    Boarding House" 10, 114–16, 121;
    "Clay" 150; "Counterparts" 143–4
Visitation convent, Paray le Monial
    70–1
Vitriol Works 36, 39–41
Volunteers 95, 230

W. & H. M. Goulding Ltd. 39
Wagner, Richard 165–7, 169, 171, 173
Waisbren MD, Burton A. 20
Waite, Arthur Edward: *A New
    Encyclopaedia of Freemasonry* 61
Walzl, Professor Florence L. 19–20,
    91–2
Wanderings of Oisin, The (Yeats) 186
Well of the Saints, The 132
Wellington Monument 232–3

West of Ireland 16, 31–2, 38, 121, 161,
    193–4, 196, 223–4, 226–7, 232,
    240–1, 246–7
Westmoreland Street 104, 143
Whaley, Buck 93–4, 98, 102
Whaley, Burnchapel 94, 98, 100
Wharf Road 7, 39
White, Luke 101
William of Orange 96, 103, 121, 154,
    230, 240
"Work in Progress" 266
Woulfe, Father Patrick: *Irish Names
    and Surnames* 16, 138, 190, 231

Yeats, W. B. 2–3, 19, 29–31, 129, 131,
    133, 136, 154, 176, 182, 190, 194,
    199, 223, 228, 259, 262, 271; "The
    Body of the Father Christian
    Rosencrux" 2, 23–4, 27, 30, 32,
    228, 251–2; *Cathleen Ni Houlihan*
    188, 202; "The Gray Rock" 192;
    Irish Fairy and Folk Tales 197;
    "Irish National Literature, III" 24,
    251; "The Mountain Tomb" 3,
    251; "Red Hanrahan's Song
    about Ireland" 3, 200; *Rosa
    Alchemica* 26; "The Tower" 194;
    "The Valley of the Black Pig"
    161–2; *The Wanderings of Oisin* 186
Yorke, Philip (third Earl of
    Hardwicke) 121
Young, Ella 136
Young Irelanders 183